The Dark Factory and the Future of Manufacturing

The world of manufacturing is undergoing significant changes driven by various factors and technological advancements. Automation and robotics technologies are revolutionizing manufacturing processes. Robotic systems are being increasingly used for repetitive and precise tasks, improving efficiency, quality, and safety. The Internet of Things (IoT) is enabling connectivity and data exchange between devices and systems. Manufacturing generates vast amounts of data and is leveraging this data through advanced analytics, providing valuable insights to optimize production processes, predict maintenance needs, and improve supply chain management.

Additive Manufacturing has also gained significant traction in manufacturing. It enables the creation of complex parts and prototypes, customization, and rapid prototyping. Supply chains are becoming more interconnected and digitally integrated. Technologies such as blockchain enable transparent and secure transactions, traceability, and efficient inventory management. These trends and others are reshaping the manufacturing industry, promoting increased efficiency, agility, and sustainability. Manufacturers must be aware, understand, and embrace these changes to stay competitive and meet the evolving demands of customers in the modern era.

This book enhances the awareness and understanding of these core technologies by explaining what they are and how they are being used in manufacturing. In addition, it provides practical suggestions on how to advance manufacturing in light of these changes. The book provides a view into the future and direction on how to navigate the journey to a more automated, smarter, and continuously learning factory. This book consolidates the major elements of the fourth industrial revolution and describes them in clear terms within the context of integrated manufacturing. It creates awareness and a fundamental understanding of the advanced technologies that are coming together to facilitate highly automated, smarter, agile, and sustainable operations.

The Dark Factory and the Future of Manufacturing

A Guide to Operational Efficiency and Competitiveness

Philip J. Gisi

Routledge
Taylor & Francis Group

A PRODUCTIVITY PRESS BOOK

First published 2024
by Routledge
605 Third Avenue, New York, NY 10158

and by Routledge
4 Park Square, Milton Park, Abingdon, Oxon, OX14 4RN

Routledge is an imprint of the Taylor & Francis Group, an informa business

© 2024 Philip J. Gisi

ISBN: 978-1-032-68748-3 (hbk)
ISBN: 978-1-032-68747-6 (pbk)
ISBN: 978-1-032-68815-2 (ebk)

DOI: 10.4324/9781032688152

Typeset in Garamond
by Deanta Global Publishing Services, Chennai, India

Contents

PART 4 SUSTAINABLE MANUFACTURING

Figures

Tables

Preface

Writing about one's work can be very satisfying and energizing as we seek ways to enhance and share our knowledge with clarity and meaning for the benefit of others. Knowledge is a collective and curious thing. The acquisition of knowledge starts at birth and continues throughout our lives, growing as we observe, read, listen, think, and interact with the world around us. It's both an active and passive process.

Writing a book about manufacturing is all about knowledge. It's about understanding the current state of the industry and where the industry is likely to go, considering technological advances and the opportunities those advances may offer in improving productivity and competitiveness. Every book starts with an idea, perhaps of what the writer believes is relevant and interesting to their intended audience. I believe many will find this topic of future factory fascinating, if not important.

In this case, I started this book knowing the future of manufacturing is changing and changing fast. Technology trends such as advanced automation, the Internet of Things (IoT), artificial intelligence, and data analytics are altering the way we think, innovate, and work to create highly automated, smart, and sustainable factories. The idea of a dark factory is a vision of the future that helps define strategic project priorities when considering the vast opportunities presented by the fourth industrial revolution.

My intent is to help shed light on what's changing and provide direction on how to navigate the challenges ahead. In the following pages, I will reveal what the factory of the future is about and provide insight into the knowledge, technologies, skills, tools, and techniques that are available, developing, and converging to help realize a digital transformation where decision-making and manufacturing optimization are heavily dependent on data mining, predictive analysis, and machine learning, among other things.

In full disclosure, about halfway through the writing of this book, I acquired access to ChatGPT. I was curious as to its potential in influencing how and what I wrote. In reality, it did not change much of what I was doing or planned to do. However, it did validate what I was doing and reaffirmed the importance of the topics covered in this book to achieve a smart and ultimately "dark" factory. At times, ChatGPT acted as my muse, sparking thoughts and stimulating ideas for further exploration and discussion. It's an impressive tool that will inevitably impact the future in ways not yet understood or imagined. This book reflects the deep learning of ChatGPT when I could not express a subject any better in my own thoughts and words.

Acknowledgments

There are many sources of knowledge that coalesce into writing a book of this nature. Those sources include many years working in industry and academia combined with reading, listening, and asking lots of questions. My primary objective in writing a book is to learn and share my knowledge with others and to pay forward the wealth of knowledge I have acquired from experts and colleagues of the past and present. Thus, the knowledge and information being shared in this manuscript is in recognition of all those who made it possible and those who will continue the tradition of sharing their knowledge with others.

I would like to thank OpenAI for sharing their valuable creation ChatGPT with me and the world; although it's not perfect, it was surprisingly resourceful in my area of questioning and very helpful in writing this book. To the reader, thank you for taking interest in this book. Building an automated, smart, and reliable factory of the future is not a trivial task. It takes knowledge, planning, execution, time, and patience. Navigating the road to "darkness" also requires an awareness and understanding of the journey ahead for all stakeholders involved. The intent of this book is to provide a vision of the future and, more importantly, a tangible roadmap on how to get there. Enjoy the book!

About the Author

Philip Gisi, PMP, SSMBB, has over 30 years' experience in the automotive, commercial, and aerospace industries. His areas of expertise include new product development, process technology, quality management, automotive electronics, and manufacturing operations. He has worked internationally in multi-cultural environments and is currently involved in project management and productivity improvements as an internal consultant at Vitesco Technologies. Phil has a Master of Science in Engineering, a Master Certificate in Project Management, Lean Management Certification from the University of Michigan, Project Management Professional (PMP) Certification, and a Six Sigma Master Black Belt (SSMBB). Phil has been sharing his experiences in project management, lean concepts, and Six Sigma process improvement as a DePaul University instructor for over 20 years and is the author of two previous books. His first book, released in 2018, is titled *Sustaining a Culture of Process Control and Continuous Improvement: The Roadmap for Efficiency and Operational Excellence*, published by the Taylor & Francis Group. His second book, also released by the same publisher in 2023, is titled *Fundamentals of Daily Shop Floor Management: A Guide for Manufacturing Optimization and Excellence*.

Introduction

Time never stops, things change, life evolves, technology advances, and people adapt. This is true with just about everything, including manufacturing. The dark age of manufacturing is nearly upon us; however, it may not be what you think. Manufacturing of the future is a vision in which most operational activities occur in a facility where equipment is doing the work once done by humans. Robots are assembling products, automated conveyors are moving parts from one station to the next while automated guided vehicles (AGVs) are transporting raw materials to the production line and taking finished goods to the warehouse for storage and transport to the customer. The idea of a dark or "lights-out" facility simply reflects the absence of light needed for people to see what they are doing since automation has nearly replaced them. Although the absence of lighting is the concept behind a dark factory, the real focus is on automation and the elimination of the human element in executing many of the traditional roles people performed in factory operations. Humans are still needed to program, maintain, and repair equipment, but this can be minimized to scheduled times if the machines and equipment used are highly reliable.

A dark factory requires lots of planning. Typical activities include a high degree of automation, the engagement of smart sensors and devices, the collection and analysis of big data, and cloud connectivity to help manage these interactions. These and many other factors must be considered when planning, converting, or building a factory of the future. This book takes on the challenging of outlining and articulating the fundamental elements required to realize a factory of the future. It highlights and describes the basic structure and approach necessary to achieve a dark factory, if only for several hours a day or several days a week initially.

There are many topics to discuss and technologies to consider when looking to augment one's awareness and knowledge of what is needed for manufacturing success in the future. In this overview, we will explore the elements of Industry 4.0 and learn how the digital age is transforming manufacturing from a physical to a digital state of operation. Finally, before leaving this introduction, a brief overview of this book is provided from which a lot more discussions will ensue. Let's get started with an overview of Industry 4.0.

Industry 4.0

The fourth industrial revolution, also known as Industry 4.0, refers to the current era of technological advancement and automation in various industries, characterized by the integration of digital technologies, data analytics, and artificial intelligence into traditional manufacturing processes. Industry 4.0 builds upon the previous industrial revolutions, which brought about significant changes in the way goods were produced, starting from the use of steam power in the first industrial revolution to mass production in the third industrial revolution. However, unlike the previous revolutions, Industry 4.0 is not just a single technology, but rather a combination of several technologies that are transforming the way products are designed, manufactured, and delivered.

Industry 4.0 technologies include IoT, cloud computing, artificial intelligence (AI), robotics, additive manufacturing, and augmented reality. These technologies work together to create a more efficient and productive manufacturing process, with increased automation and a higher level of customization. For example, with Industry 4.0, machines can communicate with each other in real-time and can be programmed to make autonomous decisions, reducing the need for human intervention. This can result in faster production, better quality control, and lower costs. Overall, Industry 4.0 is expected to revolutionize the way we live and work, creating new jobs and business opportunities while transforming the traditional manufacturing industry into a more flexible and efficient ecosystem. Now let's consider the digital age in the context of Industry 4.0 (Figure 0.1).

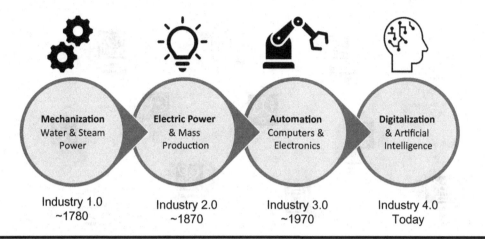

Figure 0.1 **Industrial revolutions.**

The Digital Age

The digital age has brought about significant changes in the manufacturing industry, as innovative technologies and advancements in digitalization have transformed the way products are designed, produced, and delivered to consumers. One key aspect of the digital age in manufacturing is the increased use of automation, robotics, and smart technologies. These technologies have made it possible for manufacturers to produce goods at a much faster rate and with higher levels of precision and consistency than ever before. Automation also allows for greater flexibility in manufacturing processes, making it easier for manufacturers to adapt to changing market conditions and customer demands.

Another important development in the digital age is the rise of IoT and the use of sensors and data analytics in manufacturing. IoT technologies allow manufacturers to collect vast amounts of data in every stage of the manufacturing process, from the supply chain to production to shipping and delivery. This data can be used to optimize processes, reduce waste and errors, and improve quality control. Additionally, the digital age has enabled manufacturers to use virtual and augmented reality technologies to enhance the design and development process. This allows engineers and designers to evaluate and refine products in a virtual environment before they are produced, reducing the need for expensive prototypes, and speeding up the development process. In essence, the digital age has had a profound impact on the manufacturing industry, enabling greater efficiency, flexibility, and innovation than ever before. As technology continues to evolve, it is likely

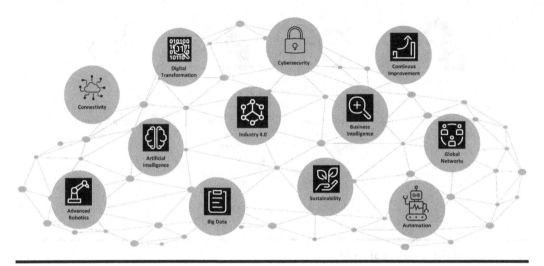

Figure 0.2   The digital age.

that we will see even more dramatic changes in the manufacturing landscape in the years to come (Figure 0.2).

Book Content

The purpose of this book is simple, to provide insight and direction on how to achieve a touchless factory, a factory in which automation dominates production and human intervention is primarily focused on equipment maintenance and repair. Although you may never achieve the ultimate goal of "lights-out" manufacturing, moving closer to it, in an incremental and meaningful way, will serve to prepare you for the future. In the fourth industrial revolution, knowledge is king. Effective implementation of proven technologies and awareness of up-and-coming opportunities, with a clear understanding of their potential impact on operational efficiency, are essential attributes of a modern-day manufacturing mindset.

Replacing humans with automation that is faster, more accurate, precise, and reliable makes sense if the cost and benefits of doing so are justified. Gone are the days of tardy employees, injury and illness, and human error from a line operation perspective. Manufacturing is being dominated by automated and reliable equipment that requires minimum maintenance, repair, and replacement. This means that workers of the future must be highly skilled, adequately compensated, and expected to maintain a level of competence commensurate with advancing technologies within their field of expertise.

In the following pages of this manuscript, we will ponder the rapidly changing face of manufacturing. In Part 1, we will consider the factory of the future and what it will look like. In doing so, Chapter 1.1 will articulate the concept of a dark factory and explore the elements of industrial automation. It will also touch on the topic of the human factor in this new frontier. A strategy in the form of a roadmap will also be provided to help visualize the journey to "darkness." Chapter 1.2 looks at Industry 4.0 and its link with the digital age in more detail. In this section, we start with an understanding of IoT and its vital role in manufacturing. Key technologies such as data analytics, digital twin, and blockchain will be reviewed in the context of achieving a dark factory along with cybersecurity, cloud, and cognitive computing.

Chapter 1.3 starts to explore the idea of digital transformation in manufacturing, moving from the physical world of objects made up of atoms to the digital realm composed of software bits and bytes used by computer programs to control operations. This is where we will discuss the smart factory and how it's transforming the way work is performed. This chapter will consider topics such as remote experts and augmented reality in shop floor activities. The last chapter in Part 1, Chapter 1.4, considers the changing mindset of manufacturing as we move from a more traditional way of thinking to one that is more flexible, modular, scalable, and sustainable when navigating toward the future.

In Part 2, we focus on strategic equipment and product line design, development, and industrialization, in the context of rapid, agile, and cost-effective solutions for modern-day automated manufacturing. Chapter 2.1 considers the manufacturing equipment needed to support advanced robotics, autonomously guided vehicles, smart sensors, and other devices required for data analytics and machine learning. Chapter 2.2 focuses on product line design, build, and integration strategies needed to support fully automated operations. This includes equipment make or buy decisions and the best approach for equipment customization to support operational flexibility, scalability, and reliability. Chapter 2.3 concentrates on equipment fabrication activities and guidelines for ease of maintenance, repair, and reuse in the context of automation and the equipment lifecycle. Chapter 2.4 focuses on product line integration by considering the best approaches for product assembly to achieve efficient and continuous product flow. This chapter will explore workstation concepts, manufacturing floor space optimization, and AGV-ready production lines, among other activities to support a "smart" manufacturing strategy. The last chapter of Part 2 (Chapter 2.5) will consider the topics of machine capability as well as product and process validation activities.

Part 3 considers product manufacturing in the digital age. In this third section, we will explore how digital technology is changing the face of shop floor management and how traditional activities need to change and adapt to a new way of working. Activities such as process standardization, data collection, and data analytics will be transformed in light of digitalization (Chapter 3.1). The traditional approach to process monitoring and control will become more efficient, automated, and remote (Chapter 3.2). Line maintenance and repair will still be required but more proactive than reactive using smart technology (Chapter 3.3). In the last chapter of Part 3 (Chapter 3.4), we will touch on the topic of continuous improvement and how this activity will evolve toward predictive maintenance and new ways of learning. These concepts and others will not only be explained, guidelines and tips will be provided to help realize and run a factory of the future.

Part 4 considers the topic of manufacturing sustainability. In this final section, we will explore key aspects of sustainable manufacturing which has become an area of interest to many stakeholders wanting to minimize the impact of manufacturing activities on the environment and climate change. Chapter 4.1 looks into water, energy, and material conservation as a manufacturing strategy and ways to enhance manufacturing recycling and reuse practices. In Chapter 4.2, we look at topics such as greenhouse emissions, air pollutants, and toxic substances in order to minimize their impact on manufacturing's environmental footprint. Renewable energy is the focus of Chapter 4.3 as we consider alternatives to fossil fuels such as solar, wind, hydropower, and geothermal energy. Chapter 4.4 tackles the subject of design for sustainability which explores a company's environmental footprint and the eco-friendly materials used in manufacturing as well as supply chain management practices. The final chapter of the book (Chapter 4.5) briefly discusses a culture of sustainable manufacturing in addition to employee awareness and collaboration necessary for its successful realization. Welcome to a new era of manufacturing!

FACTORY OF THE FUTURE

Knowledge and awareness about future manufacturing are important for several reasons. The manufacturing industry is constantly evolving with new technologies and processes. Being aware of manufacturing trends allows businesses to stay updated and adapt to advancing technologies like automation, artificial intelligence, additive manufacturing (3D printing), and the Internet of Things (IoT). This knowledge enables companies to enhance productivity, improve product quality, reduce costs, and stay competitive in the market.

Understanding manufacturing trends helps organizations make informed strategic decisions. By anticipating industry developments, businesses can plan their investments, allocate resources, and deploy production strategies accordingly. They can identify emerging markets, develop new products, and adjust their supply chains to meet future demands. Evolving manufacturing concepts such as smart factories, digitalization, and industrial robotics can significantly enhance operational efficiency and productivity. Knowledge about these advancements enables companies to optimize their manufacturing processes, streamline operations, and minimize waste. This can result in increased output, reduced lead times, and improved performance.

In light of growing concerns about environmental sustainability, manufacturers must focus on reducing waste, energy consumption, and carbon emissions. Awareness of upcoming green technologies and sustainable practices allows businesses to incorporate eco-friendly processes into manufacturing operations. This not only helps them meet regulatory requirements but also enhances their reputation and attracts environmentally conscious customers.

DOI: 10.4324/9781032688152-1

As manufacturing technologies evolve, the workforce needs to be prepared for the changing landscape. Knowledge about future manufacturing practices enables companies to identify the skills and competencies that will be in demand. They can then invest in training programs to ensure their employees are equipped to work with advanced technologies. This helps create a skilled workforce that can adapt quickly to future manufacturing requirements.

In a highly competitive global market, staying ahead of the curve is essential for businesses. Knowledge about manufacturing trends enables companies to innovate, develop new products, and deliver them faster and more efficiently. This enhances their competitiveness both domestically and internationally, allowing them to capture market share and expand their operations.

In summary, knowledge and awareness about the future of manufacturing empower businesses to embrace innovative technologies, make strategic decisions, improve efficiency, ensure sustainability, develop a skilled workforce, and stay ahead of the competition. It is crucial for companies to keep abreast of the latest manufacturing trends in order to thrive in a dynamic business environment. In Part 1 of this book, we will discuss the fundamental topics required for the journey to a smarter, more autonomous factory of the future.

Chapter 1.1

The Dark Factory: The Future of Manufacturing

What Is a Dark Factory?

Visualize a large manufacturing facility with all the equipment running and robots executing their programmed routines. Automated guided vehicles (AGVs) are roaming the facility dropping off and picking up materials at various locations in the dark. No lights, no windows, and no humans working on the factory floor. This is the idea behind a dark factory.

A dark or "lights-out" factory is a type of manufacturing facility that is fully automated and operates with little to no human intervention. In a dark factory, all production processes are controlled by robots, machines, and software, which work together to manufacture products without the need for human workers. The term "lights-out" refers to the fact that these factories can operate without any human presence, meaning that the lights can be turned off while the factory continues to run.

Dark factories will be more common in industries where high levels of precision and efficiency are required, such as the production of electronics, medical devices, and automotive components. They can operate 24/7, with no need for breaks and minimal downtime, and can produce products at a much faster rate than traditional factories.

The factory of the future is expected to be highly automated and efficient, with the use of artificial intelligence, machine learning, and the

DOI: 10.4324/9781032688152-2

Internet of Things (IoT) to create fully integrated and optimized manufacturing processes. This will lead to increased productivity, lower costs, and faster delivery times, making it possible to produce goods on demand and reduce waste. However, the implementation of a dark factory requires significant investment in automation technology and infrastructure, and is likely to have implications for employment and workforce development.

Running a high-volume, efficient manufacturing facility 24/7, with minimal labor, is the holy grail of manufacturing. This idea is being realized through the application of automation and the digitalization of the factory floor. The concept of a dark factory can be approached gradually, starting with the application of automated equipment, robotics to replace humans, and AGVs to pick up and deliver production materials. This can lead to semi-automated production lines or the eventual automation of an area, such as a warehouse or packaging operation. A factory becomes fully automated incrementally, starting with one production line, running one shift or one day without human intervention. Regardless, every automated operation will eventually require human involvement for equipment maintenance and repair. This level of engagement with automation and smart technology will require a higher level of competence that comes with knowledge and experience. Let's continue our discussion by pursuing a deeper understanding of the future factory.

Factory of the Future

A factory of the future is a highly advanced, technologically sophisticated manufacturing facility that leverages innovative technologies to improve efficiency, productivity, and quality. Such a factory would likely feature a range of advanced technologies, including robotics, automation, artificial intelligence (AI), and IoT. See Figure 1.1.1.

One of the key features of a future factory is a high degree of automation. This means that robots and other machines would perform many of the tasks that were previously done by human workers, leading to increased efficiency and reduced costs. Automation includes the use of smart machines and systems that can learn, adapt, and communicate with each other.

A fully digitalized factory is another characteristic of future manufacturing where all processes are connected through IoT and are monitored and controlled using real-time data analytics. This includes the use of sensors, machine learning algorithms, and artificial intelligence to optimize

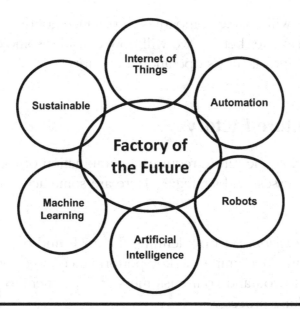

Figure 1.1.1   Factory of the future.

performance and predict equipment maintenance needs. A factory of the future will likely be designed to encourage a partnership between humans and machines, as well as between different departments and stakeholders. This includes the use of virtual and augmented reality technologies to facilitate remote collaboration and training.

Another important feature is the use of AI and machine learning to optimize production processes and predict maintenance needs. By analyzing data from sensors and other sources, these systems can identify potential problems before they occur, allowing for proactive equipment maintenance and minimizing downtime. The future is also likely to be highly connected, with sensors and IoT devices throughout the facility that provide real-time data on production processes and equipment performance. This data can be used to optimize operations, improve quality, and reduce waste.

Modern facilities will be designed with sustainability in mind. This means they will be energy-efficient, use renewable energy sources wherever possible, and prioritize the use of environmentally friendly materials and production methods. Customization will become another attribute of a future factory, meaning it will be highly flexible and able to quickly adapt to changing market demands by using modular designs, flexible production lines, and additive manufacturing techniques such as 3D printing.

Overall, the factory of the future represents a significant shift in manufacturing technology, with a focus on automation, connectivity, and sustainability that will enable companies to produce goods more efficiently and effectively than ever before. We will now consider some of the following steps to advance a facility's operational maturity.

Realizing a Future Factory

Realizing a factory of the future requires a combination of various technologies, processes, and strategies. Here are some actions that you can take.

Develop a clear vision: Start by defining the goals and objectives for your factory's future. Determine the key performance indicators (KPIs) that matter most to you and your customers and use them to guide your decision-making process.

Foster a culture of innovation: Encourage experimentation, continuous learning, and collaboration across the organization to drive innovation and stay ahead of the competition. Encourage employees to come up with new ideas and approaches that can help drive continuous improvement and keep the factory at the forefront of technological advancements.

Embrace Industry 4.0: The fourth industrial revolution or Industry 4.0 is a trend toward automation and data exchange in manufacturing technologies. It involves the use of technologies such as IoT, AI, and big data analytics to create smart factories. By adopting an Industry 4.0 mentality, you can automate your production processes, optimize your supply chain, and reduce costs.

Embrace the cloud: Cloud computing can be used to store and analyze vast amounts of data generated by a factory. This will enable real-time collaboration, remote access, and greater flexibility in managing operations.

Leverage data: Collect and analyze data for spikes, trends, and patterns across the factory. This will help you to gain insight into your operations, identify areas for improvement, and facilitate data-driven decisions.

Create a digital twin: A digital twin is a virtual replica of a physical object, allowing for the real-time simulation and optimization of targeted operations. This helps to identify potential problems before they occur and optimize manufacturing processes.

Implement lean manufacturing: Lean manufacturing is a methodology that aims to minimize waste and maximize production efficiency. By implementing lean principles, you can reduce lead times, improve product quality, and increase customer satisfaction.

Use robotics and automation: Robotics and automation can help you achieve high levels of precision, speed, and accuracy in your manufacturing processes. By using robots to perform repetitive tasks, you can reduce errors and increase efficiency. Automation can also help you achieve cost savings by reducing labor costs and improving product quality.

Exercise smart manufacturing practices: Implementing smart manufacturing practices, such as real-time monitoring and predictive maintenance, can help you optimize your processes. Predictive maintenance involves using data and analytics to predict when equipment is likely to fail. By adopting this approach, you can reduce downtime, minimize repair costs, and extend the life of your equipment.

Ensure data security: The factory of the future relies heavily on data and connectivity. Therefore, it is crucial to ensure that your data is secure. You should implement cybersecurity measures such as firewalls, encryption, and multi-factor authentication to protect your data from cyber threats.

Workforce training: As you implement new technologies and processes, it is essential to train your workforce to ensure they have the skills and knowledge to operate and maintain them. You should invest in training programs that help employees acquire new skills and stay up to date with the latest technologies.

Continuously improve: To maintain a competitive edge, you should continuously monitor and improve your production processes. You can use data analytics to identify areas of improvement and implement new strategies to optimize operations.

Design for Manufacturing

The concept behind manufacturing is changing. It's no longer just about controlling materials, assembling products, and managing people. The competitive nature of the business is expanding the manufacturing mindset to include upstream activities that include the design and building of manufacturing equipment that can be arranged into a production line concept with lean, flexible, scalable, and customization capabilities. In doing so, more control over equipment reliability, development time, and cost must be realized. Equipment reliability is a key contributor to the idea of a dark factory in that robust equipment is less likely to fail unpredictably, reducing the need for human intervention for troubleshooting and repair. Control over equipment design and build activities can significantly influence equipment reliability which is needed to sustain autonomous manufacturing.

Development time can be meaningfully impacted by the decision to build equipment internal or external to the manufacturing organization. Developing the competence and capability to design and build equipment internally may provide advantages in reuse, build time, and robustness. Unfortunately, this capability does not come cheap.

Equipment build guidelines specifying key machine characteristics such as footprint, ease of maintenance, and portability are some of the attributes that can be deployed and controlled more effectively when constructing equipment in-house versus using an external supplier.

The cost of equipment builds can be monitored and controlled more closely when specific parameters, components, and suppliers are identified in the build instructions. In addition, cost estimates tend to be more accurate while product variation is reduced. This approach can be particularly useful when targeting levels of equipment reliability and durability not commonly encountered from mainstream equipment building contractors. More details on this topic will be covered in Part 2 of this text.

Industrial Automation

Industrial automation refers to the use of advanced technologies and computer systems to control and optimize the manufacturing process. It involves the use of machines and robots to perform tasks that were once done by human operators, making production faster, more efficient, and cost-effective.

Industrial automation can be achieved through various technologies, such as programmable logic controllers (PLCs), supervisory control and data acquisition (SCADA) systems, distributed control systems (DCS), and human–machine interfaces (HMIs). These systems can be integrated to work together, providing a comprehensive solution for the control and management of industrial processes.

The benefits of industrial automation are numerous. Automation has the ability to perform repetitive tasks with precision and accuracy, thereby reducing errors and waste, increasing production speed and efficiency, reducing labor costs, and improving workplace safety. Automation can also allow for greater flexibility in manufacturing, as processes can be easily adjusted or reconfigured to accommodate changes in product design or customer demands.

Industrial automation also presents some challenges. The implementation of automation requires careful planning and design to ensure that the technology integrates seamlessly with existing manufacturing processes. The initial cost of installing automation systems can be high, and there may be a learning curve for operators and maintenance personnel. Additionally, there is the risk of job displacement as machines and robots take over tasks previously performed by humans.

Industrial automation is a crucial tool for modern manufacturing, enabling companies to achieve greater efficiency, productivity, and profitability while maintaining high product quality and safety standards. Let's look at how automated systems can be structured to achieve seamless production.

Automation System Structure

Industrial automation uses existing technologies in combination with automatic control devices such as computers and robots to execute operations and establish manufacturing controls with minimal human interaction. Modern-day automation requires various components, working in concert, to execute specific job tasks. As discussed, these components include:

- PLC
- DCS
- Field industrial devices
- Industrial communication and networks
- HMI
- SCADA
- Personal computers

To simplify this topic, let's consider automation from three different perspectives, field devices, controllers (various types), and information management (logic and design). We will begin with the lowest level, field devices.

Field Devices

Field devices comprise the physical, tangible hardware (often with software) located at the worksite or at strategic locations within the system. One of the more common devices used in the field (or manufacturing floor) are computers to monitor and control processes. To compensate for the lack of human capabilities, such as hearing and seeing, computers rely on the feedback from industrial sensors to monitor and execute the controls needed to complete their tasks. Sensors can be used to identify the presence of parts, part sizes, color, and quality (good or bad). They can also be used to create a safer and more efficient work environment through the detection of process deviations, product defects, equipment damage, and unsafe working conditions.

Controllers

Industrial automation controllers regulate the flow of data between system devices and applications according to a program or logic. Controllers monitor process and equipment inputs and respond with control status through one or more outputs commonly called control logic. Typical industrial controllers are a DCS, a PLC, and PC-based control. For example, programmable controllers are industrial computers that continuously monitor device inputs and make adjustments to control device outputs. In essence programmable logic controllers and distributed control systems are used to send, receive, and process data from sensors, control valves, and actuators as part of the control system. Personal computer controllers provide simple control systems, linking devices to applications in an industrial environment. Personal computers are easy to program and can seamlessly interface with the local area network (LAN).

Information Management

At the management level, one of the more common communication network protocols for manufacturing is the Ethernet. It's a popular application protocol within industry because it's fast, inexpensive, easy to install, and supported by various industrial networks. The management level interacts with remote devices to engage in the activity of process control, collecting real-time data through the application of various software programs. See Figure 1.1.2.

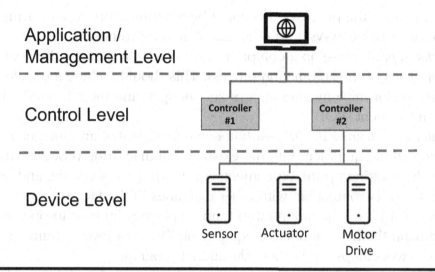

Figure 1.1.2   Automation system structure.

Human–Machine Interface (HMI)

The HMI is a critical component of industrial automation. It's a software application that enables interaction between the human operator and the machine or system, providing information to the users about the state of a system or process. It provides a window into real-time system functionality and a way for the user to instruct or control system inputs. The HMI allows humans to monitor and interact with machines to make necessary adjustments remotely or on the factory floor.

Industrial Automation – Implementation

Automating a manufacturing facility involves integrating various technologies combined with a systematic approach. Here are some steps to follow when automating a manufacturing facility.

Identify the manufacturing process: The first step in automating a manufacturing facility is to identify the manufacturing process that you want to automate. This can include any repetitive and time-consuming tasks that can be easily automated.

Determine the automation equipment: Once you have identified the process, determine the type of automation equipment that is required to automate the process. This could be anything from robotic arms to conveyor belts, AGVs, and other automated machinery.

Develop a plan: Develop a comprehensive plan that outlines the goals and objectives of the automation process. This should include a detailed timeline for implementation, a project budget, and the expected return on investment (ROI).

Install and integrate the automation equipment: Install and integrate the automation equipment into the existing manufacturing process. This involves setting up the equipment, configuring the software, and ensuring that it is compatible with other machines in the factory.

Train employees: It is important to train employees on how to operate and maintain the new automated equipment. This can involve training sessions, workshops, and other educational programs.

Monitor and optimize: Once the equipment is installed and the employees are trained, monitor the performance of the automation process regularly. This will help you identify any issues and optimize the process for maximum efficiency.

Continuous improvement: Automation is an ongoing process, so continue to identify opportunities for improvement and implement them to further optimize your manufacturing process. This involves regularly reviewing and updating the automated equipment and processes to keep up with changing business needs and technologies.

It's important to note that automating a manufacturing facility is a complex process that requires careful planning, implementation, and ongoing maintenance. Working with experienced automation professionals can help ensure project success.

The Automated Factory

The function of an automated factory can vary depending on the specific products being manufactured and the technology being used. The production process begins with designing and planning the products to be manufactured. This includes creating detailed computer-aided design (CAD) models of the products, specifying the materials to be used, and determining the sequence of manufacturing steps.

Once the product design is finalized, the factory's manufacturing system generates a detailed plan for the production process. This plan includes information such as the types of machines needed, the raw materials required, and the time necessary for each step of the process. The production process begins with the delivery of raw materials to the factory. Raw materials are loaded into the factory's automated inventory system. This system tracks the quantity and location of each material and automatically orders more when necessary. These materials can be anything from metal sheets and plastic pellets to chemicals and other components needed for the manufacturing process.

Once the raw materials are received, automated systems, such as conveyors or AGVs, transport the materials to the appropriate location in the factory where they are assembled into finished products. This process is typically done using advanced robotics and machinery that can perform highly repetitive tasks with precision and speed. Robots and other machines perform tasks such as cutting, molding, stamping, welding, and painting. The machines are controlled by a computer system that receives instructions from the manufacturing plan.

As products move through the assembly line, they are inspected by automated quality control systems to ensure they meet specific standards and specifications. Defective products are identified and removed from the production line. Automated factories use sensors and cameras to monitor the manufacturing process in real-time. These sensors can detect defects or errors in the production process and automatically make adjustments to correct them. This can include checking for defects, measuring dimensions, and performing functional tests.

Once the products have been manufactured and inspected, they are packaged and prepared for shipment. This can involve automated packing machines, labeling systems, and shipping logistics software to ensure that the products are delivered to customers efficiently and on time. The automated inventory system tracks the location of each product and automatically generates shipping labels and other necessary documentation.

Automated factories are designed to operate continuously, but maintenance and optimization are still required to ensure maximum efficiency and productivity. Computer systems monitor the performance of the machines and alert maintenance personnel when repairs are needed. Data analytics tools can also be used to analyze production data and identify areas for improvement. In essence, an automated factory is a highly efficient and productive manufacturing facility that relies on advanced technology to streamline the production process and minimize human intervention.

Warehouse Automation

There have been significant advances in warehouse material handling especially with the loading and unloading of freight from delivery vehicles. Arduous, repetitive, and injury-prone tasks are being replaced by automated loading and unloading systems. Automated devices such as robotic loaders and articulated arm loaders/unloaders are being used in warehouse operations to do the difficult work of humans. The application of advanced machine learning has enabled robotic unloaders to autonomously unload freight that varies in size and weight.

An automated manufacturing warehouse typically functions using a combination of advanced technologies such as robotics, automation, and computer systems to streamline and optimize the various processes involved in manufacturing and warehousing. Let's overview how an automated manufacturing warehouse might function.

The process starts with receiving raw materials and components from suppliers. When goods are delivered to the warehouse, they are typically scanned and logged into a computer system. This helps in tracking the inventory and ensuring that everything is properly accounted for. The materials are then stored in inventory with the help of automated inventory management systems. These systems use barcodes, radio frequency identification (RFID) tags, or other tracking technologies to monitor the movement of goods in and out of the warehouse.

Once materials are received, they are transported to different areas of the warehouse using automated material handling systems such as conveyor belts, robots, or AGVs. Storage locations may be determined by a computerized inventory management system, which helps to optimize the use of space and minimize the time required to retrieve items. These systems are programmed to move materials to the correct storage locations or to production lines for processing.

When an order is placed for a particular item, the warehouse management system (WMS) will determine the most efficient route for retrieving the item and delivering it to the appropriate location within the warehouse. This process may involve the use of automated storage and retrieval systems (AS/RS) or other types of material handling equipment, such as conveyor belts or robotic arms.

Material is then transported to the manufacturing floor via an automated transport system where the production process is managed by computer systems that ensure each step in the process is completed accurately and efficiently. After the products are manufactured and inspected, they are packed and prepared for shipment using an automated packaging system.

Products are then shipped to customers using automated shipping systems that can handle the logistics of delivering items to various locations. Throughout the entire process, data is collected and analyzed to optimize the various processes and to identify areas for improvement. This data is used to refine the manufacturing and warehousing processes to increase efficiency, reduce waste, and improve product quality.

Process Automation

Process automation is the use of technology to automate repetitive or manual tasks within a business process. It involves the use of software or hardware tools to streamline and standardize workflows, reduce errors, increase efficiency, and save time and resources.

Process automation involves several steps. First, the process is analyzed to identify opportunities for automation. This may involve mapping out the current workflow, identifying bottlenecks, and determining which tasks are best suited for automation. Next, the automation solution is designed and implemented. This may involve selecting a software tool, developing custom code, or configuring an off-the-shelf solution. The automation solution is typically integrated with other software tools or systems used within the organization.

Once the automation solution is implemented, it is tested and refined as necessary. This may involve conducting user acceptance testing to ensure the solution meets the needs of end-users and addresses any issues that arise during implementation. Finally, the automated process is monitored and maintained to ensure that it continues to function properly and meet the needs of the organization. This may involve ongoing maintenance, troubleshooting, and updates as necessary.

Robotic Process Automation (RPA)

RPA is a technology that uses software robots, also known as "bots," to automate routine, repetitive, and rule-based tasks within a business process. RPA technology is designed to mimic the actions of a human worker, such as logging into applications, copying and pasting data between systems, filling out forms, and performing calculations.

RPA bots are typically programmed using drag-and-drop interfaces that do not require coding skills, making them accessible to business users. They can be integrated with existing applications and systems to perform tasks across different departments, such as HR, finance, and customer service.

RPA is different from traditional automation technologies as it does not require significant changes to existing IT infrastructure and can be implemented quickly and cost-effectively. Additionally, RPA can reduce errors, improve productivity, and free up employees to focus on higher-level tasks.

RPA bots can be programmed to work with a wide range of software applications and can perform tasks across multiple systems. They can also be integrated with other technologies, such as artificial intelligence and machine learning, to further improve their capabilities.

The Human Factor

The factory of the future is expected to revolutionize the manufacturing industry with the integration of advanced technologies such as automation, artificial intelligence, robotics, and IoT. As a result, human labor in manufacturing is likely to be impacted in several ways. For example, many repetitive and routine tasks can be automated using robots and other advanced technologies. This will lead to a reduction in manual labor for such tasks, freeing up workers to focus on more complex and creative activities. The application of robots and other automated equipment will replace human workers required to perform dangerous tasks, resulting in a safer working environment for all.

Automation will likely eliminate many low-skilled jobs, particularly those involving repetitive manual labor. In response, factories will require workers with a different skill set than traditionally found in manufacturing. Workers with skills in programming, data analysis, and robotics are likely to be in high demand. These workers will be responsible for designing and programming advanced machinery and systems that will be used in the factory, as well as analyzing data generated by these systems to optimize factory operations and improve efficiency.

Workers will need to be trained in areas such as data analysis, machine learning, and programming. This will require a significant investment in training and education to ensure the workforce has the necessary skills to work in the new environment. While some traditional manufacturing jobs may be replaced by automation, the factory of the future will also create new job opportunities in areas such as data analysis, programming, and maintenance of advanced equipment. This will have a significant impact on human labor, requiring workers to be reskilled and upskilled to adapt to the new environment.

Strategy/Roadmap

Pursuing a strategy to achieve a dark factory requires planning, patience, and time. If the goal is not to realize a dark factory, the journey to a smarter, more automated operation is likely to be a necessary one. As discussed, a dark factory relies heavily on automation and advanced technologies such as robotics, artificial intelligence, and IoT to perform tasks that were previously done by humans. Consider the following roadmap when pursuing an automated, smart, or dark factory.

Define the scope and objectives of the journey: What products do you want to manufacture in the factory? What is the expected production output? What level of automation and machine learning do you want to achieve? These questions will help determine the size, complexity, and effort in achieving your strategy.

Evaluate the manufacturing process: Analyze the manufacturing process and determine which tasks can be automated. This includes processes such as material handling, product assembly, inspection, packaging, and shipping. This requires a thorough understanding of the process, including inputs, outputs, and bottlenecks.

Identify the right technologies: Once the manufacturing process has been evaluated, identify the right technologies that can be used to automate operations. This can include robots, automated guided vehicles, conveyor systems, and other types of automation technologies.

Set up the factory: Once you have chosen the technologies, you need to set up a new factory or revamp an existing one. This involves designing or redesigning the layout of the factory, installing the automation and robotic systems, and ensuring that they are properly integrated with each other. The automation technologies need to be integrated with each other and with the manufacturing equipment to ensure a seamless operation. This may require custom software development or the use of third-party integration tools.

Integrate the technologies: Next, integrate the selected technologies into the manufacturing process. This involves designing and implementing the necessary hardware and software systems to enable automation.

Implement the necessary infrastructure: A dark factory requires a significant investment in infrastructure, including sensors, cameras, and other IoT devices that can monitor the manufacturing process in real-time.

Test and fine-tune the systems: Before starting production, you need to test and fine-tune the automation and robotic systems to ensure that they are working properly. This involves running simulations and conducting trial runs to identify and correct any issues. Issues identified should be addressed promptly.

Implement a predictive maintenance program: A predictive maintenance program can help to reduce the risk of equipment failure and extended downtime, which is critical for a dark factory. Predictive maintenance uses sensors and analytics to predict when maintenance is required, minimizing the need for manual inspections.

Ensure cybersecurity: With an automated factory, cybersecurity is critical to prevent unauthorized access and potential data breaches. Implementing robust security measures such as firewalls, access controls, and encryption can help to protect the factory and its data. A touchless factory relies heavily on data communication between machines and systems. It's important to establish a secure network that can handle the volume of data and prevent unauthorized access.

Train the staff: While a dark factory requires minimal human intervention, it is still necessary to train the staff that will be responsible for maintaining and monitoring the automation systems. This includes training in areas such as data analysis, troubleshooting, and system maintenance.

Monitor and optimize: Once the factory is operational, it is essential to monitor the manufacturing process continuously and optimize the automation systems to ensure maximum efficiency and productivity.

Realizing that a dark factory requires a significant investment in technology, infrastructure, cybersecurity, and training. However, the benefits can be significant, including increased efficiency, improved quality, and reduced labor costs.

Key Points

- The objective of a dark factory is to minimize human intervention through automation.
- A true dark factory requires that every step of the process is automated.
- If automated equipment is designed, built, and laid out with a lean approach in mind, greater operational efficiency can be achieved.
- RPA technology can help organizations streamline their business processes.
- Automation can reduce process variation, eliminate human error, improve information flow, facilitate rapid decision-making, and redirect employees to focus on more value-added activities.
- Process automation is used to augment operational efficiency by eliminating labor-intensive, time-consuming, repetitive tasks from the workforce.
- The plant of the future will be smart, predictive, and sustainable.

Chapter 1.2

Industry 4.0: The Digital Age

Overview

The digital age in manufacturing refers to the integration of advanced digital technologies and data-driven systems into manufacturing operations. It encompasses a range of technologies such as automation, robotics, artificial intelligence (AI), Internet of Things (IoT), cloud computing, big data analytics, and additive manufacturing (3D printing). These technologies are revolutionizing the way manufacturing processes are designed, operated, and optimized.

One of the key aspects of the digital age in manufacturing is the concept of the "smart factory" or "Industry 4.0." Smart factories leverage interconnected digital systems to enable real-time communication, information sharing, and decision-making across various stages of the manufacturing process (see Figure 1.2.1). IoT sensors are used to collect data from machines, equipment, and products, which is then analyzed to gain insights and drive improvements in efficiency, quality, and productivity.

Automation plays a crucial role in the digital age of manufacturing. It involves the use of robotics and automated systems to perform repetitive and often hazardous tasks previously carried out by humans. These robots can be programmed to perform intricate operations with high precision and consistency, leading to increased productivity, reduced errors, and improved worker safety.

Artificial intelligence and machine learning algorithms are employed to analyze large volumes of manufacturing data, identify patterns, and make

DOI: 10.4324/9781032688152-3

Figure 1.2.1   Smart factory.

predictions. This enables manufacturers to optimize production processes, anticipate maintenance needs, and make data-driven decisions to enhance efficiency and quality. AI-powered systems can also enable predictive maintenance, which helps prevent equipment failures and minimize downtime.

Cloud computing provides a scalable and flexible infrastructure for storing and processing vast amounts of manufacturing data. It allows real-time access to information from any location, facilitating collaboration among geographically dispersed teams and enabling remote monitoring and control of manufacturing operations.

Big data analytics in manufacturing involves the analysis of large datasets to uncover valuable insights, optimize processes, and identify areas for improvement. By analyzing production data, manufacturers can identify bottlenecks, optimize inventory management, improve supply chain efficiency, and enhance overall operational performance.

Additive manufacturing, commonly known as 3D printing, is another key component of the digital age in manufacturing. It enables the creation of complex and customized products by adding successive layers of material based on digital designs. This technology offers advantages such as reduced waste, faster prototyping, on-demand production, and increased design flexibility.

Overall, the digital age in manufacturing represents a transformational shift in how products are designed, produced, and delivered. It offers manufacturers opportunities to improve efficiency, quality, and productivity while enabling greater customization and flexibility to meet evolving customer demands.

Internet of Things

IoT is a large network of connected objects or devices embedded with sensors and software that collect and exchange data which is analyzed for patterns and trends used to make decisions or recommendations, trigger actions, and solve problems. These objects or smart devices can be used to connect home appliances, security systems, cars, manufacturing equipment, and cities to wired or wireless networks within the internet (cloud). This application of smart devices and systems over the internet can result in the automation of tasks that can be digitally monitored or controlled, especially those that are repetitive, mundane, time-consuming, and dangerous.

The internet and web originated to provide humans with access to data and information on connected devices regardless of their geographical location. This extended level of communication allows a multitude of people to access and share information with each other, changing the way people interact. Over time, these interactions expanded to humans interfacing with machines and machine-to-machine communication. What started out with simple information and data transmissions such as emails has exploded into many facets of human and machine interactions including business marketing and commerce. This idea of interconnectivity expanded to the point where the term "Internet of Things" or IoT emerged in the early 2000s. This expansion was not only fueled by the number of people accessing the internet but the exponential addition of machines and devices using the web to communicate.

As the IoT evolves, the devices connected to it have become smarter due to the convergence of several technologies. They can be controlled by other devices such as a personal computer or mobile phone. Connectivity allows the software on these devices to be updated wirelessly. Learning devices can customize a user experience which can be further enhanced by the user accessing this data online. As an example, smart devices such as thermostats, doorbells, and motion sensors are being used at home leading to a new era of Smart Homes. The establishment of standards has enhanced the usefulness of conforming devices, facilitating coordination and one system control.

The Industrial Internet of Things (IIoT), also referred to as Industry 4.0, is a merging of the Internet of Things, automation, machine learning, sensor data, and machine-to-machine communication within industry. These various combinations of technologies are being used to facilitate predictive maintenance and enhance productivity in addition to quality control, sustainability practices, and supply chain efficiency.

Predictive maintenance is a good example of how the Internet of Things will significantly impact productivity in manufacturing by avoiding many unplanned production line stops where time is required to identify the problem, diagnose the cause, initiate repairs, and restart the line. This loss in manufacturing time can be considerable and costly. Devices embedded in manufacturing equipment such as temperature sensors, vibration detectors, and pressure gages can monitor operating parameters and warn of changing conditions flagging potential problems for investigation prior to equipment failure.

In the case of machine learning, sensors provide information to computers during normal operating conditions so that when those condition unexpectedly change, they can be detected and reacted to accordingly. Innovation in what data is collected, how it's collected, and how much is collected is changing the way we think and react within the operating environment. These advances, and many others, are possible through the industrial internet and the application of artificial intelligence.

The Manufacturing Internet of Things refers to the application of connected devices and smart sensors in the manufacturing industry to improve operational efficiency, reduce costs, and enhance product quality. In a manufacturing IoT system, devices such as sensors, robots, and machines are connected to a network that enables them to share data and communicate with each other. This data can then be used to monitor the performance of individual machines or entire production lines, optimize manufacturing processes, and improve overall productivity.

One key benefit of the manufacturing IoT is that it allows for real-time monitoring of manufacturing processes. This means that operators can quickly identify and address issues as they arise, reducing downtime and improving overall equipment effectiveness. In addition to improving operational efficiency, the manufacturing IoT can also enhance product quality by providing greater visibility into the production process. For example, sensors can be used to monitor product quality at various stages of production, allowing manufacturers to identify defects and take corrective action before products are shipped to customers. Overall, the manufacturing IoT is a powerful tool that can help manufacturers improve efficiency, reduce costs, and enhance product quality in a highly competitive industry.

Data Analytics

To remain competitive and thrive in the digital age, companies must use data to achieve agility, predict outcomes, and innovate. This can be facilitated through data analytics. Data analytics in manufacturing involves using statistical analysis and modeling techniques to extract insights from manufacturing data, which can then be used to optimize processes, improve quality, reduce costs, and increase efficiency. The manufacturing process generates a large volume of data, including production data, supply chain data, quality control data, and maintenance data, among others. With the advent of Industry 4.0 and IoT, the amount of data generated has increased exponentially, providing manufacturers with unprecedented opportunities to improve their operations.

Data analytics in manufacturing typically involves collecting data from various sources such as sensors, machines, and production lines. The data is then "cleaned" since raw data is often noisy and may contain errors. Data cleaning involves removing outliers and errors followed by preparing the data for analysis. Data analysis involves applying statistical and machine learning techniques to extract insights from the data. Insights obtained from data analysis are often presented visually to help manufacturers understand the results and make informed decisions. Some common applications of data analytics in manufacturing include the following.

Predictive maintenance: By analyzing data from sensors and other sources, you can predict when equipment is likely to fail and schedule maintenance to avoid costly downtime.

Quality control: By analyzing production data, you can identify patterns and trends that can help improve quality and reduce defects.

Supply chain optimization: By analyzing data from suppliers, you can identify inefficiencies and optimize the supply chain to reduce costs and improve delivery times.

Process optimization: By analyzing production data, you can identify bottlenecks and optimize processes to increase efficiency and reduce costs.

Customer insights: By analyzing data on customer preferences and behaviors, you can improve product design and marketing strategies to better meet customer needs.

Data analytics is a powerful tool that can help you improve operations and gain a competitive edge in the marketplace.

Digital Twin

A digital twin is a virtual model or digital copy created to accurately represent a physical object, process, service, or environment. Physical devices are outfitted with sensors used to gather data on desired functionality and performance. This data is then mathematically derived and transferred to the digital model. In turn, the digital model is used to simulate the real-world subject, collecting data used to study performance. Resulting analyses from the simulation can be used to improve or optimize the object, process, service, or environmental performance. A digital twin differs from a simulation in that it creates a rich virtual environment consisting of multiple simulations and interactive information that replicate a physical system's various processes for study from real-time data. Simulations typically focus on only one process without the benefit of real-time data. In essence, a digital twin is a computer program that simulates outcomes to predict real-world performance. These computer programs (digital twins) can then be used in concert to facilitate artificial intelligence and machine learning to improve operational performance.

As stated, a digital twin works to digitally model and simulate an object or system's real-world functionality, features, and behavior in a virtual environment. It's a virtual copy of the physical asset. The digital twin is a statistical model that uses cause and effect data to improve its accuracy over time. It's built with a human and data interface so it can be used by engineers to collect data and validate product performance before physical prototyping occurs.

There are two types of digital twin models, a statistical model and a learning model. The statistical model uses data from spreadsheets, databases, and the cloud to generate output. A learning model uses an algorithm to analyze data for patterns and trends to make decisions and predict results. Once built, these models are continuously run in an application, improving themselves over time. The application is connected to external systems through application programming interfaces (APIs) linked to external system libraries. The digital twin is the foundation of virtualization, digitally transforming the physical state to a digital format. However, we must rely on the Internet of Things to provide much of the data needed to make this a reality. Three-dimensional (3D) modeling, used to create a digital replica of a physical object, is an example of a digital twin recreating a physical object in the digital world.

In manufacturing, a digital twin is typically used to create a virtual model of a physical product, machine, or production line. It can be used to create a virtual prototype of a product before it is physically produced. This allows designers to test and refine the product design in a virtual environment, reducing the need for physical prototypes and shortening the design cycle. By creating a digital twin of a production line, manufacturers can simulate different scenarios and identify bottlenecks, inefficiencies, and opportunities for optimization. This can lead to improved productivity, reduced downtime, and lower costs.

In the case of predictive maintenance, the performance of a physical system can be monitored in real-time and compared to the digital twin, allowing engineers and technicians to detect and predict maintenance needs before they become critical. This can prevent unplanned downtime, reduce maintenance costs, and extend the lifespan of equipment.

A digital twin can also be used to simulate the production process and test the quality of a product before it is physically produced. This can help manufacturers identify potential quality issues and take corrective action before the product is released to market. Overall, digital twins offer manufacturers a powerful tool for improving product design, production efficiency, and quality control. By creating a virtual representation of physical systems, manufacturers can test and optimize their operations in a safe, cost-effective, and agile way.

Blockchain

Blockchain, also known as distributed ledger technology (DLT), originally came about as a technology to enable cryptocurrency or Bitcoin to be specific. It was used to validated and secure transactions by linking the Bitcoin owner's various transactions and storing each transaction in a block of data in sequence (or a chain) where each new block is dependent on the previous block. In doing so, it's able to keep account of the owner's total cryptocurrency value. Generally speaking, blockchain is a decentralized public digital ledger (distributed database) of transactions duplicated and distributed across a network of computer systems in a way that prevents altercation without the alignment of all subsequent (individual) blocks and network consensus. Information is separated and stored on a "chain" of interconnected blocks. The blocks of information must be aligned with the appropriate permission to be understood. Blockchain allows the sharing of information among entities (individuals) that have access to a common ledger. This decentralized approach (no network central point) to information sharing makes for a very secure and tamper-proof network. As an example, blockchain technology can be used for the secure tracking of digital information within a network.

Unlike traditional databases that use authentication to permit specific rights, distributed ledgers use a consensus approach to enable permissions. This method ensures that only transactions allowed by predetermined rules can be processed and that a transaction is associated with a specific individual. Distributed legers can ensure that an internet transaction is authentic and associated with a specific person while making manipulation of transactions nearly impossible. Distributed ledger technology has been used in many digital transactions occurring on the internet especially when complex rules can be codified into the blockchain database. The distributed ledger technology behind blockchain presents a way to store all types of data in a more secure and validated manner than traditional means. In essence, it eliminates the need to trust people.

In the context of digital transformation, blockchain technology offers several benefits that can help organizations streamline their operations and achieve greater efficiency. One of the key benefits of blockchain technology is its ability to create a secure and immutable record of transactions. This can be particularly valuable in industries where transparency and accountability are critical, such as finance, supply chain management, and healthcare. By using blockchain, organizations can ensure that every transaction is recorded and verified by multiple parties, making it virtually impossible to tamper with or alter the data. Another advantage of blockchain is its potential to reduce costs and increase efficiency. By eliminating intermediaries and automating processes, blockchain can help organizations streamline their operations and reduce the time and resources required to complete transactions. This can lead to significant cost savings and faster transaction times, which can be especially valuable in industries where speed and agility are essential. Finally, blockchain can also facilitate new business models and revenue streams by enabling organizations to create and exchange digital assets, such as cryptocurrencies or digital tokens. This can open new opportunities for organizations to monetize their products and services or to create entirely new markets and ecosystems.

Applications or "Apps"

Applications, commonly known as "apps," have played a significant role in the digital revolution. They have transformed the way we interact with technology and the world around us. Apps are software programs that are designed to run on mobile devices, such as smartphones and tablets. They can be downloaded from app stores, such as the Apple App Store and Google Play, and provide users with a variety of features and functionalities, including communication, entertainment, education, and productivity. Apps have contributed to the digital revolution in several ways. First, they have enabled people to access information and services more easily and efficiently. With apps, people can perform a variety of tasks from their mobile devices, such as ordering food, booking travel, and managing finances.

In manufacturing, apps are used to streamline production planning and scheduling by optimizing resource allocation, production sequence, and capacity planning. They help in monitoring and scheduling manufacturing processes, as well as minimizing downtime and reducing inventory costs. They have also been used to ensure quality control by monitoring and analyzing product quality data in real-time. These apps can identify quality problems early, allowing manufacturers to take corrective action before an issue becomes more significant.

Where inventory management is concerned, apps are used to manage inventory by tracking stock levels, monitoring stock movements, and automating reorder processes. This allows manufacturers to optimize inventory levels, reduce stockouts, and improve supply chain efficiency. In the case of maintenance management, apps are used to manage equipment maintenance schedules, track maintenance activities, and automate maintenance requests. This helps manufacturers reduce equipment downtime, minimize maintenance costs, and improve asset utilization.

Finally, apps are used in remote monitoring to monitor production processes and equipment remotely. This allows manufacturers to track performance in real-time and make adjustments as necessary, reducing the need for on-site personnel and improving overall efficiency. As technology continues to evolve, we can expect that apps will play an even more significant role in the future of manufacturing.

Cloud Computing

Cloud computing is the on-demand delivery of IT resources over the internet. It is an alternative to maintaining physical data centers and servers at on-site company locations. Technology services, such as computing power, storage, and databases, can be accessed wirelessly via the web, allowing the sharing of data with greater flexibility and typically lower costs than traditional on-premises alternatives. Cloud computing can be used to quickly upload large amounts of data for analysis and provide feedback for real-time problem solving and proactive decision-making.

Cloud computing services are usually provided by third-party vendors, who maintain and manage the underlying infrastructure, including servers, storage, networking, and data centers. This allows businesses and individuals to access powerful computing resources without having to invest in expensive hardware or infrastructure. Cloud computing provides several benefits to the manufacturing industry, including eliminating the need for companies to invest in expensive hardware and software systems. Instead, manufacturers can pay for computing resources, on a subscription basis, which can help reduce upfront capital expenses and ongoing maintenance costs. Cloud computing can also enable manufacturers to quickly scale their computing resources up or down to meet changing demand. This is particularly useful for organizations who experience seasonal fluctuations in demand or need to rapidly expand or contract their operations.

Cloud computing allows manufacturers to automate and streamline many of their business processes, from supply chain management to inventory tracking to production scheduling. It also can provide real-time access to data from across manufacturing operations, allowing individuals to quickly identify and respond to issues or opportunities. This can facilitate more informed decisions and improve overall performance. Another benefit is the ability to collaborate more easily with partners, suppliers, and customers, regardless of their location. This can help manufacturers reduce lead times and increase customer satisfaction. Lastly, cloud computing providers typically have robust security measures in place to protect against cyber threats and data breaches. Cloud-based systems are also easier to monitor and update, ensuring that consumers are always using the latest security protocols.

Wireless Connectivity

Wireless connectivity refers to the ability of devices to communicate with each other without the need for physical cables or wires. Instead of using wires, wireless technologies use radio waves, infrared signals, or other methods to transmit data between devices. It has enabled a wide range of devices to communicate with each other and access the internet without being physically connected to a network. Some of the most common forms of wireless connectivity include Wi-Fi, Bluetooth, cellular networks, and satellite communication.

Wi-Fi is a type of wireless connectivity that allows devices to connect to a local network and access the internet without the need for physical cables. Wi-Fi networks are typically used in homes, offices, and manufacturing facilities. Bluetooth is another type of wireless connectivity that is commonly used for short-range communication between devices. Bluetooth is often used for connecting smartphones to headphones or speakers, as well as for file transfers between devices. Cellular networks are used to provide wireless connectivity for mobile devices like smartphones and tablets. These networks use radio waves to transmit data between devices and allow users to access the internet and make phone calls from anywhere with network coverage. Satellite communication is used to provide wireless connectivity in remote areas where other types of networks are not available. Satellites orbiting the earth can provide internet access, phone service, and other forms of wireless connectivity to users in even the most remote locations.

Wireless connectivity plays a key role in modern manufacturing, enabling a wide range of applications and improving operational efficiency. It allows for the integration of various devices, machines, and sensors in the manufacturing environment, creating an interconnected network known as IIoT. IIoT enables real-time data collection, monitoring, and control of manufacturing processes, leading to improved operational visibility, predictive maintenance, and optimized production. It also enables machine-to-machine (M2M) communication where machines and equipment communicate with each other without the need for wired connections. This facilitates seamless collaboration, synchronization, and coordination between different machines, improving productivity. It also aids manufacturers in remote monitoring and control of equipment and processes. Through wireless sensors, data can be collected from machines, such as temperature, pressure, and vibration, allowing operators to monitor performance and detect anomalies in real-time. Remote control capabilities enable adjustments and interventions without physical presence, enhancing operational flexibility and reducing response times.

Radiofrequency identification (RFID) and global positioning system (GPS) are also wireless technologies that enable manufacturers to track and manage their assets efficiently. By tagging assets with wireless devices, manufacturers can locate and monitor the movement of raw materials, components, finished goods, and even tools within the manufacturing facility. This helps streamline logistics, inventory management, and supply chain operations. Wearable devices used in manufacturing also benefit from wireless connectivity by providing workers with real-time information and enhancing their safety and productivity. For example, smart glasses can provide workers with instructions, schematics, or augmented reality (AR) overlays, while wearable sensors can monitor vital signs, ergonomics, and exposure to hazardous conditions, improving safety and well-being.

Wireless connectivity enables communication and control of robots and automated systems in manufacturing environments. Through wireless networks, robots can receive instructions, exchange data, and coordinate their activities with other machines, enabling flexible and adaptive automation processes. Wireless connectivity also facilitates the use of mobile devices in manufacturing, such as smartphones and tablets, to access information, communicate, and perform tasks on the shop floor. Mobile applications can provide real-time production data, inventory updates, quality control information, and maintenance alerts, enabling workers to make informed decisions and collaborate effectively. In summary, wireless connectivity in manufacturing offers increased flexibility, improved efficiency, and enhanced data-driven decision-making, contributing to the advancement of smart factories and Industry 4.0 initiatives.

Big Data

Big data refers to the vast amounts of structured, semi-structured, and unstructured data generated by various sources such as sensors, machines, and human interactions. In the manufacturing industry, big data refers to the large amount of data generated from various processes such as production lines, quality control systems, supply chain management, and customer interactions. These datasets are typically so large and complex that traditional data processing methods are inadequate to handle them effectively. Big data is characterized by the "3 Vs":

- *Volume*: This topic involves massive amounts of data that are too large to be processed using traditional data processing tools and methods.
- *Velocity*: Data is generated and collected at an unprecedented speed, in real-time or near real-time, which poses significant challenges for data processing, storage, and analysis.
- *Variety*: Data comes in a wide variety of formats, including structured, semi-structured, and unstructured data, such as text, images, audio, and video files.

To effectively analyze and extract insights from big data, organizations typically use advanced technologies such as machine learning, artificial intelligence, and data analytic tools. Manufacturing industries have been collecting and analyzing data for decades, but the emergence of big data technologies has revolutionized the way they process and analyze this data. With big data, manufacturers can now collect and analyze data from a variety of sources, including production equipment, supply chain, logistics, and customer interactions. This data can be used to identify patterns, trends, and anomalies and to gain insights that can improve operational efficiency, reduce costs, and enhance product quality.

Some of the ways in which big data is used in manufacturing include predictive maintenance, supply chain optimization, demand forecasting, quality control, and real-time production monitoring. For example, predictive maintenance can help manufacturers identify potential issues in equipment before they occur, allowing for proactive maintenance and reduced downtime. Supply chain optimization can help manufacturers optimize inventory levels, reduce lead times, and improve delivery times, while demand forecasting can help manufacturers adjust production levels based on market demand. In short, big data has the potential to revolutionize the manufacturing industry by providing unprecedented insights and efficiencies that can lead to significant cost savings and improved product quality. See Figure 1.2.2 for the 3 Vs of big data.

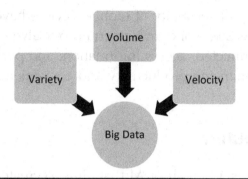

Figure 1.2.2   Big data 3 Vs.

Mobile Devices

Mobile devices are electronic devices that are designed to be portable and carried around easily. They typically have a small form factor and include smartphones, tablets, laptops, and wearables such as smartwatches and fitness trackers. Mobile devices are often equipped with wireless communication technologies such as cellular, Wi-Fi, Bluetooth, and GPS, allowing users to access the internet, communicate with others, and perform a wide range of tasks on the go. Mobile devices tend to be convenient and accessible, allowing users to stay connected and productive while on the move. The following are typical ways in which mobile devices are used in manufacturing.

- Track inventory levels, monitor stock movements, and record data related to inventory management.
- Monitor and measure the quality of products being manufactured, as well as performing inspections and collecting data related to quality control.
- Manage maintenance schedules, track equipment usage, and record maintenance data.
- Access manufacturing execution system (MES) software, allowing workers to input data, access work instructions, and track progress.
- Remotely monitor manufacturing processes, including equipment performance and product quality.
- Communicate between employees, including messaging, email, and video conferencing.
- Provide training to employees, including interactive training modules and virtual reality simulations.

The compact nature and versatility of mobile devices have revolutionized the way we communicate, work, and entertain ourselves. They have made it possible to stay connected, access information, and perform tasks from almost anywhere, enhancing productivity and convenience in our daily lives.

Cognitive Computing

Cognitive computing is a branch of AI that aims to create machines that can perform tasks that usually require human intelligence, such as understanding natural language, recognizing images, and making decisions based on complex data. Cognitive computing systems are designed to work with unstructured data, such as text, audio, and video, and can learn and adapt to new information over time. These systems use a combination of machine learning algorithms, natural language processing, computer vision, and knowledge representation to simulate human-like thinking processes. The goal of cognitive computing is to create machines that can augment human intelligence, making it easier for people to interact with and make sense of vast amounts of data.

Cognitive computing can be applied in various ways within the manufacturing industry to improve efficiency, productivity, and decision-making. Cognitive computing systems can analyze vast amounts of sensor data, images, and historical production records to identify patterns and anomalies in the manufacturing process. By continuously monitoring the production line, these systems can detect defects, predict potential quality issues, and trigger alerts for immediate action. In the discipline of predictive maintenance, cognitive computing can analyze sensor data from equipment and machinery to identify patterns indicative of potential failures or maintenance needs. By predicting maintenance requirements in advance, manufacturers can avoid unplanned downtime, optimize maintenance schedules, and reduce costs.

In the area of supply chains, cognitive computing can help optimize operations by analyzing large volumes of data related to demand, inventory levels, logistics, and supplier performance. Through the identification of patterns, demand forecasts, and potential bottlenecks, manufacturers can make informed decisions, reduce lead times, minimize stockouts, and improve supply chain efficiency.

Cognitive computing can analyze data from various sources, such as real-time production, historical records, and external factors like weather and market conditions, to optimize manufacturing processes. Cognitive computing systems can also assist in product design and development by analyzing vast amounts of data, including customer feedback, market trends, and historical performance data. These systems can generate insights, recommend design improvements, and support simulating and optimizing product performance before physical prototyping.

Collaboration between humans and machines on the shop floor is critical. By leveraging natural language processing and computer vision, workers can interact with cognitive systems using voice commands or gestures, receiving real-time instructions, guidance, or troubleshooting support. When the need for decision-making arises, cognitive computing systems can provide real-time insights and decision support to manufacturing managers. Through data integration from various sources and advanced analytics, these systems can assist in optimizing production schedules, resource allocation, and capacity planning.

Cybersecurity

Data protection and privacy are vital in the age of digital transformation. The sharing of information over the internet and among business partners creates vulnerabilities that need to be understood and addressed. Data also needs to be protected from accidental mismanagement and deliberate hacking. Cybersecurity is the practice of protecting computer systems, networks, and sensitive information from unauthorized access, theft, damage, or any other malicious activity. It involves a range of technologies, processes, and practices designed to safeguard computer networks, devices, and data from cyber threats.

Cybersecurity is critical in manufacturing because modern manufacturing operations rely heavily on computer systems and connected devices, such as robotics, sensors, and other IoT equipment. These systems and devices are often interconnected and communicate with each other through networks, which can make them vulnerable to cyber-attacks. A cybersecurity breach in a manufacturing environment can result in various consequences, including production downtime, which can lead to lost revenue and customer dissatisfaction. It can also damage a manufacture's reputation, which can lead to a loss of customer trust and ultimately impact their bottom line.

Manufacturers often have valuable intellectual property that could be compromised in a cyber-attack, leading to a loss of competitive advantage.

Cyber-attacks on manufacturing systems could result in safety risks, such as the manipulation of equipment or machines that could lead to physical harm to workers or damage to equipment. Manufacturers are part of complex supply chains that are often highly interconnected. A breach of data on one manufacturer could spread to other companies within the supply chain, leading to a disruption in production and delivery.

Clearly, it's important for manufacturers to implement robust cybersecurity measures to protect their operations, intellectual property, and reputation. These measures may include implementing firewalls and intrusion detection systems, regularly updating software and firmware, performing regular security assessments, training employees on cybersecurity best practices, and establishing incident response plans to address cybersecurity incidents. By prioritizing cybersecurity, manufacturers can mitigate the risks associated with cyber-attacks and ensure the safety, reliability, and continuity of their operations. In turn, cybersecurity activities need to be considered as part of the organization's budgeting process to warrant adequate systems and protections are in place at all times.

Key Points

- The application of digital technology will allow manufacturing companies to reduce the time and cost of product research and development while helping to satisfy unique customer requirements.
- Machine learning gets better with more data.
- Predictive maintenance will help to avoid unexpected downtime events contributing to underperformance.
- A digital twin is a virtual model of a physical object. The physical object is a construct of atoms while the digital model is composed of bits and bytes.
- A digital twin can be used to virtually represent a process or physical object and simulate real-world performance leading to improvements in process control and productivity.
- Blockchain technology can be a powerful tool for digital transformation, offering secure, transparent, and efficient transactions that can drive innovation, reduce costs, and create new business opportunities.
- Cloud computing can help manufacturers become more agile, efficient, and competitive in an increasingly complex and dynamic marketplace.

■ Cognitive computing represents an exciting area of research and development in AI, and it has the potential to revolutionize the way we interact with technology and solve complex problems.

Key Points – Internet of Things (IoT)

■ The IoT can be described as a network of connected devices, enabling the gathering of report information while being wirelessly controlled.
■ IoT sensors are hardware devices that collect data to detect changes in an environment or operating condition.
■ The IoT is composed of devices, machines, and processes that are connected through a system network that can share data and information with other machines and people.

Key Points – Smart Factory

■ Smart factories strive to reduce manual handling through the application of automation.
■ Smart factories can provide actionable data for predictive and preventive maintenance.
■ A smart factory can be broadly summarized into three areas, data acquisition, data analysis, and intelligent factory automation and learning.

Key Points – Artificial Intelligence

■ One of the defining characteristics of the industrial revolution is the advancement of AI.
■ AI is essentially a set of instructions or algorithm used to describe a process executed under certain conditions.
■ AI has been defined as "the capability of a machine to imitate intelligent human behavior."
■ Artificial intelligence, through the activity of machine learning, enables computer systems to perform human tasks such as visual perception, speech recognition, and decision-making.
■ Artificial intelligence and machine learning are used to drive automated processes that improve over time.

Key Points – Data Analytics

- Data analytics is used to provide insights into how a process is performing. Data is analyzed for patterns and trends that are used to predict machine and process behavior, solve problems, and optimize processes.
- Data analytics uses tools and statistical techniques to analyze data for patterns and trends that can be used for problem-solving, decision-making, and productivity improvement.
- Data analytics uses various tools and techniques to help people analyze raw data for actionable information.

Chapter 1.3

Digital Transformation

Overview

In its purest form, the term "digital" is the expression of signals or data as a series of digits 0 and 1. It's typically associated with technology or more specifically with computer technology. Transformation is defined as "a thorough or dramatic change in form, appearance, or function." Digital transformation in manufacturing refers to the integration of digital technologies, such as automation, artificial intelligence, and the Internet of Things (IoT), into the manufacturing process to improve efficiency, productivity, and competitiveness. It involves the use of advanced technologies to connect machines, products, and people to create a more connected and intelligent manufacturing environment. Digital transformation can encompass various aspects of manufacturing, including product design, supply chain management, production, and customer service. By leveraging data and analytics, digital transformation can enable manufacturers to optimize their operations, reduce costs, and improve quality, speed, and flexibility. It can also enable manufacturers to create new business models and revenue streams by leveraging digital technologies to offer new services and products.

Digital transformation is the progressive integration of digital technology into manufacturing processes to increase operational efficiency and the customer experience. A digital transformation of this type usually starts with system operations, as evident through the creation of digital procedures and data reports. System digitalization is often followed by automation of simple operational tasks such as temperature controllers and smart security systems. As companies mature, automation is extended to manufacturing robots, robotic process automation (RPA), and AGVs.

DOI: 10.4324/9781032688152-4

Digital transformation in manufacturing can bring significant benefits, such as increased productivity, improved quality, reduced costs, and enhanced customer satisfaction. However, it also requires careful planning and implementation to ensure that the technology is effectively integrated into the existing manufacturing process and that employees are trained to use it properly. The goal of digital transformation in manufacturing is to leverage technology to streamline operations, increase efficiency, and improve the overall performance of the manufacturing process. See Figure 1.3.1.

Physical versus Digital World

Smart technology is rooted in software-based products programmed to gather data from hardware such as sensors and other devices that are connected by a network. The network is composed of various external system elements such as data services, blockchain, analytics, and business systems linked to the digital twin. The digital twin is the conduit that links the physical hardware such as sensors collecting data from the environment with the digital world constructed as a virtual model. Let's compare the digital twin to its physical world counterpart.

The physical world refers to the tangible, material objects and spaces that exist in the world around us. It includes everything we can see, touch, and interact with in the physical realm, such as buildings, trees, mountains, oceans, animals, and people. On the other hand, the digital world refers to the intangible, virtual realm that exists within computers and other digital devices. It includes all digital information, such as software, data, files, and media, as well as the networks and communication channels that connect them. The digital world is created and controlled by humans and is not subject to the same physical laws as the physical world.

The physical and digital worlds are becoming increasingly interconnected, with digital technology permeating every aspect of modern life. For

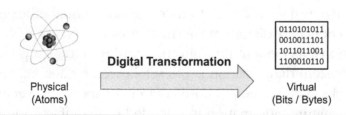

Figure 1.3.1   Digital transformation.

example, we use digital devices like smartphones, laptops, and tablets to connect with people, access information, and perform tasks in the physical world. While the physical world is finite and subject to natural limitations, the digital world is infinitely expandable and malleable. It allows for the creation of new realities, experiences, and interactions that would not be possible in the physical world. However, the digital world also poses its own challenges, such as the risk of cyber-attacks, data breaches, and online harassment.

As indicated, a digital twin is a virtual representation or a digital counterpart of a physical object, system, or process. Its purpose is to mimic and simulate the behavior, characteristics, and performance of the physical counterpart in real-time or near-real-time. To connect a digital twin to the physical world, several technologies and methods are used depending on the specific application.

Sensors embedded in the physical object or system collect real-time data about its various parameters such as temperature, pressure, motion, vibration, and more. These sensors are connected to the digital twin, allowing it to receive and process the data in order to mirror the real-world conditions. Data from various sources such as enterprise systems, databases, historical records, and external feeds can be integrated into the digital twin. This aggregated data provides a comprehensive view of the physical object or system, enhancing the accuracy and fidelity of the digital twin.

Digital twins often use standard communication protocols to exchange data between the physical object and the digital twin. These protocols enable seamless data transfer and synchronization between the two. In some cases, the digital twin can be connected to the control systems that operate the physical object. This enables the digital twin to influence and control the behavior of the physical counterpart, allowing for optimization, predictive maintenance, and testing of different scenarios without directly affecting the physical system.

Augmented reality (AR) and virtual reality (VR) technologies can be utilized to visualize and interact with the digital twin in the context of the physical environment. This enables users to overlay the digital representation onto the physical object, providing an immersive and interactive experience for monitoring, analysis, and maintenance purposes. By connecting to the physical world through these methods, the digital twin can continuously receive data, monitor and analyze the behavior of the physical counterpart, and provide insights, predictions, and simulations to optimize performance, improve efficiency, and support decision-making processes.

Smart Factory

A smart factory is a highly automated and digitized manufacturing facility that utilizes advanced technologies such as industrial robots, AGVs, digital twins, sensors, machine learning algorithms, and virtual and augmented reality to optimize production processes and increase efficiency. These technologies enable machines, equipment, and systems to communicate with each other, analyze data in real-time, and make intelligent decisions without human intervention. In a smart factory, machines and production processes are interconnected and can adapt to changing conditions to optimize production and improve product quality. This level of automation and digitization enables the factory to be more flexible, scalable, and efficient, reducing costs and increasing productivity.

Realizing a smart factory involves integrating advanced technologies and automation to optimize manufacturing processes and improve efficiency. The following is a roadmap to a smarter factory.

Define your objectives: Clearly identify your goals and objectives for implementing a smart factory. Determine the areas where you want to improve efficiency, reduce costs, enhance quality, or increase productivity.

Develop a digitalization strategy: Assess your existing processes and infrastructure, then create a strategy to digitize and automate various aspects of your factory operations. This may include deploying technologies such as IoT, robotics, AI, big data analytics, cloud computing, and other relevant technologies.

Collect and analyze data: Implement sensors and data collection devices throughout your factory floor to gather data on various parameters, including production output, machine performance, energy consumption, quality metrics, and more. Analyze this data using advanced analytics tools to gain insights and make data-driven decisions.

Implement automation and robotics: Integrate automation and robotics into your production processes to streamline operations, reduce manual labor, and improve efficiency. This can involve using robots for material handling, assembly, quality control, and other tasks. Collaborative robots (cobots) can work alongside humans, enhancing productivity and safety.

Enable connectivity and communication: Establish a robust and secure network infrastructure to connect various devices, machines, and systems within your factory. This enables real-time data exchange, remote monitoring, and control. Implement protocols and standards such as Industrial Internet of Things (IIoT), Message Queuing Telemetry Transport (MQTT), Representational State Transfer (REST), or OPC Unified Architecture (OPC UA) to facilitate seamless communication.

Implement predictive maintenance: Utilize data analytics and machine learning algorithms to predict machine failures and maintenance requirements. By monitoring equipment performance and analyzing historical data, you can identify patterns that indicate potential failures, allowing you to schedule maintenance proactively, minimizing downtime and optimizing maintenance costs.

Embrace digital twin technology: Develop digital twins, which are virtual replicas of physical assets or processes. Digital twins allow you to simulate and optimize operations, test new processes, and perform predictive analysis. They provide valuable insights for process improvement, optimization, and innovation.

Ensure cybersecurity: As you connect more devices and systems, it becomes crucial to prioritize cybersecurity. Implement robust security measures to protect your factory from cyber threats and unauthorized access. This includes firewalls, encryption, access controls, regular security audits, and employee training on cybersecurity best practices.

Foster a culture of continuous improvement: Encourage employees to adapt to new technologies and processes by providing training and education. Emphasize the importance of continuous improvement and innovation within your organization. Establish cross-functional teams to explore new technologies and identify areas for optimization.

Monitor and optimize performance: Continuously monitor key performance indicators (KPIs) to evaluate the success of your smart factory initiatives. Analyze data and identify areas where further improvements can be made. Use the insights gained to optimize processes, enhance productivity, and achieve your defined objectives.

Remember, running a smart factory is an ongoing process of innovation and adaptation. It requires a combination of technology implementation, process optimization, and employee engagement to drive continuous improvement and stay ahead in the rapidly evolving manufacturing landscape. There are several drawbacks to a smart factory including complexity associated with technology, the cost of a digital transformation, maintaining data security, and the changing requirements of the manufacturing workforce. For more information, see Side Bar: What Makes a Smart Factory Smart.

Remote Expert

A remote expert in manufacturing is a professional who provides technical guidance, troubleshooting, and support to manufacturing operations remotely, usually through a digital platform. With the advancement of technology, it has become possible to connect experts with manufacturing teams across the globe without the need for physical presence. Remote experts can assist with a wide range of manufacturing issues, such as equipment breakdowns, process optimization, and quality control.

Remote experts typically use digital communication tools such as video conferencing, AR, VR, or other remote access technologies to collaborate with on-site personnel. They can view real-time data from machines and equipment, provide instructions, and offer guidance on how to perform maintenance, diagnose problems, and fix issues. They can also remotely monitor the performance of equipment and provide feedback to improve efficiency and quality. By providing remote support, experts can diagnose issues and provide guidance without having to physically travel to the site, saving time and money.

Access to remote experts can benefit organizations that may need immediate assistance to solve problems without having the time to wait for on-site support. Availability of remote expert capability can also facilitate collaboration of team members working in different locations and time zones. Real-time collaboration of this type can help reduce downtime and unplanned business disruptions. The use of remote experts in manufacturing is a valuable tool for companies looking to streamline their operations and maintain a competitive edge in today's global marketplace, regardless of their location.

Augmented and Virtual Reality

AR and VR are two related but distinct technologies that offer immersive experiences to users. AR is a technology that overlays computer-generated digital content onto the real world, typically through the use of a mobile device's camera and screen or a wearable device like smart glasses. The digital content can include text, images, videos, 3D models, and animations, and it appears to the user as if it is part of the real world. AR is commonly used in mobile apps and games, marketing and advertising, education, and training. VR, on the other hand, is a technology that creates a completely immersive digital environment that replaces the real world. VR typically involves the use of a headset or a similar device that covers the user's eyes and ears, and sometimes includes gloves or other controllers for hand tracking and interaction. VR environments can be interactive, allowing users to move around and manipulate objects in the virtual world, and can be used for gaming, simulation, education, and training.

AR and VR are both increasingly being used in manufacturing to improve efficiency, reduce costs, and enhance safety. AR and VR can be used to train employees on equipment and procedures in a safe and controlled environment. This can reduce the risk of accidents and improve learning outcomes. AR can guide technicians through complex maintenance procedures, providing step-by-step instructions and visual aids. Workers can be given a simulated environment where they practice assembling and disassembling equipment without the risk of damaging expensive machinery or hurting themselves. This can reduce downtime and improve the accuracy of repairs.

AR/VR is used to design and prototype new products and parts. Engineers use AR/VR to visualize 3D models of products and parts and make changes in real-time. This can reduce the time and cost of producing physical prototypes. It's also been used to train workers on safety procedures and protocols. Workers can be given a simulated environment where they practice safety drills and emergency procedures, which help to improve their response time and reduce the risk of accidents. Finally, AR and VR have facilitated remote collaboration between teams working on different parts of a manufacturing process. This can reduce travel costs and improve communication. AR and VR are both rapidly evolving technologies with a wide range of applications within manufacturing operations.

Mixed Reality

Mixed reality (MR) is a technology that blends the physical world with the virtual world, creating a hybrid environment where digital content and real-world elements coexist and interact in real-time. It combines elements of both VR and AR to provide users with immersive experiences that integrate virtual objects and information seamlessly into their physical surroundings.

In mixed reality, users typically wear a head-mounted display (HMD) or use a device like smart glasses to perceive the digital content overlaid onto the real world. The technology tracks the user's movements and adjusts the virtual content, allowing for a dynamic and interactive experience.

One of the key features of mixed reality is spatial mapping, which involves mapping the physical environment in real-time. This enables the system to understand the user's surroundings, including the dimensions and geometry of objects, surfaces, and spatial relationships. By doing so, virtual objects can be precisely positioned and anchored within the real world, giving users the perception that they exist and interact with physical objects.

Mixed reality applications can range from gaming and entertainment to education, training, design, and collaboration. For example, in gaming, users can engage in immersive experiences where virtual objects and characters appear as if they are present in their physical environment. In education and training, mixed reality can be used to simulate real-world scenarios, allowing users to practice skills in a safe and controlled environment.

Mixed reality technology relies on various components such as cameras, sensors, depth-sensing technologies, and powerful computing devices to capture and process real-time data, interpret the user's actions, and generate appropriate virtual content. These components work together to create a convincing and interactive mixed reality experience.

It's important to note that the term "mixed reality" is often used interchangeably with "extended reality" (XR), which is an umbrella term that encompasses virtual reality, augmented reality, and mixed reality. XR is used to describe the spectrum of experiences that combine real and virtual elements, allowing users to interact with both worlds. Let's overview XR next.

Extended Reality

Extended Reality (XR) is a term that encompasses various technologies that merge the physical and virtual worlds to create immersive and interactive experiences. It combines VR, AR, and MR to offer users a more comprehensive and engaging digital environment. Extended reality takes these technologies a step further by integrating them into a cohesive framework. It aims to create seamless transitions between virtual, augmented, and mixed reality experiences, allowing users to move fluidly between different environments and interactive modes.

The applications of XR are wide-ranging and diverse. It is used in fields such as gaming, entertainment, education, healthcare, architecture, manufacturing, and more. In manufacturing, XR enables manufacturers to visualize and iterate product designs in virtual environments. Designers can create 3D models and examine them in VR, making it easier to identify potential flaws or improvement opportunities before physical production. This reduces costs and accelerates the prototyping phase.

XR provides immersive and interactive training experiences for manufacturing employees. With AR or VR headsets, workers can simulate complex procedures, such as assembly or machine operation, in a safe virtual environment. This improves training effectiveness, reduces risks, and enhances worker competence. XR can guide workers through assembly and maintenance processes by overlaying step-by-step instructions onto the physical workspace using AR. This helps reduce errors, speeds up the process, and enables less experienced workers to perform complex tasks with greater accuracy.

XR technologies can assist in quality control and inspection processes. AR overlays virtual information onto real-world objects, enabling inspectors to visualize specifications, compare physical objects to digital models, and highlight defects or inconsistencies more effectively. This enhances accuracy and efficiency in the inspection process.

XR can facilitate remote collaboration among geographically dispersed teams. With VR or AR, experts can virtually join a manufacturing facility and provide real-time guidance and support to on-site workers. This is particularly beneficial for troubleshooting, complex problem solving, and knowledge sharing across different locations. XR can also transform complex manufacturing data into visual representations, allowing operators and decision-makers to understand information more intuitively. For example, MR visualizations can show real-time production metrics, equipment status, or supply chain information overlaid onto physical factory floors, enabling better decision-making and process optimization.

XR interfaces can enable intuitive interactions between humans and machines. For instance, using gestures or voice commands, workers can control robotic systems, access information, or perform tasks more efficiently. XR interfaces can also provide real-time data feedback, alerting operators to potential issues or helping them optimize machine performance. XR offers opportunities for immersive training simulations, collaborative virtual meetings, interactive storytelling, virtual tourism, medical visualization, and architectural prototyping, among many other possibilities.

As XR technologies continue to advance, we can expect even more sophisticated and realistic experiences that blur the boundaries between the physical and digital worlds, opening up new avenues for creativity, productivity, and human-computer interaction.

Artificial Intelligence

AI refers to the ability of machines to perform tasks that typically require human intelligence, such as visual perception, speech recognition, decision-making, and language translation. AI systems use algorithms and statistical models to analyze and learn from large amounts of data, and they can continuously improve their performance over time. There are several approaches to building AI systems, including rule-based systems, where the machine is programmed with a set of rules to follow; supervised learning, where the machine learns from labeled data; and unsupervised learning, where the machine identifies patterns and relationships in unlabeled data.

AI is becoming increasingly important in the manufacturing industry as it can help automate and optimize various manufacturing processes. AI technologies such as machine learning, computer vision, and natural language processing can be used to extract insights from large volumes of data generated by machines and sensors and to improve decision-making in the manufacturing process. Ways in which AI is being used in manufacturing include predictive maintenance where it can monitor machines and predict when they are likely to fail, allowing maintenance to be scheduled proactively rather than reactively. This can help reduce downtime and increase efficiency. AI is also used in quality control to analyze images of products and identify defects. This can help reduce the number of defective products that are produced and improve overall quality.

Supply chain uses AI to optimize supply chain management activities by predicting demand, identifying the most efficient routes for shipping, and optimizing inventory levels. This can help reduce costs and improve efficiency. In the area of process optimization, AI is used to analyze data from sensors and machines to reduce waste and improve productivity. A common application of AI is in the control of robots on the factory floor, allowing them to perform tasks more efficiently and accurately than humans. These robots can work alongside human operators, performing repetitive and dangerous tasks and freeing up human workers to focus on more complex and creative work. AI can be used many ways in manufacturing to enhance operational efficiency and performance.

Machine Learning

Machine learning uses data and algorithms to model or simulate human behavior and learning. It has evolved due to technological advances in data storage and computer processing power. Machine learning is a type of AI that involves training computer systems to learn from data, without being explicitly programmed. Algorithms are developed using statistical methods to detect patterns and trends in large datasets that can aid in problem-solving and decision-making. In manufacturing, machine learning is used to analyze data from various sources, such as sensors, machines, and production processes, in order to identify patterns and make predictions or recommendations.

There are several ways machine learning can be applied in manufacturing. One common application is predictive maintenance. By analyzing sensor data from machines and equipment, machine learning models can predict when maintenance is needed, allowing for proactive maintenance to be performed, reducing downtime and repair costs. Another application is in the discipline of quality control. Machine learning algorithms can analyze data from sensors and cameras to identify defects in products or equipment, allowing for real-time control and adjustments to be made. Machine learning can also be used for demand forecasting, helping manufacturers optimize production and inventory levels based on predicted demand. Additionally, machine learning can be used for supply chain optimization, allowing for more efficient and cost-effective production planning and scheduling.

Overall, machine learning has the potential to revolutionize manufacturing by improving efficiency, reducing costs, and increasing quality. However, successful implementation requires access to high-quality data, effective algorithms, and skilled personnel who can analyze and interpret the results.

Before leaving this chapter, consider reading the Side Bar – Digital Maturity Model. This will provide some insight into the various states of your organization's digital maturity.

Key Points

■ A digital transformation is about converting physical objects (atoms) to digital or virtual programs (bits and bytes).

■ The physical and digital worlds are two distinct but interconnected spheres that coexist in our modern society.

■ Digital transformation in manufacturing refers to the integration of digital technologies into various aspects of the manufacturing process, from design and production to supply chain management and customer service. Digital transformation should create value for the customer and business.

■ Value is created by describing machine data as a mathematical equation, optimizing that equation, and then using the resulting information to improve equipment's operational efficiency.

■ To deliver value in digital work, one must focus on collecting the right data and transforming it into the right information.

■ A smart factory is designed to create a more agile, responsive, and competitive manufacturing environment that can meet the demands of the modern market.

■ Smart factories can lower costs, reduce downtime, and minimize waste by continuously improving manufacturing productivity. Enhancing production capacities provides opportunities for growth without further investment or the need for physical resources.

■ New technologies like augmented, virtual, and mixed realities supplement how we can view and interact with the world. They help open the mind to a whole range of new opportunities.

■ A truly smart factory is one in which real-time data is acted on to alleviate problems and improve a process with little to no human input or intervention.

■ A remote expert is typically a subject matter expert that can provide assistance and guidance virtually using collaborative tools such as live video and smart glasses connected to the internet.

■ AI can help manufacturing companies increase efficiency, reduce costs, and improve quality, making them more competitive in the global marketplace.

■ There is a vast and complex set of activities around the idea of "deep learning" which is a form of machine learning that is exploring image, speech, and face recognition.

SIDE BAR: WHAT MAKES A SMART FACTORY SMART?

A smart factory is called "smart" because it employs advanced technologies such as IoT, AI, ML, and robotics to create an interconnected and automated manufacturing environment. These technologies enable the factory to operate more efficiently, effectively, and sustainably than traditional factories. Specific characteristics that make a smart factory "smart" are as follows.

Connectivity: Smart factories use IoT to connect machines, devices, and systems throughout the factory to enable communication and data exchange.

Automation: Smart factories use robotics and automation to handle tasks that are repetitive, dangerous, or require precision.

Data analytics: Smart factories collect data from sensors and other sources to monitor and analyze the manufacturing process, enabling continuous improvement and optimization.

Predictive maintenance: Smart factories use machine learning to predict when equipment is likely to fail, allowing for proactive maintenance and reducing downtime.

Real-time monitoring and control: Smart factories use sensors and other technologies to monitor and control the manufacturing process in real-time, enabling quick responses to issues and the ability to make adjustments on the fly.

Flexibility: Smart factories are designed to be adaptable and able to quickly respond to changing production needs.

Energy efficiency: Smart factories are designed to be energy-efficient, with systems and processes optimized to minimize energy consumption and waste.

By leveraging these and other advanced technologies, smart factories can improve efficiency, productivity, quality, and sustainability, making them key to the future of manufacturing.

SIDE BAR: DIGITAL MATURITY MODEL

A digital maturity model is a framework that assesses an organization's level of digital capabilities and provides a roadmap for its digital transformation journey. It helps organizations understand their current state of digital readiness and identifies areas for improvement to enhance their digital capabilities. The model typically consists of several levels or stages, each representing a specific level of digital maturity. The stages are presented as follows.

Ad hoc: At this initial stage, organizations have limited digital capabilities and operate in an ad hoc manner. There is a lack of clear digital strategy or consistent processes. Digital initiatives are often undertaken on a case-by-case basis with no overarching coordination. This level may be characterized by the following:

■ Basic digital presence, such as a website and email.
■ Minimal integration of digital technologies.
■ Limited awareness of the potential benefits of digital transformation.

Emerging: In the emerging stage, organizations start recognizing the importance of digital transformation. They begin exploring digital technologies and experimenting with digital initiatives. Some basic processes and strategies may be established, but they are not yet fully integrated into the overall business operations. This level can be characterized by:

■ Improved digital presence with better website functionality and user experience.
■ Basic utilization of digital marketing channels.
■ Beginning to explore digital technologies and their potential.

Defined: At this operational stage or level, organizations have developed a clear digital strategy and set defined goals for digital transformation. They have established processes, policies, and guidelines for digital initiatives. Basic digital infrastructure and technologies are in place, and there is a growing awareness of the importance of data-driven decision-making. This level can be characterized by:

■ Advanced digital presence and engagement across multiple channels (website, social media, mobile apps, etc.).
■ Integration of digital technologies within core business processes.
■ Data-driven decision-making and basic analytics capabilities.

Advanced: Organizations in the advanced (or strategic) stage have significantly integrated digital technologies into their operations. They have implemented advanced data analytics and automation tools, enabling them to gain insights and improve efficiency. Digital initiatives are aligned with business goals, and there is a focus on innovation and agility. This level can be characterized by:

■ Seamless omni-channel customer experience.
■ Advanced digital technologies like AI, IoT, or cloud computing are utilized.
■ Digital strategies are aligned with overall business strategies.
■ Advanced analytics and data-driven insights drive decision-making.

Optimized: The optimized (or innovative) stage represents organizations that have achieved a high level of digital maturity. They have fully integrated digital capabilities into all aspects of their operations, creating a digital-first culture. Continuous improvement and innovation are embedded in their DNA. They leverage emerging technologies and have a proactive approach to digital transformation. Characteristics of this stage include:

■ Continuous innovation and transformation through digital technologies.
■ Agile and adaptive organizational culture that embraces change.
■ Strong digital leadership and governance.
■ Proactive experimentation with emerging technologies and business models.

It's important to note that the specific stages and characteristics of a digital maturity model may vary depending on the framework used or the industry context. Organizations can use such a model to assess their current digital capabilities, identify gaps, and develop a roadmap for their digital transformation journey, ultimately aiming to reach higher levels of maturity and reap the benefits of digital innovation.

Chapter 1.4

Design for Manufacturing Mindset

Overview

As we enter the digital age of manufacturing, organizations need to think differently. They need to move beyond the traditional understanding of manufacturing and broaden their scope of responsibility and engagement with process design, fabrication, integration, and maintenance. Complexity in automation and increasing demands in product precision and accuracy have forced modern-day manufacturers to take a greater interest in how process planning, development, and deployment are managed.

To remain competitive now and in the future, the manufacturing mindset must consider the impact of equipment design and process integration on daily production, while looking to tailor these activities toward more flexible, scalable, reliable, and sustainable operations. The focus must extend to optimizing line layout design and deployment since the cost of building and maintaining equipment used on production lines will likely impact manufacturing footprint and product lifecycle costs. If the decision to design, build, and integrate equipment is left to an external contractor, the results may not fully satisfy operational expectations. Let's take a moment to consider some of the areas where changing traditional manufacturing thinking may be important for future growth and competitiveness. See Figure 1.4.1.

DOI: 10.4324/9781032688152-5

Figure 1.4.1 The new manufacturing mindset.

Manufacturing Agility

Agile manufacturing is a flexible and adaptive approach to production that emphasizes responsiveness to customer needs and changing market conditions. It involves the use of modern technologies, such as automation, robotics, and data analytics, to create a highly efficient and flexible manufacturing system that can quickly adjust to changes in demand, product design, and production processes. In contrast to traditional manufacturing methods that rely on large-scale, long-term production runs of a single product, agile manufacturing focuses on producing smaller batches of multiple products in shorter cycles, allowing for greater flexibility and responsiveness to changing market conditions. Key principles of agile manufacturing include customer focus, flexibility, collaboration, continuous improvement, and technology enabled.

The primary focus of agile manufacturing is meeting the needs and expectations of customers by producing high-quality products that meet their changing demands. Secondary to this is the ability to quickly adapt to changing customer demands and market conditions. This requires a flexible production system that can easily adjust production processes and capacity.

Collaboration between different functions and teams within the manufacturing organization is essential to agile manufacturing as this helps to ensure that production processes are aligned with customer needs and that everyone is working toward the same goal. Continuous improvement of processes and products, along with a heavy reliance on modern technologies such as automation, robotics, and data analytics, are two other key principles of agile manufacturing with a focus on increasing efficiency, waste reduction, quality improvement, and manufacturing flexibility.

Simplicity

Simplicity in the manufacturing process and equipment design refers to the degree to which the production process and equipment are easy to understand, operate, and maintain. This can be achieved through various means, such as reducing the number of steps required in the production process, minimizing the complexity of equipment design, and using standardized components and procedures.

Simplicity is important in manufacturing because it can lead to increased efficiency, reduced costs, and improved quality. By simplifying the production process and equipment design, manufacturers can reduce the risk of errors and defects, minimize downtime, and increase throughput. Simplicity in equipment design can also improve safety in the workplace. Complex equipment designs may require specialized training and safety protocols, while simpler designs can be more easily understood and operated by a wider range of workers.

Simplification can also be achieved by optimizing the design of manufacturing equipment. This may involve using standard components that are readily available, reducing the number of custom-designed components, and making the equipment more modular. The use of modular equipment design involves breaking down the manufacturing process into smaller, self-contained modules that can be easily combined or modified as needed. By using standardized modules, manufacturers can reduce the complexity of their equipment design, streamline production, and make it easier to maintain, repair, replace, and upgrade equipment.

Another way to achieve simplicity is by adopting lean manufacturing principles. This approach emphasizes the elimination of waste and the optimization of production processes. By focusing on reducing unnecessary steps and improving efficiency, manufacturers can simplify their processes and equipment design while maintaining high quality standards. See Side Bar: Lean Manufacturing Principles for more information on this topic.

Manufacturing Process Reliability

Manufacturing process reliability refers to the ability of a manufacturing process or system to consistently produce products that meet specified quality standards and are delivered on time. It involves minimizing the risk of failures, defects, delays, and downtime in the manufacturing process and ensuring that the products are manufactured to the required specifications, in the required quantities, and within the expected time frame. Manufacturing reliability can be achieved by implementing best practices in quality control, process optimization, equipment maintenance, and supply chain management, among other areas. It is essential for maintaining customer satisfaction, reducing waste, and improving overall efficiency and profitability in the manufacturing industry.

Manufacturing reliability can be achieved through various approaches, tools, and strategies. Some of the key actions that can help improve manufacturing reliability include:

- *Process standardization*: Standardizing the manufacturing process, including equipment, materials, and procedures, can help to reduce variability and improve consistency, making it easier to achieve reliable (consistent and predictable) outputs.
- *Establishing clear quality standards*: It's important to establish clear quality standards and performance criteria for the manufacturing process, including specifications for raw materials, product design, and testing requirements.
- *Process control*: Statistical process control (SPC) techniques can help monitor and control the manufacturing process to ensure that it operates within specified limits and targets. This can help identify and address sources of variability and reduce the occurrence of defects.
- *Six Sigma*: Six Sigma is a data-driven methodology that focuses on eliminating defects and reducing variability in the manufacturing process. It involves using statistical tools and techniques to measure, analyze, and improve key process metrics.

- *Root cause analysis*: Conduct root cause analysis to identify the underlying causes of defects and errors in the manufacturing process and implement corrective actions to address them.
- *Lean manufacturing*: Implement lean manufacturing principles such as just-in-time (JIT) inventory, continuous flow, and waste reduction to streamline the manufacturing process and minimize waste.
- *Maintenance and calibration*: Regularly maintain and calibrate equipment and tools used in the manufacturing process to ensure they function correctly and accurately.
- *Total quality management*: TQM is an approach that emphasizes continuous improvement and customer satisfaction. It involves all employees in the organization and focuses on identifying and eliminating waste, improving processes, and delivering high-quality products.
- *Predictive maintenance*: Predictive maintenance involves using data and analytics to predict equipment failure and maintenance needs before they occur. This can help minimize downtime, reduce costs, and improve reliability.
- *Investing in training and development*: It is important to invest in training and development programs to ensure that employees have the necessary knowledge, skills, and expertise to perform their jobs effectively, efficiently, and consistently.
- *Continuous improvement*: Adopting a continuous improvement mindset can help to identify opportunities for improvement in the manufacturing process and implement changes that increase reliability and quality over time.
- *Technology*: Utilizing advanced technologies such as automation, robotics, and data analytics can help streamline and optimize the manufacturing process, reducing the likelihood of errors and increasing reliability.
- *Supply chain management*: Effective supply chain management, including monitoring and managing suppliers, can help to ensure that the materials and components used in the manufacturing process meet the required quality standards and specifications.

By implementing these strategies and tools, among others, manufacturers can adopt a holistic approach that addresses each of these areas, allowing companies to increase their manufacturing reliability and produce high-quality products consistently over time.

Manufacturing Equipment Reliability

Manufacturing equipment reliability is important to maximizing productivity, minimizing costs, and ensuring consistent operational quality. Investing in reliable equipment and implementing effective maintenance and monitoring strategies is critical to achieving a successful manufacturing operation. Let's consider some key practices for doing so.

Regular maintenance of manufacturing equipment is necessary to ensure it is running at optimal performance. This includes cleaning, lubrication, and inspection of equipment components to identify and fix any issues before they lead to downtime or breakdowns. It's important to establish a maintenance schedule that includes routine inspections, cleaning, and replacement of worn or damaged parts. This can help identify potential problems before they become serious issues that could result in downtime.

The condition of equipment should be monitored on a regular basis. Condition monitoring involves observing the performance and health of manufacturing equipment in real-time to detect potential issues before they lead to failure. Sensors, data analytics, and other technologies can be used to monitor the condition of machines and detect any changes or anomalies that could indicate a problem. This helps to identify issues early and allow for repairs to be made before they result in breakdowns or failures.

Invest in high-quality materials and components that are designed to withstand the stresses of manufacturing processes. Using inferior materials can result in premature wear and damage to equipment, leading to downtime and increased maintenance costs. Quality assurance programs can also help identify and address any issues with the equipment and ensure it meets all necessary standards and specifications.

All personnel should be properly trained in the operation and maintenance of equipment. This can help prevent user error and safeguard that machines are used correctly, reducing the likelihood of breakdowns. Operators should also be trained on equipment safety procedures to prevent accidents.

Consider implementing an asset management system to help track and manage manufacturing equipment, including maintenance schedules, repair history, and equipment performance data. Don't forget to regularly review and analyze data on equipment performance to identify areas for improvement. This can help optimize performance and prevent future issues.

By implementing these strategies and best practices, manufacturing equipment reliability can be improved, leading to increased productivity, reduced downtime, and higher profitability.

Manufacturing Modularity

Modularity in manufacturing process design refers to the ability to design and manufacture equipment in a way that allows for easy customization and adaptation to different production needs. This can be achieved by breaking down equipment into individual modules, which can be assembled, disassembled, and reconfigured as needed to meet specific production requirements. The use of modular equipment has several advantages in manufacturing process design. For example, it allows for greater flexibility in the production process, as modules can be added or removed depending on changes in demand or product design. This can reduce the need for costly equipment upgrades or replacements, as well as minimizing downtime during maintenance or repairs.

Modularity also simplifies equipment design and manufacturing, as individual equipment modules can be mass-produced and standardized, reducing the need for custom-made components. This can result in lower costs, faster production times, and greater reliability and consistency in equipment performance. Another benefit of modular equipment is that it can be more easily integrated with other equipment or systems, as individual modules can be designed to interface with existing components or to meet specific requirements. This can improve overall production efficiency and reduce the risk of equipment failure or downtime. Equipment modularity is an important consideration in manufacturing process design, as it offers numerous benefits in terms of flexibility, efficiency, and cost-effectiveness. By designing equipment with modularity in mind, manufacturers can ensure that their operations remain competitive and adaptable in a rapidly changing market.

The following are several tips for improving the modularity of manufacturing equipment:

- Establish equipment standards.
- Use interchangeable parts.
- Minimize dependencies between equipment workstations.
- Use common components such as connectors, fasteners, and other mechanical devices.
- Standardize interfaces and connectors to ensure compatibility across different components.
- Implement a plug-and-play approach to make it easy for users to add or remove components without the need for complex configurations or adjustments.

- Use modular enclosures that can be easily modified or expanded to accommodate different components or configurations.
- Consider compatibility with existing systems to help ensure interoperability and make it easier to integrate new components into existing systems.

As market volatility increases, modular line concepts can help manufacturing teams quickly respond to changing conditions and requirements. For example, modularity can be triggered by volume increases, a change in product design, and the introduction of a new product variant. When upgrading or modifying a line due to customer demand, duplicating bottleneck equipment, adding new processes, and installing robots/cobots for automation are common activities. Modularity is also important when product volumes drop, during ramp-down, and at a product line's end of life. At this point, unneeded equipment can be removed to reflect current demand and reused while freeing-up floor space.

The most practical approach to modularity is dedicating one piece of equipment for every process. A multi-cell concept limits modularity and standardization, leading to more complexity, increased maintenance activities, and limited reuse potential. In addition to targeting one piece of equipment for each process, avoid connecting stations together or to an in-line conveyor system since this will limit modularity. Also avoid fastening equipment to the floor and consider installing quick connects for utilities.

The goal is to integrate new equipment or remove/replace a process station in less than one working day (last good part to first good part). Practically speaking, chaku-chaku systems are particularly advantageous for implementing highly flexible modular line designs. See Figure 1.4.2 for several assembly workstation material load/unload design variants.

Scalability

Scalable manufacturing refers to a manufacturing process or system that can be easily scaled up or down to meet changing demand or production requirements. The term "scalable" refers to the ability of a manufacturing process to adapt to changes in production volume without incurring significant additional costs or requiring major changes to the production process. In a scalable manufacturing system, production capacity can be increased

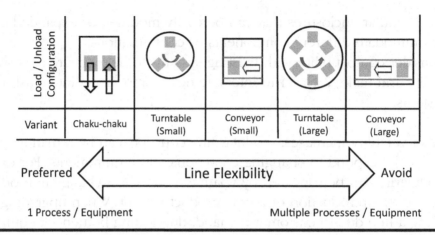

| Variant | Chaku-chaku | Turntable (Small) | Conveyor (Small) | Turntable (Large) | Conveyor (Large) |

Figure 1.4.2 Workstation load/unload design variants.

or decreased rapidly and efficiently, without compromising product quality or increasing costs per unit. This flexibility allows manufacturers to respond quickly to changes in market demand, without the need for major investments in new equipment or facilities.

Scalable manufacturing often involves the use of advanced automation and digital technologies, such as robotics, artificial intelligence, and IoT, to optimize production efficiency and reduce costs. It also relies on streamlined supply chain management, standardized production processes, and effective quality control measures to ensure consistent product quality and timely delivery.

A scalable line concept allows for adjustments to production capacity relative to changing customer demands. The objective is to create a phased approach to ramping up line volume capability based on actual demand. This can provide a significant financial advantage and minimize investment risk. Look to use as much existing equipment as possible as well as sharing equipment to utilize available capacity from other lines, especially in the early phases of production. When a unique process is required or no other good option exists, use dedicated production equipment accordingly. The number of operators used should reflect volume demands. If the line is not fully automated, start with one operator and increase the number in proportion to the increase in volume. Ensure a proper work balance as the number of operators changes.

In case of high market demand uncertainty or seasonal impacts, consider highly flexible and scalable concepts. In-line systems have scalability limitations. Also note that the less mature the technology and market, the more important it is to focus on flexibility and scalability in response to

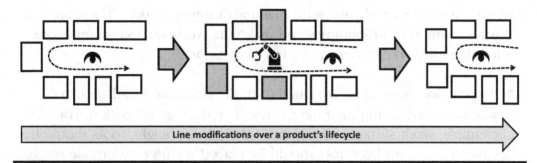

Figure 1.4.3   Example of scalability.

unexpected changes. Figure 1.4.3 visualizes a change in scalability throughout a product lifecycle.

Ergonomics

Ergonomics is the study of designing workspaces, tools, equipment, and tasks to fit the needs of the workers who use them. In manufacturing, ergonomics is important because it focuses on creating a safe and efficient work environment that promotes the health and well-being of workers, while also improving productivity and quality. Here are some specific reasons why ergonomics is important to manufacturing.

Ergonomics helps prevent workplace injuries and illnesses by reducing the physical strain on workers' bodies. By designing workstations and equipment that fit the worker's body size, height, and strength, manufacturing companies can minimize the risk of repetitive motion injuries, musculoskeletal disorders, and other workplace injuries. When workers are comfortable and not experiencing physical discomfort or pain, they can focus more on their work, leading to higher productivity levels. Ergonomic workstations and equipment also reduce the amount of time it takes to complete tasks, improving efficiency and throughput.

Ergonomics can improve the quality of the products being manufactured. For example, if a worker is less fatigued and can maintain better control over their movements, they are less likely to make mistakes or produce defective products. A comfortable and safe work environment can increase job satisfaction and reduce turnover rates. When workers feel valued and cared for, they tend to stay with the company and be more productive in their work.

Ergonomics is an essential part of the manufacturing process. By prioritizing worker safety, comfort, and well-being, companies can create a more efficient, productive, and successful manufacturing operation. There are several ways to improve ergonomics and make the workplace safer and more comfortable for workers. Here are a few suggestions:

■ Workstations should be designed to fit the needs and limitations of workers, considering their height, reach, and range of motion. For example, work surfaces should be at the proper height, tools should be easy to reach, and controls should be placed within comfortable reach.

■ Design tools and equipment to reduce the amount of force needed to operate them. This can include using ergonomic grips, minimizing the weight of tools, and reducing the need for repetitive motions.

■ Ensure workers are trained in proper ergonomic techniques, including lifting, bending, and reaching. They should also be encouraged to take regular breaks and stretch to prevent fatigue and injury.

■ Employers should regularly assess the ergonomics of workstations and tasks to identify potential problems and make necessary changes. This can be done through worker feedback, observation, and ergonomic assessments.

■ Rotate workers between different tasks to help reduce the risk of repetitive strain injuries and fatigue. This also helps prevent workers from becoming too specialized in one task, which can lead to physical strain over time.

■ Automation and robotics can reduce the need for workers to perform repetitive or physically demanding tasks.

■ Regularly monitor the work environment for potential ergonomic risks and make adjustments as necessary. This can include changing lighting, seating, temperature, or noise levels.

Implementing these strategies can aid manufacturing companies to improve ergonomics in the workplace, reduce the risk of injury and fatigue, and create a safer, more productive work environment.

Reusability

Reusability refers to the ability of a workstation or machine to be used again after it has fulfilled its initial purpose. This means that the process or equipment can be disassembled or separated from the system it is currently a part of and then reassembled or integrated into a new system or process.

Reusability is a desirable feature in manufacturing for several reasons. First, it can reduce the amount of waste generated by the production process, as components that would otherwise be discarded can be reused. Second, it can reduce the cost of manufacturing by reducing the need to produce new components, equipment, or workstations. Finally, it can also improve the efficiency and speed of production by allowing items to be easily swapped out or replaced as needed.

Reusability is also an important aspect of sustainable manufacturing, as it helps to reduce waste and conserve resources. By designing products and components that can be reused, manufacturers can reduce the amount of materials and energy needed to produce new products and minimize the environmental impact of their operations. To achieve reusability in manufacturing, designers and engineers need to carefully consider the materials, construction methods, and assembly processes used in the production of a product line or machine. They also need to ensure that the process or equipment is designed with modularization in mind, so that it can be easily disassembled and reassembled without causing damage or reducing performance. Reusability in manufacturing can be optimized in several ways.

One of the most effective ways to optimize reusability in manufacturing is to design products, processes, and components with reusability in mind. This involves using materials that can be easily disassembled and reused, designing components that can be easily removed and replaced, and minimizing the use of adhesives, fasteners, and other materials that make disassembly difficult or time consuming.

Standardizing components and processes can improve reusability by making it easier to swap out components or reuse parts across different processes. By using standardized parts and processes, manufacturers can reduce the number of unique pieces they need to employ, which can lead to cost savings and increased reusability.

Modular design involves breaking processes down into smaller, interchangeable modules that can be easily removed, replaced, or upgraded. This approach makes it simpler to reuse components, reduces waste, and can lead to faster process development and equipment integration times. In addition to modular design, proper maintenance of equipment and machinery is critical to ensuring that they last longer and can be reused. Regular maintenance helps to identify potential issues early on and address them before they become major problems.

Choosing materials that are durable and easy to clean and maintain is another crucial step toward optimizing reusability. The selection of materials should be based on their ability to withstand repeated use without degradation. Recycling materials that can't be reused can be an effective way to optimize reusability in manufacturing. By recycling materials, manufacturers can reduce the amount of waste they produce, save on raw material costs, and reduce their environmental impact. Recycling allows manufacturers to reclaim materials from old products and use them in the production of new products. This approach reduces waste and conserves natural resources.

Energy Efficiency

In a factory of the future, energy efficiency is a paramount consideration. The design and operation of such a factory should prioritize minimizing energy consumption and maximizing productivity while reducing environmental impact. In the following section, we will overview some key characteristics and practices that define energy efficiency in a factory of the future starting with smart building design.

A smart factory is designed with energy efficiency in mind, incorporating advanced building materials, insulation, and optimized layouts. The building may have features like natural lighting, efficient ventilation systems, and smart sensors to regulate energy usage based on occupancy and environmental conditions. The factory should leverage renewable energy sources to meet its power requirements. The application of solar panels, wind turbines, hydroelectric power, and other forms of clean energy generation should be employed to reduce reliance on fossil fuels and decrease greenhouse gas emissions.

Real-time energy monitoring systems can be deployed to track energy consumption throughout the factory, enabling proactive energy management. Data analytics and machine learning algorithms can analyze energy usage patterns and identify areas for optimization, allowing for continuous improvement in energy efficiency. Factories can also employ advanced, energy-efficient equipment and machinery. This includes state-of-the-art manufacturing technologies that minimize energy waste, such as intelligent robotics, energy-efficient motors, and variable speed drives. Equipment must be regularly maintained to ensure optimal performance and energy efficiency.

Waste heat produced during manufacturing processes can be captured and repurposed to heat water, generate electricity, or provide heating for other parts of the factory. By utilizing waste heat, the factory can reduce its overall energy demand and increase its overall efficiency. Energy-efficient lighting solutions like LED lights with occupancy sensors and daylight harvesting systems can be employed to minimize electricity usage for lighting. These systems automatically adjust lighting levels based on natural light availability and occupancy, reducing energy waste.

Advanced energy management systems can integrate all energy-related components, allowing for centralized control and optimization of energy usage. These systems enable load balancing, demand response, and energy storage integration, ensuring the most efficient use of available energy resources.

A smart factory fosters a culture of energy efficiency among its employees. Regular training programs and awareness campaigns can educate the workforce on energy-saving practices, encouraging them to actively participate in conserving energy and identifying improvement opportunities. Such a factory should also consider the environmental impact of its products throughout their entire lifecycle, from raw material extraction to disposal. This holistic approach helps identify areas for improvement, such as optimizing material usage, reducing waste generation, and enhancing energy efficiency during transportation and distribution.

In essence, a factory of the future is committed to ongoing research and development in energy-efficient technologies and processes. It collaborates with external partners, invests in innovation, and stays abreast of emerging trends to continually improve energy efficiency and sustainability. By implementing these energy-efficient practices, a factory of the future can achieve significant reductions in energy consumption, greenhouse gas emissions, and operating costs while maintaining high productivity levels and ensuring a sustainable future.

Sustainability

Sustainability in manufacturing refers to the development and implementation of processes and practices that reduce the negative environmental impact of manufacturing activities while maintaining or increasing productivity and profitability. Sustainable manufacturing aims to balance the needs of people, the planet, and profits, while creating products that meet customer demand. It involves a commitment to minimizing waste, reducing energy consumption, conserving natural resources, and adopting cleaner technologies throughout the manufacturing process.

Sustainability in manufacturing also involves considering the entire life-cycle of a product, from raw material extraction to disposal or recycling, and minimizing the environmental impact at every stage. Examples of sustainable manufacturing practices include using renewable energy sources such as wind and solar power, minimizing packaging and transportation waste, using eco-friendly materials and chemicals, implementing closed-loop systems to recycle and reuse materials, and using efficient manufacturing processes to reduce energy and water consumption.

Sustainable manufacturing is an essential component of creating a more sustainable future, and it requires a holistic approach that considers the social, economic, and environmental impacts of the manufacturing process. Adopting ecologically friendly manufacturing practices not only benefits the environment but also leads to cost savings and increased competitiveness by reducing waste and improving efficiency. It also helps companies satisfy regulatory requirements and meet the increasing demand from consumers for environmentally friendly products. Making the manufacturing process more sustainable involves taking measures to reduce the negative environmental impact of the production process. Here are some strategies that can be implemented:

- Adopt energy-efficient practices such as using renewable energy sources and installing energy-efficient equipment.
- Use raw materials more efficiently by reducing waste, recycling, and repurposing materials.
- Exercise water conservation practices such as recycling and reducing water waste.
- Implement recycling, waste reduction, and waste management systems.
- Reduce emissions by adopting cleaner production technologies and practices.
- Design products that are more sustainable by considering the entire life-cycle of the product, from raw material extraction to disposal.
- Work with your suppliers to ensure that they are using sustainable practices, such as reducing their carbon footprint and using sustainable materials.
- Provide training and awareness programs to employees about sustainability and encourage participation in eco-friendly practices.
- Embrace a circular economy approach which focuses on making the most of resources through recycling, repurposing, and reusing materials.
- Measure and report on your environmental impact to track progress and identify areas for improvement.

By implementing these strategies, you can make your manufacturing process more sustainable and reduce your environmental footprint.

Additive Manufacturing

Additive manufacturing, also known as 3D printing, has become increasingly popular in manufacturing due to its ability to rapidly create complex geometries and prototypes. The technology allows for the creation of parts and components by layering materials, such as plastics, metals, or ceramics, based on a digital design.

One of the key roles of 3D printing in manufacturing is the creation of custom parts and small-scale production runs. Traditional manufacturing methods, such as injection molding or computerized numerical control (CNC) machining, require expensive tooling and can be time-consuming for small orders or unique designs. 3D printing allows for the on-demand production of parts and components with minimal set-up time and cost.

In addition, 3D printing can be used to create molds for casting or injection molding, reducing the time and cost associated with traditional mold-making processes. This technology also enables the production of complex internal geometries, which are difficult or impossible to create using traditional methods.

Another important role of 3D printing in smart manufacturing is the creation of prototypes. 3D printing allows designers and engineers to quickly produce physical prototypes of their designs, enabling them to test and refine their designs before committing to expensive tooling or production runs. See Side Bar: Tips for 3D Printing.

Early Adoption of New Technologies

Awareness of new technologies and the impact of technological advancements on manufacturing productivity are essential for modern-day manufacturing. Manufacturers need the knowledge and competence necessary to understand and apply new technologies in ways that add value to bottom line profitability and performance. Industry conferences, feasibility studies, experimentation, strong supplier partnerships, and motivated employees all contribute to an environment ripe for productive change.

In summary, the topics discussed in this chapter are critical factors for success. As manufacturing businesses continue to adapt to new technologies and changing market conditions, they will need to prioritize these factors to remain competitive and profitable. By embracing concepts such as agility, simplicity, modularity, reliability, scalability, and sustainability, manufacturers can create more efficient, profitable, and sustainable businesses that are better equipped to meet the needs of their customers and market demands.

Key Points

- Agile manufacturing is a customer-focused, flexible, collaborative, and technology-enabled approach to production that emphasizes responsiveness to changing market conditions and customer needs.
- Complex workstations and equipment tend to break down often, take time to repair, and can negatively impact productivity. Focus on simplicity over complexity.
- Simplicity in the manufacturing process and equipment design can lead to significant benefits for manufacturers, including increased productivity, lower costs, and improved product quality. However, it is important to balance the desire for simplicity with other factors, such as quality, safety, and regulatory requirements.
- Reusability refers to the ability of a product or component to be used multiple times without losing its integrity or functionality.
- Modularity provides scalability in response to changing customer demands.
- If the product lifecycle (PLC) of a manufacturing line will be shorter than its depreciation period, a flexible concept with high reusability should be considered.

SIDE BAR: LEAN MANUFACTURING PRINCIPLES

- **Understand business and customer value!**
- **Design for manufacturability**: Design products that can be manufactured using existing equipment and processes, while striving to reduce the number of product components and equipment moving parts.
- **Reduce manual labor**: Automate processes whenever possible and justified.

- **Train and develop employees**: Properly trained employees can reduce errors and improve operational efficiency.
- **Material and information flow**: Strive to achieve continuous, uninterrupted material and information flow throughout the entire production process. Work to eliminate bottlenecks.
- **Focus on pull**: Establish a pull-based system where production is driven by customer demand, minimizing overproduction and excess inventory.
- **Continuous improvement:** Seek to continuously improve all aspects of the manufacturing process. Encourage a culture of continuous improvement, involving all employees in identifying and eliminating waste and inefficiencies. Consider implementing small, incremental improvements continuously to achieve significant long-term results.
- **Standardized work**: Establish standardized work procedures to eliminate variability and ensure consistent quality and productivity.
- **Just-in-time (JIT)**: Deliver the right product at the right time in the right quantity to meet customer demand, minimizing lead times and inventory.
- **Waste reduction**: Identify and eliminate all forms of waste such as overproduction, waiting time, unnecessary transportation, excess inventory, motion waste, defects, and unused employee creativity.
- **Respect for people**: Treat employees with respect, provide a safe and supportive work environment, and encourage collaboration and teamwork.

These principles serve as a foundation for lean manufacturing practices and methodologies that can be adapted and applied to various industries and sectors to achieve operational excellence.

SIDE BAR: TIPS FOR 3D PRINTING

The following are some helpful hints for 3D printing.

Understand your printer: Get familiar with the specifications and capabilities of your 3D printer. Read the user manual, learn about the optimal settings, and know the limitations of your machine.

Choose the right filament: Select the appropriate filament material for your desired print. Common options include PLA (easy to use, good for beginners), ABS (strong and durable), PETG (versatile and durable), and TPU (flexible and elastic). Each filament has its own printing requirements and characteristics.

Level the build plate: Ensuring a leveled build plate is crucial for successful prints. Follow the instructions provided by your printer's manufacturer to level the build plate correctly. This helps in achieving good adhesion and proper layering.

Calibrate extruder and nozzle: Regularly calibrate the extruder steps and check the nozzle's distance from the build plate. Accurate calibration helps in achieving precise and consistent prints.

Use a heated bed or adhesive: For better adhesion, especially with materials like ABS, consider using a heated bed. If your printer doesn't have a heated bed, use adhesive solutions like painter's tape, glue sticks, or specialized bed adhesives.

Optimize print settings: Experiment with different print settings such as layer height, print speed, infill density, and support structures to find the right balance between quality and print time. Fine-tuning these settings can greatly affect the final result.

Design considerations: When creating or choosing a 3D model, keep in mind the limitations of your printer. Avoid overhangs beyond the printer's capabilities and ensure the model has proper support structures if needed.

Support structures: For prints with overhangs or complex geometries, enable support structures. These temporary structures help to provide stability during printing and can be removed later.

Monitor prints: Keep an eye on your prints, especially during the first few layers. This allows you to catch any potential issues early on, such as poor bed adhesion or filament clogs.

Post-processing: After printing, post-process your prints as needed. This may involve removing support structures, sanding rough surfaces, or applying finishes such as primers and paints.

Maintenance and cleanliness: Regularly clean and maintain your 3D printer. Clear out any accumulated dust or debris, lubricate moving parts as per the manufacturer's instructions, and replace worn-out components when necessary.

Learn from the community: Join online communities, forums, and social media groups dedicated to 3D printing. Engage with experienced users, ask questions, and learn from their expertise. They can provide valuable insights and troubleshooting tips.

Remember, practice makes perfect. As you gain experience with 3D printing, you'll become more proficient in troubleshooting and optimizing your prints. Happy printing!

STRATEGIC PRODUCT LINE DESIGN, DEVELOPMENT, AND INSTALLATION

2

Overview

Strategic product line design, fabrication, and assembly are essential activities for product manufacturing. Traditionally these activities have been done by subcontractors who design and build equipment to meet manufacturing requirements. Often standard or "off-the-shelf" machines would be purchased, delivered, and integrated with other equipment to create a manufacturing line concept capable of producing a product that meets customer requirements. Fortunately, advances in technology have pushed the envelope of what is possible, leading to the development and fabrication of highly sophisticated and customized equipment necessary to meet increasingly demanding customer product and service requirements.

To meet higher process performance expectations, manufacturers are turning their attention to the design and development of their own equipment, building the competence and capability to design, fabricate, and integrate manufacturing equipment internally while outsourcing work that can be done more efficiently and cheaply by an external supplier. Internal resource constraints and skill-set limitations may also dictate the use of

DOI: 10.4324/9781032688152-6

external sources for equipment development and line integration activities, among other reasons.

Regardless of the situation, manufacturers are realizing that they must broaden their scope of responsibility by taking a more active role in the strategic development and assembly of process equipment in order to satisfy the technical challenges associated with modern-day products and services. Manufacturers who understand, accept, and adapt their behavior accordingly are more likely to survive and thrive in the fourth industrial revolution. Let us consider this topic in more detail in the following chapters.

Chapter 2.1

Manufacturing Equipment

Overview

There is a plethora of different types of machines, tools, and equipment used in manufacturing. The types used are dictated by the industry and advancements in technology especially in the wake of automation and smart devices. Software-based machines and equipment are becoming smarter as data is collected from sensors and other devices, analyzed, and used for problem-solving and decision-making. In the following chapter, we will consider the impact of technology on advances in manufacturing equipment and how smart, automated equipment are replacing humans while improving product quality and manufacturing productivity. Let's consider the application of industrial robots and cobots first.

Industrial Robots and Cobots

Industrial robots are being deployed in many industries to perform tasks that require greater speed, precision, and endurance. They are being used for welding, material handling, painting, assembly, and the picking and placement of components. In a warehouse setting, they are commonly used to pick, sort, package, and palletize products. In mechanical applications, they can be used for cutting, grinding, deburring, and polishing, among other things.

In many applications, robots have been deployed to mimic human activities, replacing people doing dirty, difficult, hazardous, and repetitive tasks.

DOI: 10.4324/9781032688152-7

When properly deployed, robots can eliminate human error, improve work-place accuracy, and increase productivity. The benefit of replacing a human with a robot is that the robot can work 24/7 without a break. They don't get injured or ill, complain, or make mistakes.

Although most robots are designed to work autonomously, collaborative robots or "cobots" have been designed to work safely alongside humans due to the application of sensors and other protective devices. They are easier to program than industrial robots and require minimal training. They are often deployed to reduce labor costs, especially in high-cost countries.

Robots and cobots are often the center piece for automated cell design especially when a fixed process cell concept is used. In this scenario, equipment in the cell is fixed as the robot is designed to move the product within the cell, minimizing the equipment's moving parts which are the typical source of failure due to wear and tear.

Today, millions of industrial robots have been deployed in factories around the world, with the numbers increasing every day. It's not unreasonable to expect robots to be the primary "workers" in factories of the future, with highly skilled engineers and technicians developing, deploying, maintaining, and repairing robotic equipment. Now, let us consider the application of cobots in more depth.

Collaborative Robots (Cobots)

Cobots, short for collaborative robots, are robots designed to work alongside humans in a collaborative manner. Unlike traditional industrial robots, which are typically caged or separated from human workers for safety reasons, cobots are designed to operate in close proximity to humans without the need for physical barriers.

Cobots are built with advanced sensors and programming that allow them to interact with humans safely. They are designed to be easily programmable and adaptable, allowing workers to teach them new tasks or reprogram them for different applications. Cobots are often equipped with sensors, cameras, and other perception systems that enable them to detect and respond to human presence, avoiding collisions and ensuring safe cooperation in the workplace.

The goal of cobots is to enhance productivity and efficiency in various industries by automating repetitive or dangerous tasks while working collaboratively with human workers. They can be used in a wide range of applications, such as assembly, packaging, quality control, machine tending, and material handling. Cobots are typically smaller and lighter than traditional industrial robots, making them more flexible and easier to integrate into existing workspaces.

By working alongside humans, cobots can help improve productivity, reduce the risk of workplace injuries, and allow human workers to focus on more complex and cognitive tasks. They are part of the growing field of human-robot collaboration and represent a significant advancement in robotics technology.

Cobots are employed in various ways to assist with different manufacturing tasks. They can be used for repetitive or intricate assembly tasks, such as inserting screws, applying adhesives, or connecting components. Cobots excel at handling materials, picking up objects from one location and placing them in another. This capability is also useful for sorting, packaging, or transferring items on a production line.

Cobots can be integrated with machinery to load and unload parts, monitor processes, and perform quality checks. They can ensure continuous operation and allow human workers to focus on more complex tasks. Using sensors, cameras, and AI algorithms, cobots can inspect products for defects, ensuring consistent quality. They can identify flaws, measure dimensions, or perform visual inspections at a high speed and with great accuracy.

In the case of material handling, cobots can lift and move heavy objects, reducing the risk of injury for workers. They can transport materials between workstations or assist in loading and unloading tasks. They are capable of packaging products into boxes, crates, or containers as well as palletizing goods, arranging them in an organized manner for storage or shipping. They can also perform tests and calibrations on manufactured products, carry out measurements, check product functionality, and ensure that items meet specified standards.

Cobots offer flexibility, adaptability, and the ability to work on repetitive or physically demanding tasks. Their deployment in manufacturing environments aims to optimize productivity, improve product quality, and enhance worker safety.

Robot Deployment

Robot deployment in manufacturing refers to the process of introducing and integrating robots into various stages of the manufacturing process. This deployment involves selecting suitable robotic systems, programming them, and integrating them into existing manufacturing systems to perform specific tasks. In doing so, the first step is to assess the manufacturing process and identify areas where robots can improve efficiency, productivity, and quality. This may involve analyzing repetitive or hazardous tasks, complex assembly processes, or tasks that require high precision.

Based on the identified needs, a suitable robot type is chosen. There are several types of industrial robots available, such as articulated robots, SCARA robots, delta robots, and collaborative robots (cobots). The selection depends on factors like the required payload capacity, reach, precision, speed, and environment in which the robot will operate. Once the robot type is determined, the specific tasks that the robot will perform must be defined. This includes specifying the movements, actions, and sequences required to complete the tasks. Programming languages such as Python, C++, and Java are used to program the robot's movements and actions.

The robot must then be integrated into the existing manufacturing systems. This may involve integrating the robot with other machines, conveyors, sensors, and control systems. Interfaces and protocols are established to enable communication between the robot and other equipment. While doing so, safety measures such as safety barriers, emergency stop buttons, and safety sensors are implemented to ensure the well-being of human operators working alongside the robots. Collaborative robots, designed to work alongside humans, have built-in safety features like force sensing and speed reduction when near humans.

After integration, the robot is thoroughly tested to ensure it performs the desired tasks accurately and efficiently. Adjustments and optimization are made as necessary to improve the robot's performance, cycle time, and reliability. Operators and technicians are then trained to operate and maintain the deployed robots. This includes understanding the programming interface, troubleshooting common issues, and performing regular maintenance tasks to keep the robots in optimal working condition.

Robot deployment is an ongoing process. As the manufacturing requirements evolve, the deployed robots may need to be reprogrammed or replaced with more advanced models. Continuous monitoring, data analysis, and process optimization are essential to maximize the benefits of robot deployment and identify areas for further improvement. By deploying robots in manufacturing, companies can achieve benefits such as increased productivity, improved product quality, reduced production costs, enhanced workplace safety, and the ability to manage complex tasks with precision and speed.

Consider the following key factors when looking to install a robot or cobot in your manufacturing operations:

- Actions, motions, and reach necessary to complete a task
- Size, weight, and shape of objects that will be moved or manipulated (payload)
- Speed relative to process cycle time
- Precision and repeatability
- Total installation cost (hardware, integration, operation)
- Safety
- Integration approach (internal vs. external)
- Installation knowledge and experience
- Maintenance time and costs
- Facility workspace and layout of production area

To overcome a limited workspace or improve the utilization of a robot or cobot, consider attaching it to a linear axis (extension base), enabling a seven-axis concept. Other situations that may justify this approach include a reduction of one or more robots/cobots using a seven-axis concept or the replacement of a big robot with a smaller one on a seventh axis. It's important to note that additional loading/unloading zones as well as handover operations between multiple robots/cobots could be eliminated with a seven-axis concept.

Robots and cobots are becoming the automated product handling systems of future manufacturing, providing high flexibility, reusability, standardization, and task simplification, while offering reliable and affordable solutions for many applications. Learn to integrate them into your line design and assembly practices. Traditional industrial robots are the default if you need operations to run at faster speeds and lift heavier objects than can be accommodated by cobots. Table 2.1.1 captures typical differences between an industrial robot and collaborative robot.

Automated Material-Handling Equipment

Transport equipment moves material from one location to another while positioning equipment is used to maneuver materials at a specific location.

Table 2.1.1   Industrial Robot vs. Collaborative Robot

Robot Attributes	Cobot Attributes
Autonomous (No human interaction)	**Collaborative** (Can work alongside humans)
High accuracy and precision	High accuracy and precision
Capable of heavy lifting	Weight limits compared to robots
Large reach	Limited reach compared to robots
Work faster than humans	Work slower than robots
More difficult to program	Easily reprogrammable
Equipped with safety features	Built with advanced safety features
Standalone operation	User-friendly operation(minimal training for non-experts)
Good for repetitive tasks	Good for repetitive tasks

There are five primary types of material-handling systems: Conveyors, cranes, industrial trucks, manual handling equipment, and yard ramps. Conveyors are usually stationary and are used to move a high volume of material from one point to another along a specific path such as a dock to a storage area. Cranes are commonly used when material is moved over variable terrain or within a restricted area where conveyors are not feasible. Industrial trucks, characterized as vehicles not licensed for public roads, can move material over long and variable paths not feasible for conveyors or cranes. They have the added benefit of vertical movement when equipped with lifting capabilities. Manual handling equipment is typically employed to move small loads and may be assisted by pallet trucks and trolleys. Finally, a yard ramp, typically metal and movable, is used for material loading and unloading of vehicles.

Automated handling equipment refers to machines and systems used in manufacturing to move materials and products between different stages of the production process without human intervention. These systems use a variety of technologies, such as robotics, conveyors, and AGVs, to transport, sort, and organize products.

Automated handling equipment has several advantages in manufacturing, including increased efficiency, reduced labor costs, improved safety, and higher levels of accuracy and consistency. By automating material-handling tasks, manufacturers can streamline their production processes, reduce the risk of injury to workers, and improve the overall quality of their products.

Some examples of automated handling equipment in manufacturing include the following.

Conveyor systems: These systems use belts, chains, or rollers to move materials or products along a fixed path within a manufacturing facility.

Robotic arms: These are mechanical arms with multiple joints that can be programmed to perform specific tasks, such as moving or assembling parts.

AGVs: These are self-guided vehicles that move products and materials around a factory floor, following a predetermined path.

Automated storage and retrieval systems (AS/RS): These systems use cranes or other machinery to automatically store and retrieve materials from a designated location.

Palletizers: These machines automatically stack and organize products onto pallets, making it easier to transport them.

Overall, automated handling equipment plays a critical role in modern manufacturing, helping companies increase productivity, reduce costs, and improve the quality and consistency of their products. Let's consider AGVs in more detail as they play a prominent role in the automation of material handling.

Automated Guided Vehicles

Automated guided vehicles, or AGVs for short, are transport vehicles that move material within a facility or warehouse. Vehicle navigation can result from lines or wires placed on the floor, through radio waves, vision cameras, magnets, or lasers. Material such as raw material or finished goods can be automatically picked up and moved or trailered to their assigned destination. When a trailer bed is attached to an AGV, material can be transferred or retracted from the bed using a motorized conveyor typically consisting of rollers.

In today's modern factories, AGVs are programmed to communicate with other devices to ensure product is moved smoothly throughout the factory or warehouse, whether it is being stored for future use or transport. Manufacturers that have multiple AGVs operating in a facility or area may require traffic control, managed by software, via a designated computer, to avoid collisions. There are also various charging options for AGVs, including battery swaps and automatic charging. However, it's not uncommon for the AGV's base station to have a charging system so that it's charging or maintaining its charge whenever not in use.

AGVs are commonly used in manufacturing to deliver raw materials, move work-in-process, transfer finished goods, remove scrap materials, and supply packaging materials. From a storage and distribution perspective, heavy-duty AGVs can be outfitted with automatic loading and unloading capability consisting of rollers, moving belts, lift platforms, and other devices to move material from one location to another. They are often assisted by an AS/RS in distribution centers. An AGV delivers a pallet of material to the warehouse which is met by an AS/RS that moves the pallet into a designated storage area. Finished goods can also be retrieved in the same manner when preparing a load for shipment.

AGVs are also used in manufacturing to move materials from stock to the production line, loading the line with raw materials and components for consumption and removing finished goods for transport to the packing area or warehouse. Light load AGVs can also be programmed to support product assembly by moving partially completed product through various steps of the assembly process. In this flexible manufacturing system, humans are likely to stage or place material on the AGV in the stock area; the material is delivered to the workstation and transferred by the vehicle to the station for processing. Upon task completion, the vehicle returns to retrieve the work and moves it to the next sequential workstation. In the case of line-side material supply, materials such as electronic components can be "kitted," placed in totes or trays, and delivered to a workstation for easier replenishment and process assembly.

AGV technology continues to evolve as new designs are being tested such as the installation of a robot onto an automated guided vehicle enhancing its ability to perform more complex tasks. It should be noted that there are other names given to these transport vehicles which are usually derived from the technology employed to realize them including a laser guided vehicle (LGV) and automated guided carts (AGCs). An AGC is usually a lower cost transport vehicle guided by magnetic strips or visual markers.

Autonomous vehicles in manufacturing have the potential to significantly improve efficiency, reduce costs, and improve safety in manufacturing operations. As technology continues to advance, it is likely that we will see even more widespread adoption of these vehicles in manufacturing facilities around the world.

Micro AGVs

"Micro" AGVs, or micro automated guided vehicles, are small autonomous robots that are designed to transport small loads, typically weighing less than 50 kilograms. These robots use sensors, cameras, and other technologies to navigate through a facility and can be programmed to follow specific paths or instructions. They are often used in manufacturing, warehousing, and logistics operations to transport materials, parts, or products between different locations within a facility.

Unlike larger AGVs, micro AGVs are typically designed to operate in more confined spaces and can navigate through narrow aisles or other areas where larger vehicles may not be able to operate. They are often more affordable and easier to deploy than larger AGVs, making them a popular choice for small and medium-sized businesses that want to automate their material-handling operations.

There are also versions of these transport devices being deployed in manufacturing to transport work-in-process to various bench-top assembly stations. Proximity sensors are used to relay instructions to an on-board microcontroller that directs the unit to specific assembly locations within the workstation. This is a relatively new technology expected to evolve over the coming years.

Smart Glasses

Smart glasses, also known as augmented reality glasses or AR glasses, are wearable technology devices that can display digital information, graphics, and images in front of the user's eyes. They often look like regular eyeglasses or sunglasses, but they have a built-in display, camera, and other sensors that enable them to provide an enhanced viewing experience.

The glasses use advanced technologies like cameras, microphones, and sensors to detect the user's surroundings and display digital information over the real world. This technology can be used for a variety of purposes, including navigation, entertainment, education, and communication. In manufacturing, smart glasses are used to provide workers with real-time information and instructions to help them perform tasks more efficiently and accurately. Some of the ways in which smart glasses are used in manufacturing include the training of new workers by providing step-by-step instructions on how to perform specific tasks. They can be used to guide workers through the assembly process by highlighting the correct parts and providing instructions on how to assemble them as well as to assist workers in performing maintenance tasks by providing real-time data on the status of the equipment and instructions on how to perform repairs.

Smart glasses can be used to assist workers in performing quality control checks by highlighting areas that need attention and providing instructions on how to correct any issues. Overall, smart glasses can help increase productivity and reduce errors in manufacturing by providing workers with the information they need to perform their jobs more efficiently and effectively. See Figure 2.1.1.

Sensors and Devices

At any one time, billions of devices and objects are collecting and transmitting data along the IoT, extending digital intelligence beyond dedicated devices such PCs, tablets, and smartphones. These devices can be independently connected nodes on the IoT or part of an autonomous system such as connected cars, wearable technologies, and smart buildings. At the heart of these vast digital communication networks is the application of sensors that measure real-world conditions such as light, heat, pressure, temperature, motion, and sound. Data from these sensors can be used in real-time or gathered, analyzed, and used for problem-solving and decision-making, at an appropriate time.

Sensor technology is evolving quickly in areas such as optical-sensing, machine vision, high-resolution medical diagnostics, self-regulating buildings, autonomous vehicles, personal health monitoring, and much more. Sensors are also being integrated into products for which they have not traditionally been used including light bulbs, drug-delivery devices, door

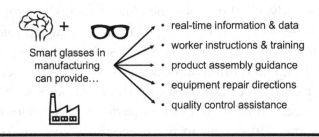

Figure 2.1.1 Benefits of using smart glasses.

locks, and meters. As sensors evolve, there is a technological push to create smaller, lower power-consumption, and network interface-capable devices. Beyond typical sensor capacitance, resistance, or output voltage, manufacturers are looking for application-ready sensor systems that can be easily connected to networks, interfaced with processors, and paired with mobile devices.

Sensors can use electrical signals to communicate imaging, optical, environmental, and audio conditions. Sensor can also be embedded with multichip technology that provides an algorithm to convert raw sensor measurements into a linear signal for digital processing or software to provide a connection to common networks like Bluetooth and Wi-Fi technologies. Sensor technology is evolving to deliver application-ready devices with algorithms that can exploit data and provide custom solutions that will change manufacturing and the world as we know it.

In the manufacturing industry, sensors and devices play a critical role in digital transformation by enabling the collection of vast amounts of data, which can then be analyzed and used to improve various aspects of the manufacturing process. Manufacturing companies use sensors and devices to gather data on various parameters, such as temperature, humidity, pressure, vibration, and other environmental factors, as well as data on the status of machines and equipment, including their performance, efficiency, and maintenance needs.

The collected data is then analyzed using various technologies, such as artificial intelligence, machine learning, and predictive analytics, to identify patterns and trends that can help optimize the manufacturing process, reduce downtime, increase productivity, and improve product quality. For example, sensors can be used to monitor the performance of machines and equipment in real-time, identifying any issues before they become major problems. Predictive analytics can be used to analyze this data and predict when maintenance is needed, reducing downtime, and improving productivity.

In addition to improving operational efficiency, sensors and devices can also be used to improve product quality. For example, sensors can be used to monitor the temperature and humidity levels during the manufacturing process, ensuring that the products are produced to the desired specifications. Overall, the use of sensors and devices in manufacturing enables companies to gather and analyze data, allowing them to make data-driven decisions that improve efficiency, productivity, and product quality, ultimately driving digital transformation in the industry.

Automated Conveyors

Conveyors are widely used in manufacturing automation to move materials or products from one point to another within a production line. They can transport parts and products to various assembly stations, where workers can perform specific tasks. This can significantly speed up the production process and reduce labor costs.

Conveyors move raw materials, such as metals, plastics, and chemicals, to the appropriate processing equipment. This reduces the need for manual handling of heavy and bulky materials, making the process safer and more efficient. They also transport finished products to packaging and shipping areas, where they can be prepared for delivery. This can be done in a highly automated manner, reducing the need for manual labor, while improving speed and accuracy.

Automated conveyors can be configured to move product at a precise time, to an exact location, to maintain a continuous process flow for product assembly. The application of conveyors in manufacturing can improve efficiency and safety if they eliminate lift trucks and other potentially dangerous equipment.

Conveyors are often used in conjunction with sensors and other monitoring equipment to inspect products for defects. This can help ensure that only high-quality products are shipped to customers. In essence, the use of conveyors in manufacturing automation can streamline production processes, reduce labor costs, and improve the quality and consistency of the final products.

There are various types of conveyors mounted on the floor and overhead including a belt conveyor, roller conveyor, motorized roller conveyor, and overhead conveyors used to move products, create buffers, and deliver products to production. Characteristics to consider in the design calculations and application of a conveyor include size, length, capacity and speed, roller diameter, power, and tension, idler spacing, type of drive unit, diameter, location, and maximum loading capacity, among other factors. The primary objective of installing an automated belt conveyor system is to achieve a fast, safe, and efficient operation and accuracy levels that cannot be achieved with manual maneuvers.

Key Points

- The integration of robots in manufacturing brings significant benefits, including increased productivity, improved efficiency, enhanced product quality, better workplace safety, cost savings, flexibility, and the ability to leverage data for optimization.

■ By harnessing the capabilities of robots, manufacturers can achieve higher levels of competitiveness, innovation, and success in today's dynamic industrial landscape.

■ Automated handling equipment plays a critical role in modern manufacturing, helping companies increase productivity, reduce costs, and improve the quality and consistency of their products.

■ The use of sensors and devices in manufacturing enables companies to gather and analyze data, allowing them to make data-driven decisions that improve efficiency, productivity, and product quality, driving digital transformation in the industry.

■ Smart glasses can help increase productivity and reduce errors in manufacturing by providing workers with the information they need to perform their jobs more efficiently and effectively.

■ The use of conveyors in manufacturing automation can streamline production processes, reduce labor costs, and improve the quality and consistency of the final products.

Chapter 2.2

Line Design, Build, and Integration Strategy

Overview

Outsourcing the design and building of equipment has been the norm for many manufacturers when the expertise was not part of a company's resources, core competence, or strategy. Under these circumstances, equipment requirements would be defined, and the purchasing department would initiate the bidding process to find the best qualified contractor to complete the work. Upon arrival, equipment would be validated and assembled into a product line by an internal engineering team or a contractor.

In today's competitive and increasingly more complex manufacturing environment, greater consideration is being given to the way equipment is designed and built as factors such as standardization, robustness, ease of maintenance/repair, and manufacturing footprint are becoming more important for achieving rapid, flexible, precise, sustainable, and reliable operations. In response, manufacturers are strengthening their internal capability to design and develop some, if not all, of their own equipment in-house. This is proving to reduce equipment development time and facilitating the application of lean, agile, and robust equipment. This knowledge is often being captured and shared with others via design guidelines rooted in best practices and lessons learned.

This approach has delivered on equipment expectations for a more agile, leaner, and smarter operating factory that has become more difficult to attain through independent contractors due to equipment complexity and

DOI: 10.4324/9781032688152-8

customization. Although there are clear benefits to acquiring this design and build capability in-house, harboring this skill set internally comes at a cost. In short, outsourcing equipment design and build services may no longer meet the needs or expectations of a world-class smart manufacturing operation, thus sparking the need to strengthen one's design and build capability in-house.

Production Concept

A manufacturing product concept refers to the initial idea or vision for a product that is to be manufactured. It encompasses the fundamental features, functions, and characteristics of the product as the basis for its design and fabrication. The concept outlines the purpose and value proposition of the product, identifies its target market, and highlights its unique selling points.

When developing a manufacturing product concept, several factors are typically considered, such as market needs, consumer preferences, technological feasibility, and competitive analysis. The concept may involve brainstorming, market research, and idea generation to determine the product's potential viability and market success.

Developing a manufacturing production concept that supports the product involves a systematic approach that begins with understanding the products to be manufactured and the processes required to support their efficient realization. When developing a production concept, you must consider the:

- Features, materials, components, and specifications of the product and product variants to be produced.
- Number of units that need to be produced over a specific time period (manufacturing capacity).
- Machines, equipment, and other resources needed for process development.
- Raw materials needed for product manufacturing.
- Manufacturing process layout and factory floor space requirements.
- Number of process steps, their sequence, and target cycle time.

Once you understand the product and process requirements, you can initiate the line design by determining the equipment needs for production. This includes deciding the most efficient way to manufacture the product when preparing a line layout within the constraints of existing standards, available floor space, reusable equipment, and workflow conditions.

Modern-day tools and techniques allow for the creation of product prototypes, conducting process simulations, and performing small-scale production runs to test design concepts for potential problems or operational inefficiencies. Once you have evaluated the product design and overall manufacturing concept and made the necessary adjustments, you can start preparations for full-scale production. It's important to note that the manufacturing concept is still at its initial stage of development. It will evolve and be refined over time as the product moves through subsequent phases of its lifecycle.

A manufacturing concept serves as a guide throughout the product development process. It helps refine the product's specifications, design elements, materials, production techniques, and the overall manufacturing strategy. The concept serves as a reference point for various stakeholders involved in product development, including engineers, designers, marketers, and production teams.

Overall, developing a production concept requires careful planning, design, testing, and ongoing refinement to ensure the manufacturing process, used to realize the product, is efficient, effective, and meets business needs. In the following pages we will overview the main activities behind the production concept.

Make or Buy Decision

In many instances, designing and building equipment in-house is cheaper, more efficient, and quicker than outsourcing equipment builds when considered over a product's lifecycle. In the development phase, decisions tend to be made faster, problems tend to get solved quicker and equipment users can provide rapid feedback on design iterations. However, fostering in-house capability to design and build equipment does not come without a price which we will discuss more later in this chapter.

Outsourcing the building of equipment has its own set of issues including potentially longer lead times, the need to provide detailed specifications, supplier management activities, as well as line latent integration concerns. Regardless, it's not unusual to take a hybrid approach to equipment acquisition including a combination of building some equipment in-house while purchasing others externally. A manufacturing equipment make or buy decision involves evaluating whether a company should produce or purchase the equipment needed for its manufacturing processes. It is a strategic decision that requires careful analysis of various factors. Here are some key considerations involved in such a decision.

Cost analysis: One of the primary factors is assessing the cost implications of making or buying equipment. This involves comparing the total costs of manufacturing the equipment in-house, including capital expenditure, labor, raw materials, maintenance, and overhead costs, with the cost of purchasing the equipment from external suppliers.

Core competencies: Evaluating the company's core competencies and strategic focus is crucial. Companies typically prefer to focus on their core activities and outsource non-core functions. If manufacturing equipment does not align with the company's core competencies, it may be more feasible to buy from specialized equipment manufacturers.

Capacity and expertise: Assessing the company's internal capacity and expertise in manufacturing equipment is important. If the company lacks the necessary technical knowledge, production capacity, or specialized skills required to manufacture the equipment efficiently, it may be more sensible to buy from established suppliers.

Time to market: Time considerations play a significant role. Developing and manufacturing equipment in-house may take longer or shorter than outsourcing depending on design, prototyping, testing, production set-up phases, and resource availability. However, buying equipment from external suppliers can sometimes expedite the process and reduce time to market especially when conventional equipment is required.

Technology and innovation: Assessing the technological advancements and innovation in the equipment market is crucial. Buying equipment externally may provide access to cutting-edge technology and advanced features that may be challenging to develop in-house.

Quality and reliability: Evaluating equipment quality and reliability requirements is essential. Buying from reputable suppliers can ensure consistent quality, reliability, and compliance with industry standards. However, in some cases, manufacturing in-house may provide better control over quality and customization options.

Supply chain considerations: Analyzing the availability and reliability of the supply chain for both in-house manufacturing and external procurement is necessary. This includes considering the availability of raw materials, components, spare parts, and the potential risks associated with supply chain disruptions.

Financial considerations: Assessing the financial impact, including investment requirements, cash flow, depreciation, tax implications, and the overall financial health of the company, is crucial. It is important to consider the long-term financial implications of the decision.

Risk management: Evaluating the risks associated with both options is necessary. Manufacturing in-house may involve risks such as technology obsolescence, production delays, and operational risks, while buying externally may involve risks such as supplier reliability, quality control, and intellectual property protection.

Scalability and flexibility: Considering the scalability and flexibility requirements is important. If the company anticipates changes in demand, production volumes, or product specifications, buying equipment externally may provide more flexibility in adapting to market dynamics.

By thoroughly evaluating these factors and conducting a comprehensive cost-benefit analysis, companies can make informed decisions on whether to make or buy manufacturing equipment that aligns with their strategic goals, resources, and competitive advantages.

In-House Equipment Design and Build Activities

Building equipment in-house has some distinct advantages in that you can initiate changes quicker and reduce build timing since you don't have to work with a subcontractor which can consume valuable time and effort. Cost savings typically occur by not having to transport heavy equipment or budget for travel expenses that may be needed to review equipment build progress and qualify equipment at the subcontractor facility. If equipment is being built in the same facility in which it will be deployed, real-time feedback from the primary users, during the development process, may provide another advantage.

An additional benefit of building equipment in-house is the ability to change the mindset of how equipment is built. One mindset shift is building equipment based on what is possible versus what's been done before. Looking at each build opportunity with fresh eyes opens the door for how certain requirements can be satisfied in the simplest and cheapest way without compromising quality and reliability. A good example of this open-minded thinking is the "fixed process cell" concept developed by a progressive automotive parts manufacturer in Texas. A significant amount of their line downtime was attributed to the wear and tear of moving parts within a process cell.

Traditionally, parts enter the work cell, stop, and allow the equipment to move about the part, performing the necessary value-adding activities. This may include process activities such as pressing, dispensing, cutting, and grinding. In a fixed process cell concept, the equipment is secured in place while the part is designed to move about the cell, often with the assistance of a cobot. In this scenario, manufacturing equipment is stationary as the part moves, virtually eliminating equipment failures associated with wear and tear. This concept is not practical for all processes but has significantly reduced downtime in those workstations where this concept can be applied.

When you choose to build some or all equipment in-house, you need to hire or develop the capability to perform the required work and retain the expertise for equipment maintenance and repair when breakdowns occur. These decisions don't come without cost, one way or another. Doing the work internally may avoid cost in outsourcing but those costs are shifted to hiring, developing, and maintaining a competent and capable workforce need to realize internal ambitions. However, having more control over equipment design, construction, and product line assembly can have a significant impact on resulting equipment reliability, manufacturing footprint, and maintainability.

Clearly, there is a cost associated with acquiring or building equipment, but it may be offset by the time and cost of subcontracting equipment development and engaging external expertise in response to equipment breakdowns. Additional benefits to building equipment and assembling them into a cohesive production line include supporting a vertical integration strategy, the high potential for capital investment savings, enhanced workforce knowledge (through experience and lessons learned), and the application of lean/sustainable machine concepts that can help minimize equipment floorspace and carbon footprint.

When build standards are defined and implemented, maintenance cost can be reduced through the more efficient management of technical resources and spare parts inventory. If you are struggling to justify the cost of building equipment internally, consider these factors:

- *Development time*: This time is likely to decrease due to easier collaboration and quicker issue response time using in-house resources.
- *Project management*: It is easier to monitor and control equipment development activities that are performed in-house than externally.
- *Application of standards*: Standards for equipment reuse, the application of common parts, and spare parts management help reduce design and build complexity in addition to costs.
- *Collaboration*: Design, development, and manufacturing stakeholders are more readily available to participate in development activities and reviews when done on-site.
- *Design changes*: Change management tends to be more agile and responsive with in-house versus outsourcing activities.
- *Mean time to repair (MTTR)*: Equipment repair response time will tend to be shorter when using internal resources versus the need to engage external support.
- *Mean time between failures (MTBF)*: Equipment reliability can improve with the application of internal best practices and lessons learned from historic equipment builds, maintenance, and repairs.
- *Spare parts management*: Less spare parts inventory and cost due to the use of common parts driven by equipment standardization.
- *Reuse*: More standardized equipment supports end-of-life reuse activities.
- *Maintenance*: Maintenance practices rapidly improve when historical experiences, best practices, and lessons learned are applied.
- *Training*: Internal training of operators and maintenance technicians by equipment builders and line integration experts.
- *Intellectual property (IP)*: Ability to retain intellectual property in-house. No need to share it externally!
- *Machine learning*: The ability to support advanced machine learning and predictive maintenance with in-house knowledge of equipment and smart devices.

Outsourcing Equipment Design and Build Activities

Outsourcing manufacturing equipment design and build activities refers to the practice of contracting external companies or specialized service providers to handle the design, development, and construction of equipment used in the manufacturing process. This outsourcing approach allows companies to leverage the expertise and capabilities of external entities, rather than developing these capabilities in-house. Outsourcing equipment design and build activities can have both pros and cons. Let's consider some advantages to start.

Cost savings: Outsourcing can often be cost-effective, especially if you're working with a company in a country with lower labor costs. You can save on hiring and training in-house designers and builders, as well as the costs associated with maintaining infrastructure and equipment.

Expertise and specialization: By outsourcing to a company that special-izes in equipment design and build, you can gain access to a team of experts with deep knowledge and experience in the field. They may have advanced technical skills and insights that can result in high-qual-ity, efficient, and innovative designs.

Risk sharing: When you outsource equipment design and build activities, you can transfer some of the risks associated with development and manufacturing to the outsourcing partner. They assume responsibil-ity for meeting quality standards, adhering to deadlines, and managing potential challenges.

There are also several potential drawbacks or disadvantages associated with outsourcing equipment design and build activities such as the following:

Loss of control: When you outsource, you may have less control over the design and build process. Communication challenges, time zone differ-ences, and cultural factors can hinder effective collaboration and deci-sion-making. This can potentially lead to misaligned expectations and results that don't fully meet your requirements.

Intellectual property concerns: Sharing proprietary information and designs with an outsourcing partner can pose risks to your IP. Ensure that you have appropriate legal agreements and safeguards in place to protect your confidential information and prevent unauthorized use or disclosure.

Quality and accountability risks: Outsourcing can introduce risks related to quality control and accountability. The outsourcing partner may not have the same level of commitment or standards as your in-house team. It's essential to establish clear expectations, quality control processes, and regular communication to mitigate these risks.

Dependency on a third party: By outsourcing, you become reliant on an external organization for critical aspects of your equipment design and build process. If the outsourcing partner faces financial or operational challenges, it could impact your projects and timelines.

Communication and coordination challenges: Effective communication is crucial for successful outsourcing. If there are language barriers, cultural differences, or geographical distance, it can be more challenging to convey requirements, provide feedback, and address issues promptly. This can potentially lead to delays and misunderstandings especially when change controls issues occur.

Unfortunately, all too often, equipment builders can become complacent, using the same approach while losing site of what's possible and practical in light of advancing technologies. In the case of external contractors, doing what's been done before by using a proven and available approach is a predictable and safe path to meeting customer requirements. However, this can stifle creativity and opportunities to produce quality equipment that is cheaper, faster to build, and more dependable. In the end, most make or buy decisions are based on price, timing, and historical performance. However, regardless of what decision you make, strive to ensure equipment builders are open minded and forward thinking when pursuing equipment building opportunities.

Build Team

Building equipment in-house takes a competent team of people consisting of experienced mechanical, automation, robotic, and controls engineers that can work with designers to develop a line concept that can be effectively and efficiently integrated together to create a seamless production line. Documentation will need to be prepared that visualizes the line layout and details the build to print requirements for the engineers and technicians tasked to complete the work. In turn, the equipment fabrication team will start to procure materials, simulate processes, and construct prototypes for evaluation and testing before line assembly activities begin. Table 2.2.1 has been prepared to outline the experience and competence needed to support an in-house design, build, and assembly team.

In additional to technical expertise, the manufacturing equipment build team should also exhibit some of these following attributes.

Table 2.2.1 Build Competencies and Experience

Competencies	Experience
Mechanical and robotics engineering	Automation concepts
	Machine design
	Cobot programming
	Safety and controls specialist
	Mechanical documentation specialist
	Computer aided design (CAD)
	Process specialist
Robotics controls engineering	Controls hardware strategy
	Programmable Logic Controller (PLC) programming
	Software and tools development
	Continuous improvement
Robotics technician	Hardware procurement
	Machine fabrication
	Additive manufacturing (3D printing)
	Electrical documentation
Automated Guided Vehicle (AGV) engineering	Automation of material delivery
	Automated warehouse

Problem-solving skills: The team should be able to identify and solve complex technical problems that may arise during the equipment build process. They should have strong analytical and troubleshooting abilities to address issues promptly and find innovative solutions.

Collaboration and communication: Effective teamwork is crucial in a manufacturing equipment build project. Team members should be skilled at collaborating, sharing information, and communicating effectively with each other. This includes listening actively, providing feedback, and working cohesively toward a common goal.

Attention to detail: Precision and attention to detail are essential attributes for a manufacturing equipment build team. They should be able to follow specifications, blueprints, and design documents accurately to ensure the equipment is built to the required standards and specifications.

Time management: The team should have excellent time management skills to meet project deadlines and milestones. They should be capable of prioritizing tasks, planning schedules, and managing resources efficiently to ensure timely completion of the equipment build.

Adaptability and flexibility: Manufacturing equipment build projects often involve unexpected challenges, changes, or evolving requirements. Team members should be adaptable and flexible, able to adjust their plans and approaches accordingly while maintaining productivity and quality.

Safety consciousness: Safety should be a top priority for the team. They should adhere to all safety protocols, guidelines, and regulations throughout the equipment build process. This includes identifying potential hazards, implementing safety measures, and promoting a safe working environment.

Quality focus: The team should have a strong commitment to quality assurance and control. They should pay attention to quality checks, inspections, and testing procedures to ensure the final product meets the required standards.

Continuous learning: Manufacturing technologies and processes evolve rapidly. A successful equipment build team should be open to learning and acquiring new skills and knowledge. They should stay up to date with the latest industry trends, best practices, and advancements to improve their effectiveness and efficiency.

Professionalism: The team should demonstrate professionalism in their conduct, interactions, and work ethic. This includes being reliable, accountable, and maintaining a positive attitude toward their responsibilities and colleagues.

These attributes will help ensure successful manufacturing equipment builds that are completed on time and within budget while adhering to all quality requirements and customer expectations.

Test Equipment and Systems

In-house development of software, in addition to hardware, can benefit the organization from a troubleshooting and equipment upgrade perspective. Standard practices in software development can lead to quicker response times to issues since software developers and programmers will already be familiar with the software code and development practices of the equipment installed.

As the degree of software content increases within manufacturing operations due to the growth in automation, smart technology, and machine learning applications, in-house knowledge of software-based operating equipment and systems will reduce the dependance on external support. This becomes particularly relevant when issues arise that demand immediate attention. Let us explore several other critical roles that test equipment and systems play in smart factory operations.

Test equipment and systems help to ensure the quality and efficiency of the manufacturing process. These systems can be designed to perform various tests and measurements on products, components, and processes to verify their compliance with quality standards and specifications. They help ensure product quality by conducting thorough inspections, functional tests, and performance evaluations.

They are also suited to verify if products meet the required specifications and standards, identifying any defects or deviations that need to be addressed before products are released. They are also used to monitor and optimize manufacturing processes. By continuously collecting data and performing real-time analysis, these systems provide insights into process efficiency, identify bottlenecks or inefficiencies, and highlight opportunities for process improvements.

Smart factories heavily rely on automation to improve productivity and reduce human errors. Test equipment and systems are integrated with automation technologies to perform testing and inspections automatically. This not only speeds up the testing process but also minimizes the need for manual intervention, reducing the risk of human errors and improving overall efficiency.

Test equipment and systems generate a vast amount of data during the testing process. This data is collected, stored, and analyzed to gain valuable insights into product performance, process efficiency, and quality trends. Advanced analytics and machine learning algorithms can be applied to this data to detect patterns, identify anomalies, predict failures, and optimize quality control strategies.

Test equipment and systems require regular maintenance and calibration to ensure their accuracy and reliability. In a smart factory, these tasks can be automated through integrated software systems that monitor the performance of the equipment, schedule maintenance activities, and track calibration records. This helps reduce downtime, optimizing equipment utilization and maintaining consistent test results.

Test systems also help establish product traceability by recording test results and associated data for each unit manufactured. This enables easy tracking of products throughout the manufacturing process and supply chain. Moreover, these systems ensure compliance with industry regulations and standards by documenting and validating that all necessary tests have been performed and the products meet the required specifications.

Overall, test equipment and systems play a vital role in a smart factory by ensuring product quality, optimizing processes, enabling automation, providing data-driven insights, ensuring compliance, and facilitating efficient maintenance and calibration.

Equipment Build/Tool Shop

Every manufacturing location is likely to have an area within it or close to the facility responsible for equipment and tooling builds, maintenance, and repair. For many plants, this is an essential team or department that can respond to urgent issues caused by unexpected equipment failures as well as managing the routine maintenance activities of the plant. A good tool/build shop is a creative department able to think on their feet and identify practical solutions to a myriad of different problems and unique situations. They can provide the needed response and flexibility to support an agile working environment while minimizing the need for external support for production or development activities. They may serve as a source for machining or 3D printing spare parts on demand, reducing the need for excess spare parts inventory. A diverse and engaged tool shop may also provide the knowledge base for training line operators on machine usage and minor maintenance activities. More on this topic will be discussed later in this book.

The competence of the build shop must reflect the needs of the process development and manufacturing teams that they serve. They must be aware of equipment standards and lean equipment guidelines that should be applied during equipment build and validation activities. The following is a brief description of tool shop activities in support manufacturing operations.

The tool shop is responsible for manufacturing or fabricating a wide range of tools and equipment used in the manufacturing process. These tools can include cutting tools, jigs, fixtures, molds, dies, gauges, and other specialized equipment. Skilled machinists and technicians use various techniques like machining, milling, turning, grinding, and heat treatment to create these tools according to specific designs and specifications.

Over time, tools can wear out or become damaged due to regular use. The tool shop provides repair and maintenance services to ensure that the tools remain in optimal working condition. This involves inspecting the tools, identifying issues or defects, and performing necessary repairs or replacements. Regular maintenance activities such as sharpening, lubrication, and calibration are also conducted to extend the lifespan of the tools and maintain their accuracy.

The tool shop may also be involved in the design and development of new tools and equipment. This includes collaborating closely with engineers, designers, and manufacturing professionals to understand their requirements and specifications. Using their expertise in tooling and fabrication processes, the tool shop team can contribute to the design process, provide input on tooling feasibility and efficiency, and help create prototypes or test components.

A tool shop typically maintains an inventory of various tools, spare parts, and consumables required for manufacturing operations. This involves cataloging, organizing, and tracking the availability of tools to ensure they are readily accessible when needed. Effective inventory management helps prevent delays in production and reduces downtime by ensuring that tools are readily available for use or repair.

The tool shop plays a critical role in ensuring the quality of manufactured products. By producing and maintaining precise and accurate tools, they contribute to the overall quality of the manufacturing process. This involves conducting quality checks, inspections, and measurements on tools to ensure they meet the required standards and specifications.

In essence, a manufacturing tool shop is a dedicated facility that supports manufacturing activities by providing essential services related to the production, repair, and maintenance of tools and equipment. It serves as a hub for tool design, fabrication, repair, and quality control, contributing to the efficiency and effectiveness of manufacturing operations.

Building for the Future

In order to realize the future vision of an automated and smart factory, manufacturing teams must work in partnership with their equipment builders and integrators regardless of whether the work is performed internally or externally. Work packages must be developed, project management plans executed, and key process indicators tracked for effective project monitoring and control. During equipment design and build activities, it's important to consider some of the following factors that are likely to influence the expected outcomes:

■ *Simplicity over complexity*: Equipment that performs multiple operations tends to experience more breakdowns due to the level of complexity. Fewer parts and fewer moving parts typically equate to less downtime and ease of repair.

■ *Standardized equipment*: Standardized equipment increases the opportunity for equipment reuse. Working with common construction materials, control units, and components allows equipment to be reused on other projects at end of life.

■ *Common (off-the-shelf) parts*: The use of common and dependable off-the-shelf parts can have a significant impact on equipment robustness and speed of repair. Customized and low-volume parts tend to be less dependable, more expensive, and difficult to get quickly when needed for urgent repairs. Common parts will be easier to procure and cheaper to maintain in the facility's spare parts inventory.

■ *Equipment reliability*: Equipment reliability starts with applying lessons learned and best practices from previous build activities and experiences gained during equipment installation, use, maintenance, and repair. Use of robust equipment components also plays a key role since the component supplier chosen and component material composition can have a significant impact on equipment reliability and durability. Maintaining a clean working environment may also help to reduce area contaminants that can accelerate equipment wear and tear. Other tips for improving equipment reliability include the elimination of moving wires, using pneumatics for actuator movements, and avoiding the use of metal on a robot's end of arm device.

■ *User feedback*: Exploit the benefit of having equipment users on site to participate in the equipment design and development process. This can have a profound impact on resulting equipment performance. The continuous interchange between designers and expected users can create an iterative development cycle that benefits everyone involved.

■ *Ease of use*: Since the equipment operator is likely to spend most of the time interacting with the equipment, ease of use becomes paramount in ensuring an ergonomically friendly experience. If the equipment is fully automated, ease of use should be replaced by ease of installation, maintenance, and repair.

■ *Ease of maintenance*: Unless equipment is highly reliable and is expected to require little to no maintenance, ease of maintenance is important. Easy access and replacement of high wear and tear components should be considered. Ensure access panels and utility lines are easily accessible without having to move equipment. A maintenance technician should not have to be a contortionist to do their job properly.

Lifecycle Engineering

Lifecycle engineering (LCE) is a sustainability-oriented product development activity that considers the technical, environmental, and economic impacts of engineering decisions on a product's lifecycle. Analysis is required to quantify sustainability with targets defined to gauge environmental impact.

ISO 14040 defines the product lifecycle as the "consecutive and interlinked stages of a product system, from raw material acquisition or generation from natural resources to final disposal." [1] This definition considers both upstream and downstream processes. Upstream processes include "the extraction and production of raw materials and manufacturing," while downstream processes include product disposal such as recycling or sending waste to a landfill. [2]

The objective of lifecycle engineering is to achieve product engineering goals with minimal impact to the environment. Several related methodologies include lifecycle assessment (LCA), design for the environment (DfE), and design for circularity (DfC). Lifecycle assessment evaluates a product's impact on the environment and potential hotspots for further consideration. Design for the environment strives to systematically reduce a product's footprint on the environment by avoiding less sustainable materials. Design for circularity focuses on reuse, remanufacturing, and a second life application, with easy end-of-life treatments.

Lifecycle assessment looks to measure a product's carbon footprint with the standard of measurement being carbon dioxide equivalents (CO_2e), where units are reported in grams or kilograms. All emissions are converted to their CO_2 equivalent based on a global warming potential (GWP). Product lifecycle phases are quantified and assessed for their GWP. See Figure 2.2.1.

The overall goal of LCA is to neutralize the impact of consumption and production on the environment while maintaining a high standard of living

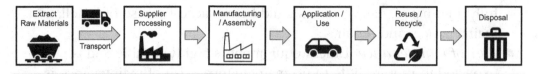

Figure 2.2.1 Product lifecycle phases.

for future generations through the conscious reduction of waste and efficient development of products and processes. The following are some tips for achieving a more sustainable future:

■ Increase your awareness of sustainability.
■ Reduce emissions and material usage through LCA design practices.
■ Favor electric over gas products.
■ Encourage clean and efficient energy usage.
■ Use recycled materials.
■ Promote sustainable requirements.
■ Design products with end-of-life environmental impact in mind.
■ Design products that are easy to maintain, repair, and recycle.

Manufacturing Simulations

Simulations use models (often computer models) to digitally replicate or imitate real-world objects, processes, and systems to understand their behavior and performance as part of a decision-making process. A model represents the object, process, or system being studied while the simulation represents the evolution of the model under changing input conditions. Simulations are increasingly used in manufacturing to optimize processes, reduce costs, and improve quality. They are used to create and test prototypes of products and parts before they are manufactured. This can help identify potential design flaws, reduce the number of physical prototypes needed, and speed up the design process. Simulations can also be used to optimize manufacturing processes, such as assembly lines, by modeling the flow of materials and identifying bottlenecks or areas for improvement. This can lead to increased efficiency, reduced waste, and lower costs.

Simulations have also been used to predict the performance and quality of products under different conditions, such as temperature, pressure, time, and stress. This can help identify potential issues and lead to improvements in product quality. From a human resource perspective, simulations can be used to train employees on manufacturing processes and procedures, allowing them to learn and practice in a safe, controlled environment. Simulations are also used to model and optimize supply chain logistics, such as inventory management and transportation planning, to reduce costs and improve efficiency.

Simulations can help quantify system capabilities such as production output, cycle time, and labor constraints under various operating conditions. It is important that the simulation model be developed and exercised using valid data and information to ensure outcome accuracy and integrity. To this end, much time and effort is spent on model verification and validation through continuous study, development, and refinement. Simulation-based technologies significantly contribute to digital manufacturing solutions since they facilitate the experimentation and validation of different products, processes, and manufacturing system configurations.

Manufacturing system simulation is a powerful, low-cost, low-risk, and effective tool for designing and evaluating manufacturing systems. Simulations help to visualize and validate product, process, and system designs. Manufacturing teams engage in modeling and analysis to gain an understanding of complex systems and their interactions with existing infrastructure.

Key Points

- Manufacturers are turning to "in-sourcing" as a more effective way to lean out their processes, increase equipment reliability, and reduce costs in product line design, development, assembly, and maintenance.
- Pursuing an internal equipment design, build, and line integration strategy has the potential to significantly reduce process development lead time and cost to realization.
- When the design and building of manufacturing line equipment remain in-house, feedback from users can be in real-time and help to evolve designs for ease of use and maintenance.
- It's important to build equipment based on what is possible and not necessarily based on what is simply available. Be creative and innovative.
- Ensure the early involvement of manufacturing team members with equipment and process designers and developers.
- Design and build small and simple automated equipment.

- Deploy proven technologies but increase equipment robustness using best practices and lessons learned.
- Capture and document best practices and lessons learned in Machine Design Guidelines which can be used for future development.
- Lifecycle management involves eco-conscious product and process development activities to achieve sustainable manufacturing.
- Lifecycle assessment considers the life of a product from material extraction, through manufacturing and product use to disposal.
- Simulations are a powerful tool for manufacturers to improve their processes, products, and bottom line.
- Technological advancements in machine learning and predictive maintenance are not only changing the paradigm of how products are produced but the availability and reliability of equipment to produce consistent quality parts efficiently.
- A tool shop is a specialized facility or workshop that is dedicated to the production, repair, and maintenance of various tools and equipment used in manufacturing and helps to ensures that the necessary tools and equipment are available and in optimal condition to support efficient and high-quality production.

References

1. ISO 14040 - International Organization for Standardization, Environmental Management: Life Cycle Assessment: Principles and Framework, vol. 14040: ISO, 2006.
2. Hauschild, M. (2018). *Life Cycle Assessment: Theory and Practice*. Basel, Switzerland: Springer International Publishing AG, 2018.

Chapter 2.3

Equipment Fabrication

Overview

Equipment fabrication in manufacturing refers to the process of creating custom machinery, tools, or equipment used in the production and assembly of various products. This fabrication process involves designing, engineering, and constructing specialized equipment to meet specific manufacturing requirements.

The first step is to understand the manufacturing needs and requirements. This includes evaluating the production process, identifying the limitations of existing equipment, and determining the desired specifications for the new equipment. Based on the requirements, a team of engineers and designers develops a detailed design for the equipment. This involves creating 2D and 3D models, conducting feasibility studies, and performing simulations to ensure optimal performance.

Once the design is finalized, suitable materials are selected for construction. Factors such as strength, durability, and cost are considered during this stage. Commonly used materials include metals like steel or aluminum, as well as various plastics and composites. The fabrication process begins with the preparation of raw materials, such as cutting, shaping, or molding them into the required forms. Various manufacturing techniques are employed, including machining, welding, casting, forging, or additive manufacturing (3D printing). Skilled technicians or specialized fabrication facilities carry out these processes.

Once individual components are fabricated, they are assembled to create the complete equipment. This involves fitting and aligning different parts,

DOI: 10.4324/9781032688152-9

attaching fasteners, and integrating electrical or electronic components if necessary. Proper calibration and testing are performed to ensure the equipment functions correctly. Throughout the fabrication process, quality control measures are implemented to ensure the equipment meets specified standards. Inspections, testing, and quality checks are conducted at different stages to verify dimensions, tolerances, functionality, and safety.

Manufacturing line equipment must be compact, cost competitive, easy to use, easy to maintain, and reliable. Production line machines and corresponding equipment must also be designed for automation as cobots and autonomous guided vehicles become an integral part of the workplace. These things can only happen effectively when a well-planned approach to line design and execution is exercised.

In-House Equipment Fabrication

The ability to design and build production line equipment in-house can sharpen the competitive edge needed to survive and thrive in manufacturing. Innovative equipment designs, unique to a manufacturer's operating needs, can be realized more quickly and with fewer defects if the people who create the designs work in concert with equipment fabricators and users under one roof to realize standard and customized product line layout requirements. This is an ideal scenario which can optimize the interaction of key stakeholders when creating a new or next generation production line. Simulations can be evaluated, prototypes built, workstations exercised, and data collected to assess equipment capability and product line capacity for production readiness.

There are several benefits to building and assembling equipment in-house, the first being a significant cost saving in overall line investment, depending on equipment complexity, parts availability, and internal expertise. If lean and intelligent automation techniques are applied, in addition to the establishment of equipment build standards, the equipment lifetime savings can be even greater. Benefits are not only financial; shorter project execution times and quick responses to issues before and after start of production (SOP) can be achieved. Additional benefits can also include rapid equipment transfer to production and the real-time sharing of operational knowledge to the production team responsible for equipment use, repair, and maintenance. One final benefit that can be realized, if pursued with vigor, is increased equipment robustness driven by design decisions related to equipment construction and component selection based on experimentation and lessons learned. These topics are discussed in more detail elsewhere in this manuscript.

Keep in mind that equipment fabrication is not a trivial task. It takes talented and experienced individuals with the right problem-solving acumen and foresight to realize what is possible versus simply using what's available. Equipment is easier to fabricate, maintain, and repair when standards for construction and components are defined and readily available in-house or from a local source. Application of lean design concepts, ergonomic practices, quick utility disconnects (for equipment mobility), and easy access panels for maintenance can all contribute to a cost-effective investment over the life of a production line and its equipment.

A good in-house equipment build/tool maintenance shop can facilitate cost-effective construction by minimizing the need for a formal change control process through direct communication with designers and expected users. The impact of requesting and evaluating changes when outsourcing equipment builds can slow down the development and assembly process without even considering the potential cost associated with each change. When building internally, intellectual property can be better protected, and lessons learned can be applied to design builds by those who understand their origin and impact.

Building in-house equipment takes engineers, technicians, programmers, and machinists. To initiate an in-house build strategy, start with acquiring the expertise and skill set required for the activity. Standardizing machine and component usage will help simplify this activity. In addition, start building strong relationships with key suppliers to aid with in-house equipment builds and externally subcontracted work. It's likely that your equipment fabrication strategy will be a combination of internal support, based on available competence and resources, as well as external expertise when costs are lower or the required expertise is not available. Don't forget to include some type of key process indicator (KPI) tracking for the equipment development activities since timely realization of equipment fabrication and line assembly is essential for hitting the target dates for the start of production.

Outsourcing Equipment Fabrication

When outsourcing equipment fabrication, significant attention must be given to documenting construction details to avoid confusion, excessive questions, and unexpected changes due to unclear expectations. Unanticipated questions and clarification of requirements will likely add time to the existing build schedule leading to project delays in equipment completion and delivery. More up-front work is likely to be required when outsourcing to ensure requirements are properly and completely defined, clearly documented, properly executed, and adequately realized. See Table 2.3.1 to review a list of equipment build activities that should be considered regardless of executing an internal or external equipment build plan.

One other cost adder to consider when outsourcing is proper equipment packaging and shipment to the designated location. These costs should be included in the project budget and have the potential to be significant based on the size and fragility of the equipment being transported.

A good equipment build and line integration project manager is recommended to oversee outsourcing activities to ensure project milestones are met, requirements are correctly completed on time, and the final product is verified as meeting contractional requirements and stakeholder expectations. Relying on a contractor to complete the work specified without periodic monitoring and control can create unnecessary risk during the outsourcing process. Figure 2.3.1 outlines a typical high-level equipment lifecycle process.

Tool Shop Fabrication Capabilities

As discussed previously, a good machine/tool shop is one of the most important areas in the factory for equipment building, repair, and maintenance. It's where ingenuity and creativity work in concert to realize industrial equipment designs, solve unexpected equipment problems, and implement robust solutions. When competent machinists have capable equipment, quality tools, and access to experienced engineers and technicians, a qualified team of people can apply their craft with efficiency, while significantly reducing operational cost throughout equipment and product line lifecycles. This can only be done by maintaining employee competence and department capability.

The machines and tools that occupy the factory floor can vary significantly based on the industry and type of manufacturing processes being employed. Equipment reliability can also vary depending on the equipment supplier and build quality. Equipment warranties and maintenance contracts can help manage equipment lifetime costs. Regardless, it is wise to have a

Table 2.3.1   Equipment Build Activities Checklist

Phases	Equipment Build Activities Checklist
Make vs. buy decision	Project charter prepared/team defined
	Equipment make vs. buy analysis performed
	Project kickoff – KPIs defined
	Identify industrialization milestones (design freeze, PV, SOP)
Production concept	Production concept assessment
	Design for manufacturing initiated
	Boundary conditions of line/station identified
	Workstation processes defined
	Definition of new, unique, difficult (NUD) requirements
	Known long-lead-time components defined
	Known long-lead-time components ordered
	PFMEA draft started
	Preliminary line layout prepared
	Floorspace constraints considered
	Transportation system defined (conveyor, pallet size, etc.)
	Machine/station cycle time determined
	Concept acceptance review
Equipment process planning	Equipment specification drafted
	Budget defined (WBS elements available for procurement)
	Process equipment defined with KPIs
	Prepare equipment validation plan
	Review existing design guidelines
	Product drawings available with tolerances, process specifications defined
	Product prototypes available
	PFMEA initial release
	Logistics concept (input of material from supplier to customer)
	Prototypes available
	Resources assigned

(Continued)

Table 2.3.1 (Continued) Equipment Build Activities Checklist

Phases	Equipment Build Activities Checklist
Equipment procurement, build, and line integration	Work package data storage completed
	Design for manufacturing review/updated
	Equipment BOM completed for procurement and build
	Equipment and line integration
Equipment release	Final acceptance (requirements) review meeting
	Execution of equipment station validation plan
	Monitor KPIs
	Hand-off of equipment responsibility to production
	Prepare the equipment manual
	Spare parts list prepared
	Maintenance procedures completed
	Best practices/lessons learned documented

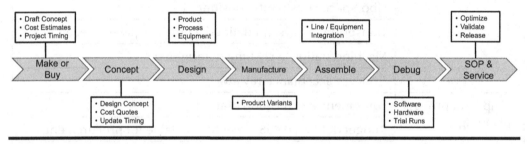

Figure 2.3.1 Equipment lifecycle process.

team equipped and capable to support unexpected machine breakdowns especially when production equipment availability is essential to meet challenging production output targets.

A modern-day manufacturing machine shop typically utilizes a variety of equipment and machinery to perform various machining and fabrication operations. Some common types of equipment found in a modern machine shop include the following.

CNC machines: Computer numerical control (CNC) machines are automated tools that use computer programming to control the movements of the machine. These machines can perform precise machining operations such as milling, turning, drilling, and grinding. CNC machines include CNC mills, CNC lathes, CNC routers, and CNC grinders.

Manual machines: Although CNC machines are prevalent, many machine shops still use manual machines for certain tasks. Manual machines require the operator to control the movements and operations of the machine manually. Examples include manual mills, lathes, drill presses, and surface grinders.

Milling machines: Milling machines are used to remove material from a workpiece using rotary cutters. They can perform various operations such as face milling, end milling, drilling, and tapping. Common types of milling machines include vertical mills, horizontal mills, and universal mills.

Lathes: Lathes are used to rotate a workpiece while a cutting tool is applied to shape it symmetrically. They are commonly used for cylindrical turning, facing, threading, and grooving operations. Types of lathes include engine lathes, turret lathes, and CNC lathes.

Grinding machines: Grinding machines are used to remove material from a workpiece by abrasive action. They can achieve high surface finish and dimensional accuracy. Grinding machines include surface grinders, cylindrical grinders, centerless grinders, and tool and cutter grinders.

Drilling machines: Drilling machines are used to create holes in workpieces. They can perform various drilling operations such as drilling, reaming, countersinking, and tapping. Drilling machines include bench drills, radial drills, and CNC drilling machines.

Sawing machines: Sawing machines are used for cutting workpieces into desired lengths or shapes. They include bandsaws, circular saws, and abrasive cutoff saws.

Welding and fabrication equipment: Machine shops often have welding and fabrication equipment for joining and manipulating metal parts. This includes welding machines (MIG, TIG, arc welding), plasma cutters, and bending machines.

Metrology equipment: Machine shops employ various metrology equipment for quality control and measurement purposes. This includes coordinate measuring machines (CMMs), height gauges, micrometers, calipers, and dial indicators.

Tooling and accessories: Machine shops require a wide range of tooling and accessories such as cutting tools (end mills, drills, inserts), tool holders, holding devices (vices, clamps), rotary tables, and tool pre-setters.

If repair is a focus of the shop, having common spare parts and spare part kits available can help reduce the time for needed repairs. For example, the in-house fabrication of cobot grippers, typically by 3D printing, can save significant time and money on modifications and repair. A shop capable of mechanical repairs can focus on valve type repairs while electronic repair shops can assist with electronic drives. A good tool shop, equipped with the appropriate team members and work items, can be a true asset to the design, build, and assembly effort.

Equipment Build Standards

Standardized equipment refers to the use of common or identical machinery, tools, and equipment across different production lines or manufacturing facilities. In manufacturing, standardized equipment is essential for achieving uniformity and quality in the production of goods. This is because the use of the same equipment across different facilities or production lines allows for better control over the production process, reduces the likelihood of errors, and enables easier maintenance and repair.

Standardized equipment can be achieved through a variety of means, such as the adoption of industry standards, the use of modular equipment designs, and the implementation of standard operating procedures. It is also important that the equipment is properly calibrated and maintained to ensure that it operates at peak performance. Using standardized equipment in manufacturing has numerous benefits, including the following:

Consistency: Standardized equipment ensures that the production process is consistent and reliable. This is because the equipment is designed to operate in a specific manner, and this consistency ensures that products are of the same quality every time they are produced.

Efficiency: Standardized equipment helps to streamline the manufacturing process, which can result in increased efficiency. Equipment that is standardized is often designed to operate at maximum efficiency, which can reduce production time and costs.

Safety: Standardized equipment can be designed with safety features that reduce the risk of accidents or injuries. This helps to protect workers and minimize the potential for liability issues.

Cost-effectiveness: Standardized equipment is often designed to be modular, allowing for easy maintenance and replacement of individual parts.

This can reduce repair costs, downtime, and minimize the need for specialized expertise or training.

Scalability: Standardized equipment can be replicated or expanded to accommodate changing production needs, allowing for greater scalability and flexibility in manufacturing processes.

The following are tips to consider when designing and fabricating smart, lean equipment for product manufacturing and assembly.

■ Follow a smart, minimalist equipment design by removing all unnecessary parts. Focus on equipment robustness and value.
■ Remove items like cabinets, top frames, and covers which restrict accessibility to equipment. Allow for an open design which facilitates efficient and direct part handling from one station to the next. See Figure 2.3.2.
■ Keep equipment extremely simple by minimizing moving parts.
■ Minimize safety-related components on the machine. Instead, focus on safety protocols for the entire work area or line.
■ Consider material loading from the back side of the equipment.
■ Service and maintenance areas should be at the back or front of the machine with no side access, allowing for close side by side equipment placement.
■ Use standard control boxes, electrical cabinets, pneumatics panels, and human-machine interfaces.

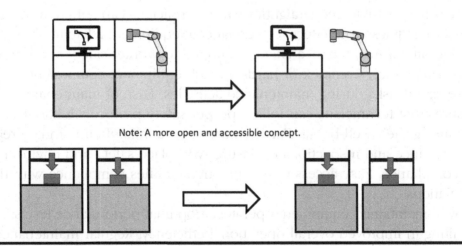

Note: A more open and accessible concept.

Figure 2.3.2   Equipment design considerations.

- Standardize pallet size to limit tooling changes needed for new products.
- Create a library of standard process modules for the simulation of new applications.

Ease of Equipment Maintenance

Equipment maintenance is essential to prevent unexpected break-downs and minimize production downtime. When equipment is easy to maintain, technicians can quickly access critical components, perform routine inspections, and carry out preventive maintenance tasks efficiently. This proactive approach helps identify potential issues early on, allowing for timely repairs or replacements and reducing the risk of unplanned downtime.

Timely maintenance can help avoid costly repairs or equipment replacement. By ensuring that equipment is easy to maintain, manufacturers can reduce labor costs associated with maintenance activities. Technicians can perform tasks swiftly and effectively, minimizing the time and effort required. Additionally, regular maintenance prolongs equipment lifespan, reducing the need for premature replacements and resulting in long-term cost savings.

Equipment reliability is crucial for maintaining consistent production output and meeting customer demands. Well-maintained machinery experiences fewer breakdowns and malfunctions, leading to improved overall equipment effectiveness (OEE) and productivity. When maintenance tasks are easily accessible and straightforward, technicians can adhere to maintenance schedules more effectively, enhancing equipment reliability.

Equipment maintenance is closely linked to worker safety and regulatory compliance. Complex or hard-to-reach equipment components can pose safety risks during maintenance activities. Ease of maintenance ensures that technicians can follow proper safety protocols without compromising their well-being. Furthermore, regulations often mandate regular maintenance and inspections to ensure workplace safety and environmental compliance. Easy access to equipment simplifies compliance with these regulations.

Well-maintained equipment operates at optimal performance levels, resulting in improved overall operational efficiency. Regular maintenance, including cleaning, lubrication, and calibration, ensures that equipment operates as intended. When maintenance tasks are easily performed, technicians can complete them more frequently and with greater precision, maximizing equipment efficiency and minimizing energy consumption.

In the event of equipment failure or performance issues, easy maintenance access facilitates troubleshooting. Technicians can quickly identify the root cause of the problem, perform diagnostics, and resolve issues promptly. Easy-to-maintain equipment often includes diagnostic features or access points that facilitate the identification and resolution of problems, reducing downtime and minimizing the impact on production.

The following are some tips to make equipment maintenance easier in manufacturing.

Maintenance schedule: Develop a maintenance schedule that outlines the maintenance tasks that need to be performed and when they need to be done. This will help ensure that maintenance is performed on a regular basis.

Train employees: Provide training to employees on how to properly maintain and operate equipment. This will help them identify potential issues and address them before they become major problems.

Clean equipment: Regularly cleaning equipment will not only help prevent breakdowns, but it will also extend equipment life. This includes cleaning and replacing filters, as well as keeping the equipment free from debris and dust.

The right tools: Ensure that employees have access to the right tools and equipment needed for maintenance tasks. Using the wrong tools can damage equipment, so it's important to use the appropriate tools for each task.

Preventive maintenance: In addition to regular maintenance, consider implementing a preventive maintenance program that includes regular inspections and equipment maintenance. This will help identify potential issues before they become bigger problems.

Accurate records: Keep accurate records of all maintenance performed, including any repairs or replacement parts used. This will help you track maintenance schedules, identify recurring issues, and maintain an accurate inventory of spare parts.

Assess equipment: Conduct regular equipment assessments to identify any potential issues or areas for improvement. This can help you identify where maintenance or upgrades may be needed, ultimately reducing downtime and improving overall efficiency.

By implementing these tips, you can make equipment maintenance easier in manufacturing and help ensure the smooth operation of your facilities. Overall, by prioritizing ease of equipment maintenance, manufacturers can ensure smooth operations, minimize downtime, reduce costs, enhance safety, and improve overall productivity and efficiency in their manufacturing processes. Reference Side Bar: Manufacturing Equipment Design Guidelines for more information on this topic.

Key Points

- Optimize resource efficiency by ensuring machinists support both fabrication and maintenance efforts.
- Consider machine capability (cost, time, resources) when designing and developing manufacturing equipment, production lines, and products in-house while being mindful of managing the outsourcing of these same activities.
- Strive to improve investment costs and reduce development time. Prepare an equipment fabrication and assembly plan.
- The value of using standardized equipment in manufacturing is that it can help to ensure consistent, efficient, safe, and cost-effective production processes that can be adapted to meet changing needs and requirements.
- Highly reliable equipment can be achieved by minimizing moving parts and reducing equipment wear and tear that leads to unexpected downtime.

SIDE BAR: MANUFACTURING EQUIPMENT DESIGN GUIDELINES

The following are general guidelines for designing manufacturing equipment:

- Safety should always be the top priority when designing manufacturing equipment. Make sure that all moving parts are properly guarded and that the equipment meets all relevant safety standards.
- Equipment should be designed with the user in mind such as minimizing physical strain on operators. This also includes designing the

equipment with adjustable height, minimizing the need for heavy lifting, and ensuring that operators can perform tasks comfortably and safely.

■ Equipment should be designed to maximize efficiency. This includes designing the equipment with optimal workflows, reducing set-up time, and using automation where possible.

■ Equipment should be designed to be easily accessible for maintenance and repair. This includes providing access panels, designing equipment with easy-to-replace parts, and ensuring that maintenance procedures can be performed quickly and easily.

■ Materials used in manufacturing equipment should be carefully selected to ensure that they are appropriate for the application and can withstand the stresses of the manufacturing process.

■ Equipment should be designed with modularity in mind, allowing for easy customization and modification as needed. This can include designing equipment with interchangeable parts or modular components that can be easily swapped out.

■ Equipment should be designed to be reliable and durable. This means using high-quality materials and components and designing the equipment to withstand the stresses of intended use.

■ Consider the environmental impact of the equipment, such as energy consumption, emissions, and waste generation, and design the equipment to minimize its impact.

These are just some general guidelines. There are likely additional considerations depending on the specific type of equipment and the environment in which it's being used.

Chapter 2.4

Production Line Integration/Assembly

Overview

Manufacturing line equipment assembly is the process of building and integrating various machines, tools, and components into a cohesive system that facilitates the production of goods on an assembly line. It involves designing, constructing, and connecting diverse types of equipment to ensure smooth and efficient manufacturing operations.

The first step is to develop a detailed design and layout for the manufacturing line. This includes determining the sequence of operations, the types of equipment required, and the overall flow of materials and products. The design process also considers factors such as ergonomics, safety, and production targets.

Once the design is finalized, the necessary equipment and components are built or procured. This may involve purchasing standard machinery or customizing existing equipment to suit specific production requirements. Equipment selection is based on factors such as production volume, product specifications, and technological capabilities.

The mechanical assembly phase involves physically assembling the equipment and machinery. This includes integrating various mechanical components such as motors, conveyors, robotic arms, sensors, and actuators. Skilled technicians or assembly teams perform this task, following detailed instructions and using appropriate tools and techniques.

Manufacturing lines often require electrical and electronic systems for control, automation, and monitoring purposes. This phase involves wiring,

DOI: 10.4324/9781032688152-10

connecting, and integrating electrical panels, sensors, programmable logic controllers (PLCs), human-machine interfaces (HMIs), and other electronic components. These systems ensure synchronization, communication, and precise control of the equipment during production.

Once the assembly is complete, thorough testing and calibration are conducted to ensure that all the equipment and systems are functioning correctly. This involves running simulated production cycles, verifying the accuracy of measurements, and fine-tuning parameters for optimal performance. Any issues or malfunctions are identified and rectified during this phase.

After successful testing, the manufacturing line equipment is installed in the production facility. This includes positioning the equipment in the designated locations, aligning conveyors, connecting utilities such as power and air supply, and ensuring proper integration with existing infrastructure. Once installed, the entire system is commissioned, and further adjustments are made to optimize performance and efficiency.

Operators and maintenance personnel are trained on how to operate, maintain, and troubleshoot the manufacturing line equipment. Documentation such as user manuals, standard operating procedures (SOPs), and maintenance schedules are created to guide personnel in their respective roles. Training and documentation are crucial for ensuring safe and efficient operation, reducing downtime, and maximizing productivity.

Manufacturing line equipment assembly is a complex process that requires coordination among various teams, including design engineers, technicians, electricians, and automation specialists. By following systematic procedures and ensuring proper integration and testing, manufacturers can create efficient and reliable production lines capable of meeting their production targets and quality standards. See Side Bar: Product Line Assembly Overview for more information.

SIDE BAR: PRODUCT LINE ASSEMBLY OVERVIEW

Assembling equipment into a manufacturing production line requires careful planning and attention to detail. It starts with determining what equipment is needed for your specific manufacturing process. This might include machinery such as conveyors, mixers, and packaging machines. Next, plan the layout of the production line. Consider the flow of materials and products, as well as the space required for each piece of equipment. Prepare the site where the production line will be installed. This might involve clearing the area, installing flooring and walls, and providing utilities such as electricity, water, and gas.

When ready, install each piece of equipment according to the layout plan. Follow the manufacturer's instructions for installation and wiring. Ensure that the equipment is level and properly anchored. Connect the equipment to each other and to any necessary utilities, such as power and water. Evaluate each piece of equipment to ensure that it is functioning properly. Once the equipment is installed, optimize the production line by adjusting the speed and flow of the equipment to maximize efficiency. Make any necessary adjustments to the layout or equipment placement to ensure that the production line is operating at its full potential.

It's important to train operators on how to use the equipment safely and efficiently. Provide ongoing training to ensure that operators are up to date on best practices and new technology. Finally, continuously monitor the performance of the production line to ensure that it is operating at maximum efficiency. Make any necessary adjustments or repairs to keep the equipment running smoothly.

Production Line Concepts

There are several types of manufacturing lines, each designed to produce different types of products at different volumes. Some common types of manufacturing lines are as follows.

Assembly line: This is a production line where products are assembled using a series of stations where workers perform different tasks in sequence. The assembly line is typically used for producing large quantities of standardized products with a high degree of consistency.

Continuous production line: This is a manufacturing line that operates continuously, with products flowing through the production process without interruption. This type of line is often used for producing high volumes of products with minimal variation in the production process.

Batch production line: This is a manufacturing line that produces a specific quantity of a product at a time, with each batch being identical in terms of design and specifications. This type of line is often used for producing smaller quantities of products with greater customization.

Cellular manufacturing: This is a production line that is organized into groups of workstations or cells, each of which is responsible for producing a specific product or component. This type of line is often used for producing a variety of customized products with high efficiency and flexibility.

Flexible manufacturing line: This is a production line that is capable of quickly changing its production process to accommodate different product designs or specifications. This type of line is often used for producing a variety of products with short production runs and frequent design changes.

Job shop manufacturing lines: These are used to produce highly customized products with complex manufacturing processes. The line is highly flexible, with workers and equipment being reconfigured as needed for each new product.

The type of manufacturing line chosen depends on the product being produced, the volume required, and the level of customization needed.

Workstation Concepts

In automated manufacturing, there are several concepts and approaches for product assembly and test workstations. The following are some commonly used concepts.

Sequential assembly: This concept involves a linear arrangement of workstations, where each workstation is responsible for performing a specific assembly or testing task. The product moves from one workstation to another in a sequential manner until the entire assembly or testing process is completed.

Parallel assembly: In this concept, multiple workstations operate simultaneously, and each workstation is responsible for performing a specific assembly or testing operation. The product is divided into sub-assemblies or modules, and each module is processed independently at different workstations. Parallel assembly allows for increased throughput and reduced cycle times.

Cellular manufacturing: Cellular manufacturing involves grouping workstations into cells, where each cell is responsible for manufacturing a specific product or product family. The cells are designed to be self-contained and capable of producing a complete product or sub-assembly. This concept improves efficiency by reducing material handling and streamlining the flow of work.

Flexible assembly systems: Flexible assembly systems are designed to handle a variety of product configurations and variations. These systems use reconfigurable workstations and equipment that can be easily adjusted or programmed to accommodate different product designs or specifications. This concept is particularly useful in industries where product customization or frequent product changes are common.

Automated testing stations: Automated testing stations are dedicated workstations designed specifically for product testing and quality control. These stations often incorporate specialized equipment, sensors, and software to perform various tests and inspections on the products. Automated testing stations can be integrated into assembly lines or operated as standalone units to ensure product quality and compliance with specifications.

In-line and end-of-line testing: In-line testing involves performing tests and inspections at various stages of the assembly process, typically integrated within the assembly line. This allows for real-time monitoring and early detection of defects. End-of-line testing, on the other hand, occurs after the final assembly is completed. It involves comprehensive testing and verification to ensure the finished product meets all the required specifications before it is shipped or packaged.

These are just a few examples of assembly and test workstation concepts in automated manufacturing. The choice of concept depends on factors such as the product complexity, volume, customization requirements, and desired production efficiency. Manufacturers often employ a combination of these concepts to optimize their assembly and testing processes.

Mixed Line Concept

Mixed line production is a manufacturing concept that involves the integration of multiple product models or variants on a single production line. In traditional production systems, each product typically has its dedicated assembly line, resulting in separate lines for different models or variants. However, in mixed line production, multiple product models are assembled on a single line, allowing for increased flexibility and efficiency in the manufacturing process.

The main idea behind mixed line production is to minimize the need for separate production lines for each product variant, thereby reducing costs, optimizing resource utilization, and improving overall productivity. By consolidating the assembly process onto a shared line, manufacturers can achieve economies of scale and eliminate the redundancy associated with maintaining multiple lines.

The first step is to design the products in a way that allows for commonality and compatibility among different models or variants. This involves identifying shared components, standardized modules, and flexible design features that can accommodate variations. The production line must be configured to accommodate the different product models or variants. This may involve arranging workstations, tools, equipment, and materials in a manner that allows for smooth transitions between different product configurations.

The production schedule is carefully planned to ensure that the right combination of products is assembled on the line at any given time. The sequencing of products is optimized to minimize changeovers and maximize efficiency. When transitioning from one product model to another, changeovers and set-ups are performed to reconfigure the line accordingly. This may involve adjusting equipment settings, reprogramming automated systems, and changing tooling or fixtures. Efficient changeover procedures are crucial to minimize downtime.

Mixed line production relies on flexible manufacturing systems that can adapt to different product configurations quickly. This may include modular assembly stations, adjustable tooling, robotic automation, and advanced software control systems.

Note that a "hybrid" line concept may be required when a significant difference in cycle times exists within production line workstations or between product variants. High process time differences require multiple units of single stations or multiple test stations with adapters. For example, an assembly process with a relatively low cycle time (~12 seconds) may need several test systems (or a test system with multiple adapters) due to a significantly higher test cycle time.

The benefits of mixed line production include increased production flexibility, reduced floor space requirements, improved resource utilization, shorter lead times, and lower costs associated with operating multiple dedicated lines. However, implementing mixed line production requires careful planning, coordination, and investment in equipment, automation, and workforce training to ensure smooth operations and maximize the advantages of this concept.

Decoupling Process Workflow (Buffers)

A manufacturing process decoupling buffer is a technique used to improve efficiency and reduce waste by breaking up dependencies between dissimilar stages of a production process. The goal is to create a more flexible and adaptable manufacturing system that can better respond to changes in demand or production requirements.

The term "decoupling buffer" in this context refers to the use of intermediate buffers or storage areas between different stages of the manufacturing process. These buffers allow each stage to operate independently, without having to wait for the previous stage to complete its work. For example, in a traditional assembly line, each station is dependent on the previous station to complete its work before passing the product to the next station. This creates a rigid and inflexible system that can be slow to adapt to changes in demand or production requirements.

In a decoupling buffer-based system, each station has its own buffer or storage area, which allows it to continue operating even if the previous station is not ready. This reduces the impact of bottlenecks or slowdowns in the production process and can improve overall efficiency and throughput. Overall, the use of process decoupling buffers is a key technique in the field of lean manufacturing, which aims to optimize production processes and minimize waste.

Decoupling points can be defined by several conditions:

■ Bottleneck processes
■ Machine or process capability
■ Work-in-process (WIP) areas
■ An operator's work distribution
■ Handover points
■ Execution of periodic tasks (such as the exchange of boxes, a regular cleaning step, or a weight check to verify proper machine functionality)

Buffer material can be created by running necessary operations during a break, while the line is stopped, during downtime or overtime, if needed. Reworked material can also be introduced as buffer material when appropriate.

If employing decoupling buffers to regulate the impact of process variation or minor equipment stops on operating performance, be mindful to keep the amount and size of buffers in balance with the working environment. Strive to minimize or eliminate the need for buffers over time.

Manufacturing Floor Space Optimization

In manufacturing, the efficient use of space is key especially when floor space is in high demand and expensive. A compact approach to line layout is a best practice, regardless of current space availability. When designing a product line with the goal of minimizing floor space usage, there are several guidelines you can follow to optimize efficiency and maximize the use of available space. Start by standardizing components, materials, and processes across the product line as much as possible. By reducing variations, you can streamline production and minimize the number of unique set-ups required, which can help optimize floor space utilization.

Embrace modular design principles to create products that share common modules or sub-assemblies. This approach allows for greater flexibility and interchangeability while reducing the overall number of unique components. It also simplifies inventory management and production planning.

Design products with a focus on minimizing their physical footprint. Optimize the arrangement of components and internal structures to ensure efficient use of space. Consider factors like component placement, stacking possibilities, and ergonomic considerations to achieve a compact design.

Maximize the use of vertical space by designing products that can be stacked or stored vertically. Utilize racks, shelves, or automated storage systems to take advantage of the height of the facility. This approach allows you to maximize storage capacity without significantly increasing the floor area.

Apply lean manufacturing principles, such as just-in-time (JIT) production and kanban systems, to reduce excess inventory and minimize the need for storage space. By implementing efficient production processes, you can reduce work-in-progress inventory and optimize the flow of materials, resulting in reduced floor space requirements.

Analyze the production workflow and identify opportunities to improve efficiency. Minimize unnecessary movement or transportation of materials and products within the production line. Optimize the layout of workstations, assembly lines, and equipment to reduce bottlenecks and streamline the production process.

Implement flexible manufacturing systems that allow for quick change-overs and adaptability to different product configurations. This approach enables you to produce multiple products within a smaller space, as the same production line can be reconfigured for various products as needed.

Utilize computer-aided design (CAD) software and simulation tools to visualize and optimize the layout of the production line. By simulating different scenarios, you can identify the most efficient arrangement of equipment and workstations, ensuring effective space utilization.

Establish a culture of continuous improvement within your organization. Regularly review and analyze production data, gather feedback from employees, and implement suggestions for optimizing floor space usage. Encourage collaboration and communication among team members to foster innovative ideas for space-saving solutions. Several other tactical tips include:

- Placing workstations as close together as possible to avoid empty space between equipment. Open space between equipment consumes valuable floor space and becomes a default storage area, creating clutter.
- Position the deepest equipment in long "U-shape" lines at the front of the line to optimize space consumption.
- Keep the inside width of a U-shape product line as small as possible without violating any standard or regulatory rules.
- Design narrow, single-process stations with the intent to supply material from behind the machine.

By following these design guidelines, you can minimize product line floor space usage, improve efficiency, and optimize the overall utilization of your manufacturing facility.

Equipment Mobility

Mobile equipment allows for greater flexibility in production processes. It enables manufacturers to easily reconfigure their production lines, rearrange equipment layouts, and adapt to changing product requirements. This flexibility is particularly crucial in industries that deal with frequent product changes, customized orders, or evolving market demands.

Mobile manufacturing equipment can be easily moved to different locations in a factory or to different facilities, providing flexibility in the production process. This can allow for faster reconfiguration of the manufacturing line and greater adaptability to changes in product demand or design. This flexibility is especially useful in industries where demand or production requirements change frequently.

Manufacturing facilities often have limited space, and mobile equipment helps optimize space utilization. It allows manufacturers to maximize the use of available floor space by repositioning equipment as needed. Mobile equipment can be moved out of the way when not in use or relocated to accommodate new production processes or expansions.

Mobile equipment can also simplify maintenance and repair tasks. When equipment breaks down, it can be moved to a dedicated maintenance area without disrupting the entire production line. This reduces the impact of maintenance activities on overall production and minimizes downtime. Additionally, mobile equipment can be easily replaced or substituted with backup units if necessary, ensuring continuous operation.

Making manufacturing equipment mobile typically involves modifying the equipment to be easily moved or relocated from one place to another. Before making any modifications, it is important to determine the specific mobility requirements of the equipment. This includes factors such as how frequently the equipment needs to be moved, the distance it needs to travel, and the terrain it will be moving on.

Wheels can be used to enhance mobility. The type of wheels used will depend on the weight of the equipment and the terrain it will be moving on. For lighter equipment, casters or swivel wheels may be sufficient, while heavier equipment may require larger, more durable wheels. To move the equipment, it may be necessary to add handles or lifting points to the equipment. This will make it easier to lift or maneuver the equipment into position.

Modular equipment is designed to be easily moved and reconfigured. This type of equipment consists of multiple modules that can be quickly assembled and disassembled, making it easy to transport and set up in different locations. Once the equipment is in place, it is important to ensure that it stays put. Installing locking mechanisms such as brakes or clamps will prevent the equipment from moving or sliding during use. Also consider power and utility requirements. Depending on the equipment, it may be necessary to modify power and utility connections to make them easily detachable and mobile.

Overall, equipment mobility in manufacturing offers increased flexibility, improved efficiency, optimized space utilization, simplified maintenance, enhanced safety, and better alignment with lean manufacturing principles. It empowers manufacturers to respond swiftly to market changes, maximize productivity, and maintain a competitive edge in today's dynamic manufacturing landscape.

Production Line Material Supply

Material supply in a production line refers to the process of maintaining a continuous and reliable flow of materials to each workstation or operation along the production line. This ensures that the production process runs smoothly and efficiently.

Material supply or replenishment to the production line should be automated and performed without interrupting production. Plan sufficient equipment autonomy to avoid production stops due to replenishment delays. Material replenishment tasks that cannot be automated should be performed by material handlers or other support staff until automation becomes possible. Strive to make each line autonomous AGV ready. The following are tips for ensuring a smooth and continuous supply of material for production.

- Accurate demand forecasting is crucial for effective material supply. Analyze historical data, market trends, and customer orders to forecast demand accurately. This will help you plan your material requirements and avoid shortages or excess inventory.
- Install kanban systems to replenish materials only when needed. This reduces carrying costs and optimizes space utilization.
- Develop standardized processes for material handling, storage, and retrieval. Clearly define procedures for receiving, inspecting, and storing materials. This reduces errors, minimizes waste, and improves overall efficiency.
- Organize materials in a staged area near the production line. This allows quick and easy access to frequently used items, reducing the time required for material retrieval and minimizing line downtime.
- Use visual cues such as color-coded bins, labels, and signs to clearly identify different materials, their quantities, and their locations. This improves visibility, reduces errors, and helps employees quickly locate and retrieve the required materials.

- Implement error-proofing techniques to prevent material supply mistakes. For example, use barcode scanning or RFID technology to ensure the correct materials are picked and delivered to the production line.
- Utilize technology and real-time monitoring systems to track material usage, inventory levels, and delivery status. This enables proactive identification of potential supply issues, allowing you to take corrective actions in a timely manner.

Additional tips for line side replenishment of materials supplied in different ways are as follows.

Small Components

- One time set-up by batch (~2 hours) or frequent material supply from outside the line (equipment back-side).
- Install simple pick and place equipment or a cobot.
- Supply in a tube or tray to make pick and place using a cobot simple.
- For bulk material, consider automation with 3D camera support.
- Consider kitting material if practical.

PCB Magazines

- Transport by automated guided vehicle.
- Automatic loading/unloading with an automated guided vehicle.
   Note: The production line must be AGV ready for material drop-off and pick-up activities.

Boxes

- Transport by automated guided vehicle.
- Consider a karakuri solution using gravity (for single box handover). See Side Bar: Karakuri Solution.
- Consider a powered conveyor handover (for stacked boxes).

Pallets

- Transport by automated guided vehicle.
- Line integration with automated palletizing/depalletizing.

By implementing these tips, you can improve the efficiency and reliability of your material supply process, ultimately enhancing your manufacturing production line.

SIDE BAR: KARAKURI SOLUTION

Karakuri is a term derived from the Japanese word "Karakuri ningyō," which translates to "mechanical puppet" or "trick device." In the context of manufacturing, karakuri refers to the use of mechanical or low-tech solutions to automate tasks or improve efficiency without relying on complex or expensive machinery.

Karakuri systems typically involve simple, gravity-driven mechanisms, pulleys, springs, and other mechanical components to achieve automation. These systems leverage the principles of physics and gravity to perform specific functions, such as transferring parts, sorting materials, or completing assembly processes.

One of the key characteristics of karakuri in manufacturing is its simplicity and reliance on existing resources. Instead of investing in expensive automated equipment, karakuri encourages the use of everyday objects or basic components to create efficient and cost-effective solutions. This approach can be particularly beneficial for small-scale or low-budget manufacturing operations.

Karakuri systems often focus on eliminating waste, reducing manual labor, and improving safety in the production process. By automating repetitive or physically demanding tasks, they can enhance productivity, reduce errors, and free up workers to focus on more complex or value-added activities.

The concept of karakuri originated in Japan and has gained recognition worldwide as a lean manufacturing technique. It aligns with the principles of the Toyota Production System and has been adopted by various industries to enhance efficiency and competitiveness.

AGV-Ready Production Lines

Automated Guided Vehicles (AGV) can provide touchless material flow in production. These autonomous transport vehicles can reduce manual work, speed up transport of raw materials to the line, and move finished goods from production to the warehouse for storage and delivery. Factors to consider for material movement by AGV are material handover height, factory spacing for AGV docking, and clearly defining replenishment points (e.g., conveyor). Avoid using only one point for multiple parts as this can create unnecessary complexity.

When delivering material to a manual workstation, consider having the autonomous AGV deliver its load to the operator's point of use. In the case of an automated workstation, fully integrate the autonomous AGV material handover into the line, considering a de-stacking mechanism if the transported material lot is greater than what the machine can handle. Plan at least one buffer position (waiting load carrier) besides the "active" position (load carrier in use) to avoid machine-to-AGV dependency.

Manufacturing Operators

Manual workplaces should be concentrated in one area to minimize the waste of motion (walking), WIP inventory, and transport. It is difficult to maintain a balanced operator workload when individual operations are concentrated in manual work areas that are separated from each other. Where possible, place automated process equipment and line segments behind manual workstations to minimize waste due to walking distances and material handling. See Figure 2.4.1.

Whenever value-added, use operators to perform production tasks such as monitoring robotic lines, assembling or inserting components (especially flexible parts), handling complex tasks (high variability and flexibility), and picking bulk material. Where feasible, use robots and cobot for simple handling operations, pick and place, and easy repetitive tasks. The application of robots/cobots will increase with advancements in technology, including machine learning and handling dexterity. If not robotics, continuously look for smart and basic automation solutions to manage simple, mundane, and repetitive manufacturing tasks.

Key Points

- Focus on simple and efficient solutions to optimize line investment.
- Highly flexible and reusable solutions are generally preferred.
- Modular lines will facilitate fast and easy modifications and scalable line concepts.

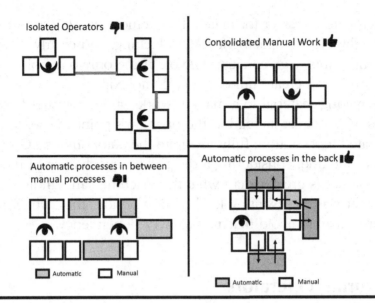

Figure 2.4.1 Operator positioning.

■ Avoid remote sub-processes or workplaces that require manual handling.

■ Strive to perform all manufacturing processes on the line transportation system to avoid additional loading and unloading work-in-process to other positions.

■ Avoid obstacles that could hinder or restrict the movement of operators within the production line or the automated transport of materials throughout the facility. Ensure walkways and working areas remain clear, clean, and orderly.

■ Manufacturing equipment mobility can improve flexibility, efficiency, space utilization, and maintenance in manufacturing operations, making it a useful option for many industries.

Chapter 2.5

Product Line Validation

Overview

Manufacturing product line validation is a process of verifying that a manufacturing process is capable of consistently producing products that meet the desired quality standards and specifications. This process involves a series of tests and checks to ensure that the manufacturing processes and equipment are operating correctly and that the finished products meet the desired quality criteria. Product line validation typically involves several activities such as the following:

Design validation: This stage involves testing the product design to ensure that it meets the functional requirements and is suitable for production.

Process validation: This stage involves testing the manufacturing process to ensure that it is capable of consistently producing products that meet the desired quality standards and specifications.

Production validation: This stage involves testing a sample of products from the production line to ensure they meet the required specifications and functional requirements.

Product performance validation: This stage involves testing the product under real-world conditions to ensure it performs as expected and meets customer needs.

The validation process is essential for ensuring that the manufacturing processes are robust and capable of producing high-quality products consistently. By validating the manufacturing processes and equipment, manufacturers can identify potential issues early on, make necessary adjustments,

DOI: 10.4324/9781032688152-11

and reduce the risk of defects and production failures. Ultimately, manufacturing product line validation helps ensure that customers receive products that meet their expectations and are of the highest quality. See Figure 2.5.1 for a visual depiction of this subject.

Machine Capability

A subcategory of product line qualification is the verification of machines and equipment being used to perform their specific task or operation within certain specifications or tolerances. Machine capability is a measure of a machine's ability to produce output that meets the required quality standards consistently over time.

The capability of a machine or piece of equipment is determined by several factors such as its design, construction, and maintenance. For instance, a machine's design determines its maximum output capacity, the range of parameters it can operate under, and the accuracy and precision of its output. Its construction determines the level of durability, robustness, and resistance to wear and tear.

In addition, machine and equipment maintenance determines its ability to preserve its performance over time. Regular maintenance and calibration ensure that machines and other equipment operate within their desired specifications, and that any wear or damage is addressed before it affects the machine's output quality.

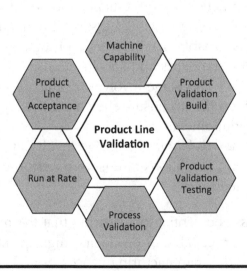

Figure 2.5.1 Product line validation.

Machine capability is usually expressed in terms of its capability index or Cpk, which is a statistical measure of how well the machine is able to meet the required specifications or tolerances. A higher Cpk value indicates a higher level of machine capability and a lower likelihood of producing defective products. It's important to calibrate the equipment before performing a Cpk analysis to ensure the equipment is performing at its optimal level. If the equipment falls short of expectation, consider adjusting, upgrading, or replacing the equipment if necessary. Other options to consider are as follows:

■ Analyze the process to identify the specific areas or factors causing a low Cpk. This may involve examining raw materials, equipment settings, process parameters, or human factors.

■ Conduct a statistical analysis of the process variables to understand their distribution, variation, and relationship to the desired specifications. Tools such as control charts, histograms, scatter plots, or regression analysis can be useful in this stage.

■ Determine the sources of variation in the process and work to reduce them. This can involve optimizing equipment settings, improving calibration, tightening tolerances, or addressing issues related to material quality.

■ Implement or enhance process controls to achieve and ensure consistency and stability. This may include revising standard operating procedures (SOPs), implementing automated controls, or adding inspection and feedback loops.

■ Contact the equipment suppliers for suggestions on how to improve equipment capability. They may have some suggestions based on their understanding and experience with equipment performance.

Remember that addressing a low Cpk is an iterative process. It may require incremental improvement to achieve the desired level of equipment capability over time.

Product Validation Build

Product validation build refers to a version of a product that is developed specifically for the purpose of testing and validating its features, functionality, and usability. The product validation build is typically created after the initial development of a product, but before it is released for serial production.

The purpose of this build is to ensure that the product is functioning correctly, meets the intended requirements, and satisfies the needs of the target audience. It is also an opportunity to collect feedback from users, identify defects, and make any necessary changes or adjustments to the product before its final release. The units built are commonly tested by a team of quality assurance (QA) engineers, who are responsible for identifying any issues or bugs in the product. Once the issues have been identified, the development team can work to resolve them and make any necessary improvements to the process or product.

Product Validation Testing

The validation testing process typically involves a series of tests that are designed to evaluate the product's functionality, durability, reliability, and safety. These tests may include the following:

Functional testing: This involves testing the product's performance and functionality to ensure that it meets the required specifications and operates as intended.

Durability testing: This involves subjecting the product to various stress tests to evaluate its durability and ensure that it can withstand normal use.

Reliability testing: This involves testing the product's reliability by subjecting it to a series of tests that simulate normal use over an extended period of time.

Safety testing: This involves testing the product's safety features to ensure that it meets the required safety standards and regulations.

Quality testing: This involves testing the product's overall quality to ensure that it meets the required quality standards.

Once testing is complete, the manufacturer can make any necessary adjustments to the process or product to ensure that it meets the required standards. Once the product passes the validation testing phase, it can be released with confidence that it will perform as intended and meet customer expectations.

Process Validation

Validating a manufacturing process involves verifying that the process consistently produces products that meet certain specifications. To validate a manufacturing process, you must first identify the process parameters that can affect product quality. These parameters include things like temperature, pressure, time, and humidity.

Next, determine process capability by collecting data on the parameters identified and the quality of the products produced. You can use statistical process control (SPC) methods such as control charts, process capability studies, and Six Sigma techniques to analyze the data.

Identify potential failure modes in the manufacturing process that could cause defects or non-conformance with the specifications. You can use tools like Failure Mode and Effects Analysis (FMEA) to identify potential failure modes and their impact on the process.

It's also important to develop a plan that outlines the steps to validate the manufacturing process. This plan should include the testing methods, acceptance criteria, and the sample size for each test. Conduct testing on the manufacturing process to verify that it consistently produces products that meet the specifications. This may involve testing samples of the product for physical, chemical, or other properties.

Once complete, analyze the test results and compare them to the acceptance criteria in the validation plan. If the results meet the acceptance criteria, the manufacturing process is considered validated.

Upon validation, it's critical to implement controls that will ensure the manufacturing process continues to produce products that meet specifications. This may involve implementing process controls, monitoring the process, and conducting periodic audits to verify that the process remains stable and capable over time.

Run at Rate

In manufacturing, a "run at rate" refers to a production test run that is conducted at the intended speed and volume of the production line. This test run is designed to validate the process and ensure that the production line is able to produce a specific quantity of products consistently and efficiently within a certain time frame, while meeting all quality and performance specifications.

The purpose of a run at rate is to validate the performance of the production line under actual operating conditions and to identify any potential issues or bottlenecks that may impact the overall efficiency and productivity of the line. This test run allows manufacturers to refine their processes, identify any issues, and make necessary adjustments before beginning full-scale production.

During a run at rate, production engineers and quality control personnel monitor the performance of the production line closely to ensure all equipment is functioning properly, all necessary materials and components are available, and the final product meets all required quality and performance standards. Once the run at rate is successfully completed, manufacturers can be confident that their production line is ready for full-scale production and that it can efficiently produce products at the required speed and volume while maintaining the defined quality standards.

The purpose of this testing is to identify any defects or issues with the product that could affect its performance or safety. Parts built during the run at rate may be used for product validation testing.

Product Line Acceptance and Approval

A manufacturing line is typically considered qualified for production when it has undergone a series of tests, inspections, and evaluations to ensure that it can consistently produce high-quality products that meet the required specifications and standards.

The specific criteria for qualifying a manufacturing line for production may vary depending on the industry, product type, and regulatory requirements. Some common factors that are often considered in product line approval include:

- Equipment and tooling validation. This may involve testing equipment and tooling for accuracy, precision, and reliability.
- Process validation. This may involve testing the process for consistency, reliability, and repeatability.
- Quality control. This may involve implementing statistical process control, visual inspection, and other quality control measures and methods.
- Training and documentation. This may involve ensuring that personnel who operate and maintain the manufacturing line are trained and

qualified to do so. All relevant documentation, such as standard operating procedures, work instructions, and equipment manuals, are in place and up to date.

Once all the acceptance factors have been adequately addressed and the manufacturing line has been validated, it can be considered qualified for production. However, ongoing monitoring and evaluation are necessary to ensure that the manufacturing line continues to meet the required standards over time.

Key Points

- Product line validation activities are critical to ensuring the product line is reliable, safe, and meets the needs of the customers, while also complying with applicable regulations and standards.
- Machine capability is a crucial factor in determining the quality and consistency of a machine's output, and it is essential to ensure that machines are designed, constructed, and maintained to meet the required specifications and tolerances.
- Manufacturing product validation testing is the process of testing a product during the manufacturing phase to ensure that it meets certain standards and specifications before it is released to the market.

MANUFACTURING IN THE DIGITAL AGE

3

In Part 3, we will focus on the start-up, stability, capability, and control of automated manufacturing systems in smart factories. These practices will not deviate significantly from the activities found in many modern factories today. However, the degree of automation, the maturity of AI, and the rate of machine learning will digitally transform these activities over time. This transformation will reflect the complexity of equipment, systems, and skills of the manufacturing team and the improvements pursued within operations. This section will reflect the changing face of manufacturing operations in the digital age and explore how employees interface and adapt to a more automated, smarter, and sustainable manufacturing environment.

In the process execution phase of manufacturing (Chapter 3.1), we will discuss the need to establish the process stability and capability of manufacturing processes along with maintaining the automated and smart equipment that makes it happen. Once process stability and capability are established, the manufacturing team focus will shift to the monitoring and control of equipment and processes to maintain production output at peak performance (Chapter 3.2). This becomes easier and more automated with the application of smart devices and systems used for this purpose.

We will continue our discussion of process control in Chapter 3.3 by focusing on the critical activity for line maintenance and equipment repair. In this chapter, we will stress the importance of maintenance and the preparation needed for rapid response to downtime issues. However, we cannot leave this last section without discussing the ongoing activities necessary to

DOI: 10.4324/9781032688152-12

capture best practices and lessons learned along with the need for a robust change management system (Chapter 3.4). It's vital to capture and harness this knowledge to gain a deeper understanding of the process and use it to continuously improve and optimize process performance on the never-ending journey to operational excellence.

Chapter 3.1

Process Execution

Overview

Process execution in automated manufacturing involves the use of specialized equipment, control systems, and software to carry out various manufacturing tasks with minimal human intervention. The process typically begins with the creation of a design or specification that outlines the product's requirements, materials, and production processes. This information is then used to program the automated equipment and systems to perform the necessary tasks.

Once the equipment and systems are programmed, the manufacturing process can begin. Automated systems use sensors and other feedback mechanisms to monitor production and ensure that the products are being manufactured to the required specifications. These systems can also make adjustments in real-time to ensure that the products meet the necessary quality standards.

Throughout the process, the equipment and systems communicate with each other and with a central control system, which coordinates and manages overall production. The control system can provide operators with real-time information on the status of the manufacturing process, including the progress of each task and any issues that need to be addressed. Let's consider process execution from the start of production (SOP).

DOI: 10.4324/9781032688152-13

Start of Production

"Start of production" (SOP) is a critical milestone in the manufacturing process as it signals the start of full-scale production, which requires significant investment in materials, equipment, and labor. Prior to the SOP, several stages of development occur including prototyping, testing, and validation to ensure that the product meets the required specifications and quality standards.

Before the start of production, manufacturers typically conduct extensive planning, design, and engineering work to ensure that the product is manufactured efficiently and effectively. This involves creating a production plan, determining the necessary resources, and developing the necessary processes, tools, and equipment for production.

Once the planning is complete, the manufacturer will typically conduct a pre-production trial run to test and refine the production process. This involves producing a small number of units to ensure that the manufacturing process is efficient and to identify any issues that need to be addressed before mass production begins.

Once the trial run is successful, the manufacturer will officially announce the start of production and begin mass producing the product. This involves producing a large number of units according to the established production plan, using the tools and equipment that were developed during the planning phase.

At the SOP, the manufacturing process is typically optimized to ensure efficiency, quality, and consistency. This may involve fine-tuning the assembly line, training the workforce, and implementing quality control measures to identify and rectify any defects or issues that arise during production. There are several key characteristics that are typically associated with the start of production:

Design finalization: Before the start of production, the product design must be finalized and approved for manufacture. This includes all design details such as materials, dimensions, tolerances, and production processes.

Tooling and equipment preparation: Once the design is finalized, the necessary tooling and equipment must be prepared for production. This may involve creating custom molds, dies, or jigs, as well as setting up assembly lines and other production equipment.

Production planning and scheduling: A production plan and schedule must be developed to ensure that the necessary resources and manpower are in place to begin production. This may involve coordinating with suppliers for raw materials, hiring and training new workers, and optimizing production processes.

Execution: This is the actual process of manufacturing the product, which may involve several steps, such as assembly, testing, and packaging.

Quality control: Quality controls must be in place to ensure that the product meets all necessary specifications and standards. This may involve setting up testing protocols, conducting inspections, and implementing quality assurance procedures.

Delivery: This is the process of getting the product to the customer.

The start-up process requires close monitoring for abnormalities and deviations from standards as these events are most likely to occur at the start of process execution. The following are several tips to consider at production start-up.

- Ensure all necessary resources, equipment, and materials are available at the start of production.
- Provide comprehensive training to operators, technicians, and supervisors. Ensure that they are familiar with the production processes, safety protocols, and quality standards.
- Make sure all equipment is properly calibrated, tested, and in good working condition.
- Establish preventive maintenance procedures to minimize downtime and ensure optimal performance.
- Define quality control checkpoints at various stages of production and establish procedures for inspecting, testing, and validating products.
- Build relationships with reliable suppliers.
- Monitor inventory levels to prevent any disruptions in process execution.
- Conduct safety training sessions and enforce safety practices to minimize the risk of accidents or injuries.
- Regularly assess key performance indicators (KPIs). Identify any issues or bottlenecks early and take corrective actions promptly.
- Seek feedback from employees and other key stakeholders for improvement opportunities.

- Use information gathered at SOP to refine your production processes, address any shortcomings, and make necessary adjustments for future production cycles.

Overall, the start of production is a critical milestone in the manufacturing process and requires careful planning and preparation to ensure that the product is produced efficiently and meets all necessary quality standards.

SOP is a time of great potential for problems. There are many things that can go wrong such as equipment breakdowns, quality issues, and delays in the supply chain. It is important to have a plan in place and resources available to deal with these problems. It is also a time of great opportunity. The start of production is a chance for the company to make a good impression on its customers and establish itself as a reliable supplier. By executing the start of production smoothly and efficiently, the company can build customer loyalty and create a positive reputation.

Standardization

One of the core principles for realizing process stability, simplicity, modularity, scalability, and other critical manufacturing practices in the digital ages is standardization. This includes the standardization of manufacturing equipment and daily operational practices.

Standardization is crucial to manufacturing because it ensures that products are made consistently to the same specifications, with the same level of quality, and according to recognized industry standards. This helps to ensure that products meet the needs of customers, are safe to use, and can be produced efficiently and cost-effectively.

By having established standards for materials, processes, and finished products, manufacturers can ensure that the quality of their products is consistent and meets industry standards. This helps reduce defects and errors in the manufacturing process, which can save time and money and improve customer satisfaction.

Smart factories typically consist of a diverse range of interconnected devices, machines, and systems that need to work together seamlessly. Standardization ensures that these components can communicate and exchange data effectively, regardless of their manufacturer or specific implementation. It allows for the integration of various technologies and ensures interoperability across different parts of the factory, enabling efficient collaboration and coordination.

Standardization promotes efficiency by establishing common protocols, formats, and interfaces. This streamlines operations, reduces complexity, and simplifies maintenance and troubleshooting processes. When systems and devices are standardized, it becomes easier to scale up or modify the factory without significant disruptions. It also facilitates the reuse of components and solutions, enhancing flexibility in adapting to changing production requirements.

Smart factories generate vast amounts of data from sensors, machines, and other connected devices. Standardization of data formats and protocols allows for consistent collection, storage, and analysis of this data. It enables data integration from various sources, making it easier to derive valuable insights, identify patterns, and optimize production processes. Standardization also facilitates the implementation of advanced analytics techniques such as machine learning and artificial intelligence, enabling predictive maintenance, quality control, and process optimization.

Standardization ensures that components and subsystems within smart factories are interchangeable and replaceable. This feature enables easier upgrades, repairs, and maintenance activities. If a particular component becomes obsolete or needs to be replaced, standardized interfaces and protocols simplify the replacement process, minimizing downtime and disruption to operations.

Standardization also plays a crucial role in ensuring the safety and security of smart factories. By adhering to established standards, manufacturers can implement robust security measures and protocols to protect critical systems and sensitive data. Standardized security practices reduce vulnerabilities, enhance system resilience, and provide a framework for addressing emerging threats. Furthermore, standardized safety protocols help ensure compliance with regulations and mitigate risks associated with machinery, processes, and worker well-being.

Standardization encourages collaboration and knowledge sharing among different stakeholders in the manufacturing ecosystem. When everyone follows common standards, it becomes easier to share best practices, experiences, and innovations. Manufacturers, suppliers, and technology providers can collaborate more effectively, fostering an environment of continuous improvement and innovation in the smart factory domain.

Standardization in smart factories promotes interoperability, efficiency, flexibility, data management, safety, security, and collaboration. It establishes a common foundation for seamless integration, optimized operations, and the realization of the full potential of smart manufacturing technologies. However, let's consider some potential drawbacks to standardization if not deployed mindfully.

Standardization Drawbacks

Standardization is not a manufacturing panacea. There are drawbacks to too much standardization. Standardization aims to streamline production by creating uniform processes, parts, and products. However, this can limit the ability to customize products to meet specific customer requirements. Customization often requires deviations from standardized processes, which can increase costs and complexity.

Standardization emphasizes consistency and conformity, which may stifle innovation. When manufacturers are bound by rigid standards, they may be less inclined to explore new ideas, technologies, or manufacturing methods that could potentially improve products or processes.

Standardization often assumes a homogenous market with uniform customer needs. However, customer preferences can vary significantly across regions, cultures, and individual preferences. Standardized products may fail to address unique market demands, leading to missed opportunities and reduced competitiveness.

Standardized manufacturing systems are designed to be stable and efficient, but they can become less adaptable to changing market conditions or technological advancements. Implementing modifications or incorporating new technologies into existing standardized processes may be challenging and time-consuming. Achieving standardization often requires significant investment in equipment, training, and reconfiguration of production systems. Small and medium-sized manufacturers may face challenges in implementing standardization due to the high upfront costs involved.

In rapidly evolving industries, standardization may lead to the risk of products or processes becoming obsolete. If manufacturers are too heavily reliant on standardized methods and fail to adapt to emerging trends, they may lose relevance in the market.

Standardization can foster a "one-size-fits-all" mentality, which may discourage creative problem-solving and the pursuit of unique approaches. It can also limit diversity in the marketplace, as smaller manufacturers may struggle to compete with larger companies that benefit from economies of scale.

It's important to note that while standardization has its drawbacks, it also provides numerous benefits such as improved quality control, cost savings through economies of scale, simplified supply chains, and enhanced interoperability. The suitability of standardization depends on the specific industry, market conditions, and business objectives.

Data Collection and Analysis

Data collection and analysis play a key role in automated manufacturing. Automated manufacturing systems generate a large amount of data at every stage of the production process, and this data can be used to optimize the production process, reduce costs, and improve product quality. Data management in smart factories refers to the process of collecting, organizing, and interpreting data generated by various systems and sensors within a factory environment.

Smart factories utilize advanced technologies such as the Internet of Things (IoT), artificial intelligence (AI), and machine learning (ML) to gather data from machines, production lines, and other sources. The collected data is then analyzed to gain insights, optimize operations, and make informed decisions to improve efficiency, productivity, and quality in the factory.

Data Collection

Data collection in smart factories refers to the process of gathering and analyzing various types of data from the manufacturing environment to drive insights and optimize operations. Smart factories leverage IoT, automation, and advanced analytics to collect data from interconnected devices, sensors, and machines deployed throughout the manufacturing process.

Smart factories are equipped with a network of sensors and devices embedded in machines, equipment, and production lines. These sensors can monitor various parameters such as temperature, pressure, humidity, speed, vibration, and energy consumption. They collect real-time data and transmit it to a central data repository for further analysis.

IoT enables connectivity and communication between devices and systems. It allows machines, equipment, and other components to share data and collaborate with each other. IoT devices play a crucial role in data collection by providing a continuous stream of information from different points within the manufacturing process.

Data logging involves recording and storing data from sensors and devices at regular intervals. It captures historical data, which can be used for analysis, monitoring trends, and detecting anomalies. Data logging may occur locally within individual devices or centrally in a dedicated server or cloud-based storage system.

In smart factories, edge computing is often employed to perform data collection and initial data processing at the edge of the network, close to the data sources. This approach reduces latency and network bandwidth requirements. Edge devices preprocess and filter data, extracting relevant information before transmitting it to higher-level systems for further analysis.

Smart factories rely on robust networking infrastructure to enable seamless communication between devices, sensors, machines, and backend systems. Wired or wireless networks are used to transmit data to central servers, cloud platforms, or local data processing units. This connectivity ensures that data flows continuously and securely across the factory.

Collected data is typically stored in centralized data repositories or cloud-based platforms. These storage systems provide scalable and secure environments to handle large volumes of data generated by smart factories. Proper data management practices are implemented to ensure data integrity, security, and compliance with regulations.

Once the data is collected and stored, advanced analytics techniques such as machine learning, artificial intelligence, and statistical analysis are applied to derive insights. These analyses can identify patterns, correlations, anomalies, and performance trends. The insights obtained can help optimize production processes, improve quality control, predict maintenance needs, and make data-driven decisions.

Data collection in smart factories enables real-time monitoring and control of various manufacturing parameters. By continuously collecting and analyzing data, operators and automated systems can track the performance of machines, identify bottlenecks, and take proactive measures to optimize production efficiency and reduce downtime.

Overall, data collection in smart factories forms the foundation for data-driven decision-making, process optimization, and continuous improvement in manufacturing operations. By harnessing the power of data, smart factories can achieve higher productivity, quality, and flexibility while enabling predictive and proactive maintenance.

Data Analysis

Smart factories generate vast amounts of data from different sources, including machines, sensors, production lines, and employee interactions. This data can include machine performance metrics, operational parameters, production rates, energy consumption, environmental conditions, and more. The data is collected in real-time and stored in a centralized database or cloud infrastructure.

The collected data is often diverse and comes from various systems and devices. Data integration involves consolidating and organizing the data from different sources into a unified format. This step ensures that data from different machines and processes can be analyzed collectively, enabling a holistic view of the factory operations. Raw data collected from smart factories may contain inconsistencies, errors, or noise. Data preprocessing involves cleaning, filtering, and transforming the data to improve its quality and usefulness for analysis. This step may include removing outliers, handling missing values, normalizing data, and performing other data cleansing techniques.

Descriptive analytics focuses on summarizing and visualizing historical data to gain insights into past performance and trends. This involves generating reports, dashboards, and data visualizations that provide a clear understanding of KPIs, production rates, downtime, energy consumption patterns, and other relevant metrics. Descriptive analytics helps identify areas for improvement and supports real-time monitoring of factory operations.

Predictive analytics leverages historical data and statistical modeling techniques to make predictions and forecasts about future outcomes. Machine learning algorithms are commonly used to analyze patterns in the data and generate predictive models. For example, predictive analytics can help predict machine failures, identify maintenance needs, optimize production schedules, and forecast demand. These insights enable proactive decision-making and reduce the likelihood of unplanned downtime or disruptions.

Prescriptive analytics takes the analysis a step further by recommending optimal actions or decisions to achieve desired outcomes. It combines historical data, predictive models, and optimization algorithms to provide actionable insights. For instance, prescriptive analytics can suggest the most efficient production schedule, optimal resource allocation, or energy-saving strategies. By incorporating real-time data, prescriptive analytics enables dynamic decision-making and adaptive control of factory operations.

Data analysis in smart factories is an iterative process aimed at continuous improvement. By monitoring and analyzing data on an ongoing basis, smart factories can identify bottlenecks, inefficiencies, or emerging issues in real-time. This allows for timely interventions, process optimizations, and the implementation of corrective actions. Through continuous improvement, smart factories can enhance productivity, quality, and overall performance over time.

Data analysis in smart factories leverages advanced technologies to collect, integrate, and analyze data generated within the factory environment. It encompasses descriptive, predictive, and prescriptive analytics to gain insights, make predictions, and optimize operations. By harnessing the power of data, smart factories can achieve higher efficiency, reduce costs, improve product quality, and drive innovation in manufacturing processes.

Daily Shop Floor Management

Daily shop floor management is a practice that aims to optimize the performance of manufacturing processes by focusing on the daily activities of shop floor personnel (see Figure 3.1.1). The current direction of daily shop floor management is toward the implementation of digital technologies that can help automate and streamline shop floor operations.

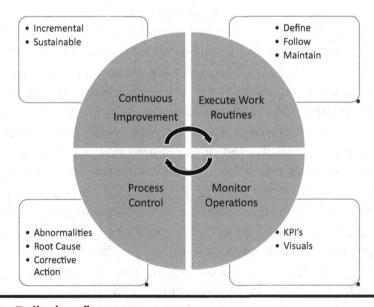

Figure 3.1.1   Daily shop floor management.

One of the key trends in this area is the use of real-time data analytics to monitor and optimize shop floor performance. By collecting data from various sensors and systems on the shop floor, manufacturers can gain insights into how their processes are performing in real-time. This allows them to quickly identify and address any issues that may arise, as well as optimize their processes to improve efficiency and quality.

Another trend in daily shop floor management is the use of mobile devices and cloud-based applications to enable better communication and collaboration between shop floor personnel and management. This allows for more effective and timely decision-making, as well as improved coordination between different departments and teams. Let's take a closer look into some the key aspects of daily shop floor management.

The abundance of data generated by smart factories is analyzed using advanced analytics techniques and AI algorithms. This data-driven approach helps to identify patterns, optimize operations, predict maintenance needs, and make informed decisions to improve efficiency and quality. Real-time feedback allows for early detection of defects and deviations, enabling timely corrective actions. Additionally, traceability systems track and record product information to ensure compliance, facilitate recalls, and enhance customer satisfaction.

Data visualization techniques are utilized to present critical information in an intuitive and easy-to-understand manner. Graphs, charts, and dashboards provide real-time updates on KPIs, production targets, and quality metrics. Reports generated by the system enable managers to track progress, identify trends, and take proactive measures to improve performance.

While automation and robotics play a significant role, human workers remain essential in smart factories. Workers collaborate with machines, oversee operations, perform complex tasks, handle exceptions, and utilize their expertise to solve problems that require human intervention.

Smart factories must work with their supply chains to ensure seamless coordination and synchronization. Real-time data exchange with suppliers and customers facilitates efficient inventory management, demand forecasting, and order fulfillment, resulting in reduced lead times and optimized logistics.

In addition, factories should focus on continuous improvement through the use of data analytics, performance metrics, and real-time feedback. Managers analyze data to identify bottlenecks, inefficiencies, and quality issues. They can then make data-driven decisions to optimize processes, reduce waste, and enhance overall performance. Optimizing the use of resources, such as energy, raw materials, and manpower, is also necessary in this new age. Intelligent systems monitor resource consumption and provide insights to identify opportunities for efficiency improvements, cost reduction, and sustainability.

As smart factories introduce advanced technologies, the workforce needs to be trained and upskilled accordingly. Providing training programs to employees ensures they can effectively operate, maintain, and manage the new technologies, contributing to the success of the smart factory.

Overall, daily shop floor management in a smart factory focuses on leveraging technology, automation, and data-driven insights to enhance productivity, optimize processes, and achieve operational excellence. By harnessing the power of digitalization, smart factories aim to achieve higher efficiency, quality, and agility in manufacturing operations.

Key Points

- Standardization plays a critical role in ensuring that products are of high quality, efficient to manufacture, and safe to use. It's important to establish a common language and set of expectations within manufacturing and promote consistency and reliability across operations.
- Data collection and analysis are important to automated manufacturing. By analyzing data in real-time and using advanced analytics, manufacturers can optimize their manufacturing processes, reduce costs, and improve product quality and consistency.
- Effective management of a smart factory involves a holistic approach that combines technology, data analysis, human expertise, and continuous improvement strategies to optimize operations, enhance productivity, and drive innovation.

Chapter 3.2

Process Monitoring and Control

Overview

Process monitoring and control are essential to automated manufacturing. They involve the use of sensors, actuators, and control systems to monitor and regulate various aspects of the manufacturing process. The process begins with the collection of data from sensors that are placed throughout the manufacturing system. These sensors can measure a variety of parameters, such as temperature, pressure, and flow rate. The data is then transmitted to a central control system, which analyzes the information and determines if any adjustments need to be made to the process.

The control system uses algorithms and decision-making rules to make these adjustments, which can include adjusting the speed of production equipment, altering the amount of raw materials being used, or changing the temperature or pressure of the manufacturing environment. The control system can also alert human operators if any issues arise that require their attention.

One of the key benefits of process monitoring and control in automated manufacturing is that it helps ensure consistent product quality. By monitoring the process and making adjustments as needed, manufacturers can minimize variations in the product and reduce the likelihood of defects. This can result in higher customer satisfaction and lower production costs. See Figure 3.2.1.

Key Process Indicators

Key process indicators (KPIs) are measurements used to evaluate the performance of a manufacturing process and identify areas that require improvement. KPIs are used to monitor and control various aspects of the manufacturing process, including production efficiency, quality control, and inventory management.

KPIs can be used to monitor production efficiency by measuring the number of units produced per hour, the amount of time it takes to produce each unit, and the percentage of units that meet quality standards. By tracking these KPIs, manufacturers can identify bottlenecks in the production process and implement measures to increase efficiency and reduce waste. KPIs can also be used to monitor the quality of the products being produced. This can include measures such as the percentage of products that meet quality standards, the number of defects per unit produced, and the amount of rework required. By tracking these KPIs, manufacturers can identify areas where quality control needs to be improved and take corrective action.

KPIs can be used to monitor inventory levels and ensure that the right amount of raw materials and finished products are available at the right time. This can include measures such as inventory turnover, days of inventory on hand, and order lead time. By tracking these KPIs, manufacturers can identify potential supply chain issues and take action to prevent stockouts or excess inventory. There are several common KPIs used in manufacturing. Let's briefly review some.

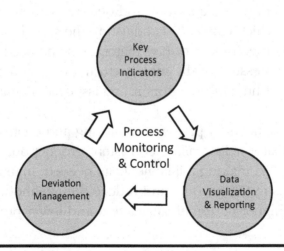

Figure 3.2.1   Process monitoring and control.

Overall equipment effectiveness (OEE): OEE is a metric that measures the overall productivity of a manufacturing process. It considers three factors: availability (the percentage of time that equipment is available for use), performance (the speed at which equipment operates), and quality (the percentage of good products produced). See Side Bar: Improving OEE for more information on this KPI.

Cycle time: Cycle time is the amount of time it takes for a process to complete from start to finish. It helps manufacturers identify areas where they can improve efficiency and reduce waste.

Yield: Yield measures the percentage of good products produced compared to the total number of products produced. It helps manufacturers identify areas where they can improve product quality.

Downtime: Downtime measures the amount of time that equipment is not available for use. It helps manufacturers identify areas where they can improve equipment maintenance and reduce production interruptions.

Defect rate: Defect rate measures the percentage of defective products produced compared to the total number of products produced. It helps manufacturers identify areas where they can improve product quality and reduce waste.

By monitoring these KPIs, among others, and taking appropriate actions based on the insights gained, manufacturers can improve their processes and ultimately increase their profitability.

Data Visualization and Reporting

Data visualization and reporting are critical components of smart manufacturing systems. These systems collect a vast amount of data about every aspect of the manufacturing process, from raw material inputs to final product output. The challenge is to make sense of this data and turn it into actionable insights that can help improve production efficiency, reduce waste, and increase overall profitability.

Data visualization refers to the graphical representation of data using charts, graphs, and other visual aids. This process can help make complex data more accessible and easier to understand. For example, a line chart could be used to show how the production volume changes over time, or a bar chart could be used to show how different machines contribute to the overall production output.

Reporting, on the other hand, involves summarizing and presenting data in a structured way that allows decision-makers to quickly identify trends, patterns, and outliers. Reports can be generated on a regular basis, such as daily or weekly, or on an ad hoc basis, such as when a specific problem arises that requires investigation. Let's consider how this topic of data visualization and reporting is changing in the digital age by reviewing several scenarios that previously would not have been possible prior to the digital revolution starting with interactive visualization.

Interactive visualizations: Digital tools and platforms enable the creation of interactive visualizations, where users can explore and interact with the data. This interactivity allows users to drill down into details, filter information, and gain deeper insights.

Real-time updates: With the advent of real-time data collection and analysis, visualization tools can now display information as it is being generated. This capability is particularly useful in applications such as financial dashboards, production monitoring, and live tracking of events.

Big data visualization: As datasets continue to grow in size and complexity, data visualization techniques have adapted to handle big data. Advanced algorithms, parallel processing, and cloud computing enable the visualization of large-scale data, facilitating pattern identification and trend analysis.

Data storytelling: Data visualization is no longer limited to presenting isolated charts or graphs. Modern tools allow users to create interactive narratives by combining multiple visualizations, text, and multimedia elements. This approach enables the effective communication of complex insights and data-driven stories.

Machine learning and AI integration: Data visualization in the digital age often involves the integration of machine learning and artificial intelligence (AI) techniques. These technologies can automatically analyze data, identify patterns, and suggest visual representations that best convey the insights hidden within the data.

Mobile and responsive design: With the widespread use of mobile devices, data visualization and reporting have adapted to provide responsive and mobile-friendly experiences. Dashboards and reports are designed to be accessible and optimized for different screen sizes, allowing users to access and interact with visualizations on the go.

Data security and privacy: As data becomes increasingly valuable, ensuring the security and privacy of data visualization and reporting is crucial. Robust security measures, encryption techniques, and compliance with data protection regulations are integral to safeguarding sensitive information.

It's clear that data visualization and reporting in the digital age have evolved to accommodate larger and more complex data sets, incorporate interactivity and real-time updates, leverage AI and machine learning capabilities, and prioritize mobile accessibility and data security. These advancements enable organizations and individuals to derive meaningful insights, make informed decisions, and effectively communicate data-driven narratives.

Deviation Management

Deviation management in manufacturing refers to the process of identifying, managing, and resolving deviations or anomalies that occur during the manufacturing process. Deviations are any events or circumstances that deviate from the normal or expected operation of the manufacturing process, which could impact product quality, safety, or regulatory compliance.

In smart manufacturing, deviations can occur for various reasons such as equipment malfunction, material quality issues, software glitches, or operator error. Deviation management aims to minimize the impact of these deviations by implementing corrective and preventive actions to ensure that the manufacturing process stays within acceptable limits.

The deviation management process typically involves several steps. The first is to identify any deviation from the normal manufacturing process. This can be done through various means, including real-time monitoring, data analysis, or visual inspection. Once a deviation is identified, it needs to be evaluated to determine the potential impact on the product quality, safety, or regulatory compliance. The next step is to identify the root cause of the deviation. This involves analyzing data, conducting experiments, or performing interviews to determine the underlying cause of the abnormalities.

Based on root cause analysis, corrective and preventive actions can be implemented to address the deviation and prevent it from happening in the future. After implementing corrective and preventive actions, the manufacturing process should be monitored and tracked to ensure that the deviation does not occur again.

Deviation management is critical in smart manufacturing as it helps ensure the final product meets quality and safety standards while complying with regulatory requirements. It also helps minimize the risk of product recalls, customer complaints, and legal issues. See Figure 3.2.2.

Key Points

- KPIs provide manufacturers with a way to monitor and control various aspects of the manufacturing process. By tracking these metrics, manufacturers can identify areas where improvements are needed and take action to optimize their operations.
- Data visualization and reporting in the digital age leverage advanced technology, interactive features, real-time updates, and storytelling techniques to transform raw data into actionable insights. It enhances data comprehension, facilitates decision-making, and promotes collaboration among users in an increasingly data-driven world.
- Deviation management in automated manufacturing ensures that any deviations or variations are promptly identified, analyzed, and addressed, thereby maintaining the desired quality, efficiency, and reliability of the manufacturing process and the produced goods. It helps in minimizing production defects, improving product consistency, and maintaining compliance with industry standards and regulations.

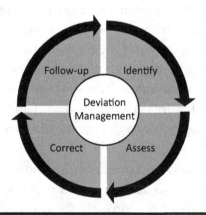

Figure 3.2.2   Deviation management.

SIDE BAR: IMPROVING OEE

Improving the OEE of a manufacturing line involves optimizing various aspects of the production process. OEE is a measure of how effectively a manufacturing asset is utilized to produce quality products within the scheduled production time. To improve OEE, you can focus on the following areas.

AVAILABILITY

- Minimize equipment breakdowns and downtime by implementing preventive maintenance programs.
- Conduct regular inspections and promptly address any potential issues to prevent unplanned stops.
- Optimize changeover times between product runs to reduce idle time.

PERFORMANCE

- Enhance equipment efficiency by optimizing operating parameters and settings.
- Streamline production processes to minimize cycle times and increase throughput.
- Identify and eliminate bottlenecks in the workflow to ensure smooth operations.

QUALITY

- Implement quality control measures to reduce defects and rework.
- Train operators to follow standardized work instructions and perform quality checks.
- Use statistical process control techniques to monitor and maintain consistent product quality.

OPERATOR INVOLVEMENT

- Involve operators in problem-solving and continuous improvement efforts.
- Empower them to make decisions and take ownership of their work areas.
- Provide training and resources to enhance their skills and knowledge.

DATA ANALYSIS

■ Collect and analyze data on machine performance, downtime, and defects.

■ Identify recurring issues and root causes to implement targeted improvements.

■ Use real-time monitoring systems and predictive analytics to anticipate and prevent failures.

OVERALL PROCESS OPTIMIZATION

■ Implement lean manufacturing principles to eliminate waste and streamline workflows.

■ Optimize material flow and reduce inventory levels through just-in-time (JIT) practices.

■ Continuously seek opportunities for process improvement and innovation.

EMPLOYEE ENGAGEMENT

■ Foster a culture of continuous improvement and encourage employee feedback.

■ Recognize and reward employees for their contributions to productivity and quality.

■ Promote effective communication and collaboration between teams and departments.

Remember that improving OEE is an ongoing process that requires continuous monitoring, analysis, and adaptation. By focusing on availability, performance, quality, operator involvement, data analysis, overall process optimization, and employee engagement, you can work toward maximizing the efficiency and effectiveness of your manufacturing line.

Chapter 3.3

Line Maintenance and Equipment Repair

Equipment Reliability

Touchless manufacturing relies heavily on the reliable performance of machines and equipment. Automated manufacturing often involves complex processes where large and small deviations in machine performance can result in significant quality issues. Therefore, reliable equipment can help ensure that the manufacturing process consistently produces high-quality products, which is critical for maintaining customer satisfaction and a positive reputation in the market.

The quality of the finished product is directly linked to the performance of the machines. Unreliable equipment can result in variations in production output, which can negatively impact the consistency and quality of the final product. Consistency is important in manufacturing, particularly when it comes to meeting quality standards and customer expectations.

Unexpected downtime can stop production, causing delays in meeting deadlines, reducing productivity, and ultimately affecting the bottom line. Reliable equipment helps ensure that the production process runs smoothly without interruptions, minimizing downtime. Unreliable equipment can lead to increased maintenance and repair costs, as well as higher replacement costs. Investing in reliable equipment reduces the need for frequent repairs, maintenance, and replacements, leading to long-term cost savings.

DOI: 10.4324/9781032688152-15

Improving equipment reliability in manufacturing is key to maximizing productivity and reducing downtime. Here are some strategies you can employ to enhance equipment reliability:

■ Develop a comprehensive preventive maintenance plan that includes regular inspections, cleaning, lubrication, and calibration of equipment. This proactive approach helps identify and address potential issues before they turn into major problems.

■ Ensure that your employees receive proper training on equipment operation, maintenance, and troubleshooting techniques. Well-trained staff can detect early signs of equipment failure, follow maintenance procedures, and address minor issues promptly.

■ Utilize condition monitoring techniques such as vibration analysis, thermography, oil analysis, and equipment inspections. These methods help detect anomalies and potential failures, allowing you to take corrective actions proactively.

■ Maintain an inventory of critical spare parts and establish a system for tracking usage, reordering, and restocking. This helps minimize downtime by ensuring quick availability of essential components when needed.

■ Avoid overloading or underutilizing equipment. Strive for a balanced workload distribution to prevent excessive wear and stress on specific machines. Regularly review production schedules and equipment capacities to ensure optimal utilization.

■ Cleanliness is crucial for equipment reliability. Implement effective cleaning procedures, removing dirt, debris, and contaminants that can cause damage or affect performance. Encourage proper housekeeping practices to maintain a clean and organized manufacturing environment.

■ Encourage all employees to take ownership of equipment reliability. Foster a culture where individuals are accountable for following maintenance procedures, promptly reporting issues, and suggesting improvements. Recognize and reward proactive behavior in equipment care.

■ Collect and analyze data on equipment performance, downtime, and maintenance activities. Utilize this information to identify patterns, determine root causes of failures, and make data-driven decisions for process improvements and equipment upgrades.

■ Engage with equipment suppliers to understand recommended maintenance practices, access technical support, and stay informed about updates and improvements. Suppliers can provide valuable insights into optimizing equipment reliability.

Remember that continuous improvement is key. Regularly review and refine your strategies, monitor results, and involve cross-functional teams to drive equipment reliability improvements in your manufacturing processes.

Equipment Reliability Metrics

In manufacturing, there are several key equipment reliability metrics that can help assess the performance and efficiency of equipment. Here are some commonly used metrics:

Mean time between failures (MTBF): MTBF measures the average time interval between two consecutive equipment failures. It indicates the reliability and uptime of the equipment. A higher MTBF value suggests greater reliability and longer periods of uninterrupted operation.

Mean time to repair (MTTR): MTTR calculates the average time required to repair failed equipment and bring it back to full operation. A lower MTTR indicates quicker repairs and reduced downtime, contributing to higher overall equipment reliability.

Overall equipment effectiveness (OEE): OEE provides a comprehensive assessment of equipment performance, considering availability, performance efficiency, and quality output. It is calculated as the product of availability, performance, and quality rates and is often displayed as a percentage. OEE offers insights into equipment reliability, utilization, and productivity.

Failure rate: Failure rate refers to the frequency at which equipment failures occur within a specified period. It is typically measured in failures per unit of time and helps identify the rate at which equipment is failing. Lower failure rates indicate improved reliability.

Mean time to failure (MTTF): MTTF calculates the average time until an equipment failure occurs. It is often used for equipment that undergoes preventive maintenance or is replaced after a fixed operating period. A higher MTTF indicates increased reliability and longer periods between failures.

Availability: Availability measures the percentage of time that equipment is available for production. It considers planned and unplanned downtime, including maintenance activities. Higher availability values signify improved equipment reliability.

Utilization: Utilization evaluates the extent to which equipment is used during the production process. It compares the actual operating time to the total available time. High utilization suggests efficient and effective use of equipment, contributing to overall reliability.

Remember that the selection of specific metrics depends on the nature of the manufacturing process, equipment types, and industry standards. It's essential to choose metrics that align with your organization's goals and objectives and track them consistently to monitor equipment reliability effectively.

Predictive Maintenance

Predictive maintenance is a proactive maintenance strategy that relies on real-time data and analytics to predict when equipment failures are likely to occur and take appropriate actions to prevent those failures from happening. In smart manufacturing, predictive maintenance can be used to anticipate and prevent equipment breakdowns, optimize production schedules, and minimize downtime.

To implement predictive maintenance in automated manufacturing, sensors and other monitoring devices are installed on machines to collect data on their performance. This data is then analyzed using machine learning algorithms to identify patterns and anomalies that could indicate impending equipment failure. Based on these insights, maintenance teams can schedule repairs and replacements in advance, reducing the likelihood of unplanned downtime and improving overall equipment effectiveness.

In addition to reducing the costs associated with equipment breakdowns and unplanned maintenance, predictive maintenance can also help manufacturers optimize their production processes by identifying opportunities for efficiency improvements. For example, by analyzing data on equipment usage and performance, manufacturers can identify bottlenecks in their production lines and adjust schedules and processes to maximize throughput and minimize waste.

Predictive maintenance is a powerful tool for improving the reliability, efficiency, and profitability of automated manufacturing operations. By leveraging real-time data and advanced analytics, manufacturers can proactively identify and address potential equipment issues before they become serious problems, minimizing downtime and maximizing productivity. See Figure 3.3.1 for predictive maintenance benefits.

Predictive Analytics

Predictive analytics is a subset of data analytics that uses statistical algorithms, machine learning, and artificial intelligence techniques to analyze data and make predictions about future events or behaviors. It involves the use of historical data to identify patterns and relationships, which are then used to make predictions about future outcomes. Predictive analytics can be applied to a wide range of fields, including finance, marketing, healthcare, and manufacturing.

Predictive analytics in manufacturing involves using data analysis techniques to make predictions about future events and trends in manufacturing processes. This helps manufacturers to identify potential problems before they occur, improve efficiency, reduce waste, and make better decisions. Some common applications of predictive analytics in manufacturing include the monitoring of equipment in real-time to detect potential equipment failures before they occur. This helps manufacturers schedule maintenance at the most convenient time, reduce downtime, and improve overall equipment effectiveness.

Predictive analytics can also aid in identifying potential quality issues before they occur by analyzing data from sensors, production lines, and

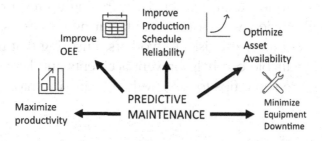

Figure 3.3.1   Predictive maintenance benefits.

other sources. This can lead to improvements in product quality and waste reduction. It can also be used to forecast demand, optimize inventory levels, and identify potential supply chain disruptions. This can result in reduced inventory carrying costs, improved delivery times, and increased customer satisfaction.

Production planning can apply predictive analytics to forecast production capacity, identify bottlenecks, and optimize production schedules, helping to improve efficiency, reduce waste, and increase output. Overall, predictive analytics is a powerful tool for manufacturers looking to optimize their operations, reduce costs, and improve product quality.

Spare Parts Management

Effective spare parts management is fundamental for ensuring smooth and uninterrupted operations in manufacturing. In a factory, downtime due to equipment failure can be extremely costly. Efficient spare parts management ensures that critical components are always available and can be replaced quickly, minimizing the risk of extended downtime.

Regular maintenance and timely replacement of worn-out parts can help extend the lifespan of expensive equipment. With proper spare parts management, maintenance and repairs can be done promptly, preventing equipment from deteriorating further and reducing the need for costly replacements. Keeping an inventory of spare parts can be expensive, but running out of critical parts can lead to costly downtime and delays. An effective spare parts management system can strike a balance between having sufficient inventory to minimize downtime without excessive inventory that ties up capital.

An effective spare parts management system can help reduce the time and effort required to locate and order parts, freeing up resources and improving overall efficiency. In some manufacturing processes, equipment failure can pose serious safety risks to workers. Ensuring that the right spare parts are always available can help prevent accidents and keep workers safe.

The following are some tips to effectively manage inventory of spare parts.

■ Maintain an accurate and up-to-date inventory of spare parts and components. This includes tracking stock levels, lead times for ordering, and identifying critical parts that may require emergency ordering.

- Procure spare parts from reliable suppliers, negotiating favorable pricing and ensuring timely delivery.
- Ensure that equipment maintenance schedules are regularly reviewed and any necessary spare parts are ordered well in advance of scheduled maintenance or repairs.
- Properly store and handle spare parts to ensure their quality and longevity. This includes ensuring that parts are stored in the correct conditions (e.g., temperature, humidity) and implementing appropriate handling procedures.
- Track equipment downtime and maintenance costs to identify patterns and optimize spare parts inventory levels and ordering processes.

Effective spare parts management can help manufacturers minimize equipment downtime, reduce maintenance costs, and improve overall equipment reliability and performance. By ensuring that the necessary spare parts are always available when needed, manufacturers can keep their production lines running smoothly and avoid costly delays.

3D Printing for Maintenance and Repair

3D printing, also known as additive manufacturing, can play a significant role in supporting equipment maintenance and repair in manufacturing. One of the most valuable applications of 3D printing is the ability to produce spare parts on demand. Rather than relying on traditional supply chains and waiting for parts to be shipped, manufacturers can use 3D printing to produce components locally and quickly. This reduces downtime and enables faster repairs, improving overall equipment maintenance.

3D printing allows for rapid prototyping and customization of parts. When repairing or maintaining equipment, customized components may be required to fit specific requirements. 3D printing enables the production of these parts with ease, ensuring a precise fit and reducing the need for extensive modifications or adaptations. This technology can also be used to create specialized tooling and fixtures needed for maintenance and repair tasks. These tools can be tailored to the specific requirements of the equipment, making the repair process more efficient and accurate. Additionally, 3D-printed jigs and fixtures can assist in positioning and aligning components during repairs, improving the overall quality of maintenance work.

In situations where replacement parts are not readily available, 3D scanning and reverse engineering techniques can be employed. A damaged or worn-out part can be scanned and a digital model created. This model can then be used to 3D print an exact replica, enabling the repair or maintenance of equipment even when the original parts are no longer produced.

Another interesting aspect of 3D printing is that manufacturers have the flexibility to experiment with different materials and optimize them for specific maintenance and repair applications. This can lead to the development of materials with enhanced properties, such as increased durability or improved resistance to wear and corrosion, resulting in longer-lasting repairs.

In smart manufacturing environments, 3D printers can be integrated into a network and remotely controlled. This allows for decentralized production, where spare parts can be printed on-site or at local service centers. Remote printing reduces lead times and shipping costs, ensuring a faster response to maintenance and repair needs.

In short, 3D printing can revolutionize equipment maintenance and repair in smart manufacturing by providing on-demand part production, customization capabilities, specialized tooling, reverse engineering solutions, material advancements, and decentralized manufacturing. These benefits lead to reduced downtime, improved efficiency, and enhanced productivity in the maintenance and repair processes.

Key Points

- Equipment reliability is essential in automated manufacturing, as it ensures that the production process runs smoothly, delivers consistent quality, is cost-effective, and is safe for workers.
- Spare parts management is a critical aspect of maintaining manufacturing equipment uptime and minimizing downtime. It involves ensuring that the necessary spare parts and components required for equipment repairs or maintenance are available when needed. A well-designed spare parts management system can help ensure that an automated manufacturing facility operates smoothly, efficiently, and safely.
- 3D printing has the potential to revolutionize automated manufacturing by providing greater design flexibility, faster prototyping, and on-demand production capabilities.

Chapter 3.4

Continuous Improvement

Overview

Continuous improvement is a philosophy and approach aimed at constantly improving processes, products, and services through ongoing and incremental changes. In smart factories, continuous improvement involves the use of data and advanced analytics to identify areas for improvement, optimize operations, and enhance overall efficiency.

Smart factories are highly automated and interconnected manufacturing facilities that rely on advanced technologies such as the Internet of Things, artificial intelligence, and machine learning. These technologies generate vast amounts of data, which can be used to gain insights into the performance of machines, processes, and systems.

Continuous improvement in smart factories involves using this data to monitor and analyze various aspects of the manufacturing process, such as production rates, energy consumption, maintenance requirements, and quality control. Based on these insights, adjustments can be made to optimize performance and reduce waste, errors, and downtime. For example, a smart factory may use sensors and machine learning algorithms to monitor the performance of a production line. If the data shows that a particular machine is consistently underperforming or consuming more energy than it should, adjustments can be made to optimize its performance and reduce energy consumption. Similarly, if the data shows that a particular process is generating a high rate of defects, changes can lead to improved quality control and waste reduction.

DOI: 10.4324/9781032688152-16

Continuous improvement in smart factories is an ongoing process that involves constant monitoring, analysis, and refinement. By leveraging data and advanced analytics, manufacturers can optimize their operations, reduce costs, and enhance their competitiveness in the marketplace. Let's look at how best practices and lessons learned can contribute to continuous improvement, making a factory smarter. See Figure 3.4.1 for more information.

Lessons Learned

Lessons learned refer to the knowledge, insights, and experiences gained from past experiences, projects, or activities. These lessons provide valuable feedback and guidance that can be used to improve performance, reduce errors, and enhance overall efficiency. Lessons learned help identify areas where improvements are needed. By reviewing past experiences, organizations can learn from their mistakes and identify opportunities where processes, procedures, and systems can be improved. Regularly reviewing lessons learned and making changes based on those lessons creates a culture of learning within an organization.

From a manufacturing perspective, lessons learned provide insights into process inefficiencies, bottlenecks, and areas for improvement. By analyzing past experiences, manufacturers can identify optimization opportunities, streamline workflows, eliminate waste, and enhance overall operational efficiency. From a quality control perspective, lessons learned from quality issues, defects, or customer complaints can help identify root causes and implement corrective actions. By understanding the factors that led to quality

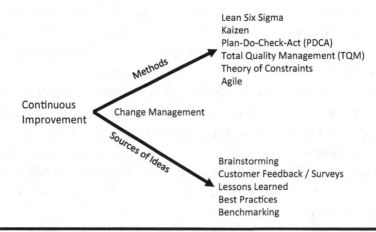

Figure 3.4.1 Continuous improvement methods and sources of ideas.

issues in the past, manufacturers can enhance their quality assurance processes, improve product reliability, and reduce defects.

Lessons learned foster a culture of continuous improvement within organizations. By reflecting on past experiences, companies can identify opportunities for innovation, adopt best practices, and implement changes that lead to ongoing enhancements in products, processes, and systems. Lessons learned often highlight potential risks and their consequences. By studying past failures or mistakes, manufacturers can develop risk mitigation strategies, implement preventive measures, and enhance safety protocols. This helps reduce the likelihood of future incidents, such as accidents, product recalls, or supply chain disruptions.

Lessons learned promote knowledge sharing and transfer within manufacturing organizations. By documenting and disseminating lessons learned across teams, departments, or even industry networks, companies can leverage collective wisdom, avoid repeating past mistakes, and accelerate problem-solving processes. Lessons learned also provide valuable information for decision-making. When faced with new challenges or opportunities, manufacturers can refer to past experiences and outcomes to make better-informed decisions, select appropriate strategies, and anticipate potential obstacles.

In the area of training and development, lessons learned can contribute to employee training and development. Manufacturers can extract valuable insights from past projects or initiatives and use them to enhance training programs, educate employees about potential pitfalls, and foster a culture of learning and improvement.

Through the process of actively capturing, analyzing, and applying lessons learned, manufacturing organizations can drive continuous improvement, reduce costs, enhance product quality, optimize processes, mitigate risks, and foster a culture of innovation and excellence.

Tips for Gathering Lessons Learned

The following are some tips for gathering and leveraging lessons learned for continuous improvement.

- *Conduct post-project or post-production reviews*: After completing a manufacturing project or a specific production run, gather the relevant stakeholders to review the process and outcomes. Discuss what worked well, what didn't, and identify areas for improvement. Encourage open and honest feedback from all participants.

■ *Document successes and failures*: Maintain a detailed record of each project or production run, including key metrics, milestones, challenges faced, and outcomes achieved. Document both successes and failures and analyze them to extract valuable insights.

■ *Analyze data and metrics*: Utilize data analytics and performance metrics to identify patterns, trends, and anomalies. Analyze factors such as production efficiency, downtime, quality control, customer feedback, and any other relevant data points. Look for correlations and causal relationships between different variables to identify areas of improvement.

■ *Foster a culture of continuous improvement*: Encourage all employees, from the production floor to the management level, to actively participate in identifying lessons learned. Foster a culture that values learning from mistakes and sharing best practices. Promote open communication channels to enable knowledge sharing and cross-functional collaboration.

■ *Engage frontline workers*: Frontline workers have valuable insights into the manufacturing process and are often the first to identify issues or bottlenecks. Involve them in the lessons learned process by conducting regular feedback sessions or establishing suggestion programs. Their input can help identify operational inefficiencies and potential improvements.

■ *Benchmark against industry standards*: Compare your manufacturing processes, performance metrics, and outcomes against industry benchmarks and best practices. This will help you identify gaps and areas where improvements can be made. Attend industry conferences and workshops, or engage with industry associations to learn from others and stay up-to-date with the latest trends.

■ *Engage with customers and suppliers*: Seek feedback from customers regarding product quality, delivery times, and overall satisfaction. Understand their pain points and expectations to identify areas where improvements can be made. Similarly, communicate with suppliers to address any issues related to materials, components, or logistics. Collaborating with external stakeholders can provide valuable insights into your manufacturing processes.

■ *Learn from the competition*: Monitor your competitors and the broader industry to learn from their successes and failures. Analyze their strategies, technology adoption, and innovations. Identify areas where you can implement similar improvements or differentiate yourself.

■ *Create a lessons learned repository*: Establish a centralized repository or knowledge management system to document and store lessons learned. This can be in the form of reports, case studies, or process documents. Make it easily accessible to employees so they can learn from past experiences and apply those lessons to future projects or production runs.

■ *Regularly revisit and update lessons learned*: Lessons learned should not be a one-time activity. Regularly revisit your repository, update it with new insights, and incorporate the lessons into your manufacturing processes and training programs.

Remember, the goal is to foster a culture of continuous improvement and to implement the identified lessons to drive positive change in your manufacturing operations.

Best Practices

Best practices can contribute significantly to continuous improvement by providing a set of established and proven methods, techniques, and approaches that have been tested and refined over time. By following best practices, organizations can achieve better results, avoid mistakes, reduce risks, and improve their overall performance. Best practices can help drive process standards, making operations more consistent and predictable. They can also help organizations improve efficiency by providing guidance on the most effective ways to accomplish tasks. This can lead to reduced costs, increased productivity, and better overall quality. They can also stimulate collaboration and knowledge sharing among team members, identifying opportunities for improvement, and developing new and innovative solutions.

Best practices can be acquired by benchmarking industry leaders. Study industry leader processes, systems, and practices to identify what sets them apart and make them successful. This can provide valuable insights that you can adapt to your own organization. Also consider evaluating your existing manufacturing processes and operations for best practices which can be deployed in other areas of your organization where applicable.

Involve your employees in identifying and implementing best practices. They are often the ones closest to the processes and can provide valuable insights and ideas. Encourage open communication, conduct brainstorming sessions, and establish feedback mechanisms to gather input from your workforce. In addition, encourage employees to engage with industry associations, attend conferences, and network with experts in their field. These interactions can provide access to valuable resources, knowledge-sharing opportunities, and case studies of successful implementations.

Invest in training and educating your workforce on best practices in manufacturing. Provide opportunities for employees to enhance their skills, learn about new technologies, and stay updated on industry trends. This will help build a knowledgeable and adaptable workforce that can drive the implementation of best practices. Best practices are not static, and the manufacturing landscape is constantly evolving. Regularly review and update your practices to ensure they remain relevant and aligned with industry standards. Stay informed about emerging technologies, methodologies, and regulatory changes that may impact your operations.

Best practices are constantly evolving as new technologies, methodologies, and approaches emerge. By staying up to date on the latest best practices, organizations can continue to learn and improve over time. Best practices provide a framework for organizations to continuously assess and improve their processes and performance. By adopting and implementing best practices, organizations can achieve greater efficiency, effectiveness, and success over time.

Identifying Best Practices

The following are some guidelines to help identify and adopt best practices:

- Benchmark your operations against industry leaders. Look at successful companies in your industry and study their manufacturing processes.
- Conduct internal process audits to identify areas for improvement. Evaluate the effectiveness of your current practices and compare them to industry standards or benchmarks.
- Encourage open communication and collaboration within your organization. Conduct employee surveys, hold brainstorming sessions, or establish suggestion programs to gather insights and ideas.

- Encourage employees to seek better ways of doing things and provide them with the necessary training and resources.
- Implement data collection and analysis systems to gather accurate and detailed information about your manufacturing processes.
- Attend industry conferences and seminars to understand the latest trends, technologies, and best practices in the field. Network with industry experts and peers who can provide valuable insights.
- Engage with your suppliers and manufacturing partners to understand their best practices. Foster strong relationships and open lines of communication with your supply chain network to exchange knowledge and learn from each other.
- Stay informed about emerging technologies and automation solutions in the manufacturing industry.
- Stay updated with industry publications, journals, and online resources that focus on manufacturing.

Remember that every organization is unique, and the best practices that work for one may not directly apply to another. Tailor the identified best practices to fit your specific manufacturing processes, resources, and goals. Continuously evaluate and adapt your practices to remain competitive in the ever-evolving manufacturing landscape.

Change Management

Continuous improvement requires constant change which must be effectively managed. Change management in a smart factory involves assessing the impact of the proposed change, planning for implementation, communicating the change to stakeholders, and monitoring and evaluating the outcomes. A well-executed change management plan can help mitigate potential risks, avoid disruptions to operations, and ensure that employees are adequately prepared for the changes ahead.

Implementing a smart factory requires significant changes to manufacturing processes, organizational structure, and workforce roles and responsibilities. A smart factory involves the integration of advanced technologies such as the Internet of Things, artificial intelligence, and robotics to create a fully automated production system. Implementing such a complex system requires careful planning and coordination. Effective change management is essential to ensure a smooth transition and successful adoption of new processes and technologies.

Smart factories require a high level of technical knowledge and skills, which may be different from those required in traditional manufacturing. Implementing new technologies and processes can cause disruptions in production. Effective change management minimizes downtime by ensuring that changes are properly planned, tested, and executed. Change management also ensures that employees receive proper training and are equipped with the necessary skills to work with new technologies and processes.

Investing in a smart factory is a significant financial commitment. Effective change management ensures that the implementation is successful and the new processes and technologies are adopted by the workforce, leading to a positive return on investment.

Change management helps to identify and manage any resistance to change within the organization. This is important because employees may be resistant to new technologies or processes, which can affect their ability to work effectively. It also fosters communication between management, employees, and other stakeholders, ensuring that everyone is on the same page. It aids in managing expectations, addressing concerns, and keeping everyone informed throughout the transition.

Change management is critical in a smart factory because it is deployed to ensure that the implementation of new technologies and processes is well-planned, communicated effectively, and optimized for maximum efficiency and productivity. Let's consider several ways to effectively manage change in manufacturing.

Effective Change Control

Effective change control is crucial for ensuring smooth and controlled transitions in any organization. Here are some ways to help you manage change effectively:

Establish a formal change control process: Develop a structured and well-documented change control process that outlines the steps, roles, and responsibilities involved in managing changes. This process should define how changes are initiated, assessed, approved, implemented, and reviewed.

Define clear criteria for change evaluation: Establish specific criteria for evaluating proposed changes. This ensures that every change is assessed based on its impact, risks, benefits, and alignment with organizational goals. Clear evaluation criteria help in prioritizing and making informed decisions about which changes should be implemented.

Involve relevant stakeholders: Identify and involve all relevant stakeholders throughout the change control process. This includes individuals or departments affected by the change, subject matter experts, project managers, and executive sponsors. Collaboration and input from stakeholders help in gaining buy-in, addressing concerns, and ensuring successful implementation.

Communicate effectively: Effective communication is essential to managing change successfully. Clearly communicate the reasons for the change, its expected outcomes, and the impact it may have on individuals or departments. Ensure that the communication channels are open, transparent, and timely, allowing for feedback and addressing questions or concerns.

Conduct impact assessments: Before implementing any change, perform thorough impact assessments to identify potential risks and dependencies. Assess the effects of the change on people, processes, systems, and the overall organization. This helps in planning mitigation strategies, resource allocation, and addressing any unintended consequences.

Prioritize changes: In situations where multiple changes are proposed, prioritize them based on their urgency, importance, and alignment with strategic objectives. Consider the potential benefits, risks, and dependencies associated with each change. This allows for effective resource allocation and ensures that critical changes are addressed promptly.

Document and track changes: Maintain a centralized repository to document all change requests, evaluations, approvals, and implementation details. Use a change management tool or system to track the status of changes, assign tasks, and monitor progress. Proper documentation and tracking facilitate accountability, provide historical context, and support knowledge transfer.

Test and validate changes: Before implementing changes in a production environment, conduct thorough testing and validation. This ensures that the changes are properly implemented, do not introduce new issues, and align with the desired outcomes. Utilize testing environments, conduct pilot projects, or employ other appropriate validation methods.

Monitor and review changes: Continuously monitor the implemented changes to assess their effectiveness and ensure desired outcomes are achieved. Establish metrics and key performance indicators (KPIs) to measure the impact of changes. Regularly review and analyze the results to identify opportunities for improvement and make necessary adjustments.

Learn from experience: Promote a culture of learning and improvement within your organization. Encourage feedback from stakeholders and incorporate lessons learned from past change initiatives. Embrace a mindset of continuous improvement to refine your change control process and increase its effectiveness over time.

By following these practices, you can enhance your change control management activities and increase the likelihood of successful and well-managed changes within your organization.

Key Points

- Implementing best practices in manufacturing is an ongoing process. It requires commitment, collaboration, and a willingness to adapt and improve continuously.
- Lessons learned are a valuable tool for continuous improvement. By analyzing past experiences and applying the knowledge gained, organizations can identify areas for improvement, enhance processes, encourage best practices, and foster a culture of continuous improvement.
- Best practices can play a vital role in supporting continuous improvement by providing a benchmark for performance, a roadmap for achieving goals, a standard for consistency, and a framework for innovation and learning.
- Change management is essential for the successful implementation of a smart factory as it helps to minimize resistance to change, ensures proper training, reduces downtime, and improves communication.

SUSTAINABLE MANUFACTURING

4

Overview

In manufacturing, sustainability refers to the practice of producing goods in a way that minimizes negative environmental impacts, conserves resources, and promotes long-term economic viability. It involves considering the entire lifecycle of a product, from raw material extraction to disposal, and implementing strategies to reduce waste, energy consumption, and pollution throughout the manufacturing process. In the last section of this book, we will discuss key aspects of sustainable manufacturing, including the following topics.

Resource efficiency: Sustainable manufacturing aims to optimize the use of resources such as energy, water, and raw materials. This involves reducing waste, improving energy efficiency, and implementing recycling and reuse strategies.

Pollution prevention: This topic focuses on minimizing or eliminating the release of harmful substances and pollutants into the environment. This can be achieved by using cleaner production technologies, adopting green chemistry principles, and implementing effective waste management systems.

Renewable energy: Sustainable manufacturers prioritize the use of renewable energy sources such as solar, wind, or hydropower to power their

DOI: 10.4324/9781032688152-17

production processes. This reduces reliance on fossil fuels and lowers greenhouse gas emissions.

Design for sustainability: The concept of design for sustainability involves considering environmental and social factors during the product design phase. This includes selecting eco-friendly materials, designing for durability and recyclability, and minimizing the overall environmental footprint of the product.

Supply chain management: Sustainable manufacturing extends beyond individual facilities and encompasses the entire supply chain. Manufacturers work closely with suppliers to ensure sustainable sourcing practices, ethical labor conditions, and reduced transportation impacts.

Lifecycle assessment: Manufacturers conduct lifecycle assessments (LCAs) to evaluate the environmental impacts of their products throughout their entire lifecycle. LCAs help identify areas for improvement and guide decision-making to reduce environmental burdens.

Stakeholder engagement: Sustainable manufacturing involves engaging with various stakeholders such as employees, customers, suppliers, and communities. This collaboration helps foster innovation, transparency, and accountability and ensures that social and environmental concerns are addressed.

Benefits of sustainable manufacturing include reduced environmental pollution, conservation of resources, cost savings through improved efficiency, enhanced brand reputation, and compliance with regulatory requirements. By adopting sustainable practices, manufacturers contribute to a more environmentally responsible and socially conscious industrial sector.

Chapter 4.1

Resource Efficiency

Sustainable manufacturing aims to optimize the use of resources such as water, energy, and raw materials. This involves adopting efficient production techniques, implementing recycling and waste reduction programs, and exploring alternative materials that are renewable or have a lower environmental impact. See Figure 4.1.1.

Water Conservation

Water conservation in manufacturing refers to the implementation of strategies and practices aimed at reducing water consumption and improving the overall efficiency of water usage within industrial processes. Manufacturing operations often require significant amounts of water for various purposes, such as cleaning, cooling, heating, and as a component in the production of goods. However, due to the increasing scarcity of freshwater resources and the growing awareness of environmental sustainability, companies are increasingly focused on conserving water in their manufacturing operations.

Water conservation in manufacturing offers several benefits, both for the environment and for the companies themselves. Water is a finite resource, and conserving it helps preserve the environment. By reducing water consumption and minimizing wastewater discharge, manufacturing facilities can contribute to the conservation of local water sources, ecosystems, and overall water availability. This promotes sustainability and helps protect the planet's natural resources.

DOI: 10.4324/9781032688152-18

Figure 4.1.1   Resource efficiency.

Implementing water conservation measures can lead to significant cost savings for manufacturing companies. By reducing water usage, businesses can lower their water bills and wastewater treatment expenses. Additionally, optimizing water management systems often involves identifying and fixing leaks and inefficiencies, which can further reduce operational costs.

Water conservation and energy efficiency go hand in hand. Treating and distributing water requires energy, so reducing water consumption also means reducing energy consumption. By implementing water-saving strategies, manufacturing facilities can decrease their energy usage, resulting in cost savings and a reduced carbon footprint. Many regions have strict regulations regarding water usage and wastewater discharge. By practicing water conservation, manufacturing companies can ensure compliance with these regulations, avoiding fines, penalties, and reputational damage. Implementing efficient water management practices also demonstrates a commitment to environmental responsibility, which can enhance a company's image and reputation.

Water conservation efforts often involve treating and reusing water within manufacturing processes. By implementing advanced treatment technologies, companies can recycle and reuse water, leading to improved water quality. This can have a positive impact on downstream ecosystems, local communities, and overall water resources. Dependence on water-intensive processes can pose a risk to manufacturing operations, particularly in areas prone to water scarcity or drought. By implementing water conservation practices, companies can reduce their vulnerability to water shortages and disruptions in the water supply. This enhances business continuity and minimizes operational risks.

Embracing water conservation can drive innovation within manufacturing processes. Companies may explore alternative water sources, implement water-efficient technologies, and optimize production methods to reduce water usage. These efforts often lead to increased operational efficiency, improved product quality, and a competitive advantage in the market.

Overall, water conservation in manufacturing offers numerous benefits, including environmental protection, cost savings, regulatory compliance, energy efficiency, improved water quality, risk mitigation, and opportunities for innovation. By prioritizing water conservation, manufacturing companies can contribute to a more sustainable and responsible future.

Tips for Reducing Water Consumption

- Assess your facility's water usage patterns and identify areas of high consumption. This will help you pinpoint specific areas where you can focus your efforts and make targeted improvements.
- Regularly inspect and maintain your equipment, machinery, and pipelines to identify and fix leaks or malfunctions promptly. Even minor leaks can result in significant water wastage over time.
- Consider upgrading your manufacturing equipment to more water-efficient models. Look for technologies that optimize water usage without compromising productivity. For example, low-flow nozzles, high-pressure cleaning systems, and water recycling systems can significantly reduce water consumption.
- Cooling systems often account for a large portion of water usage in manufacturing facilities. Implement measures like optimizing cooling tower operations, using efficient heat exchangers, and monitoring water chemistry to minimize water losses through evaporation and drift.
- Evaluate opportunities to recycle and reuse water within your facility. Wastewater treatment systems can help purify and reuse water for non-potable applications such as equipment cleaning or landscape irrigation.
- Educate your employees about the importance of water conservation and involve them in your conservation efforts. Encourage simple practices such as turning off taps when not in use, reporting leaks, and using water-efficient methods for cleaning and maintenance.

- Analyze your manufacturing processes to identify areas where water consumption can be minimized without compromising product quality. Explore alternative production methods that require less water or adopt closed-loop systems to minimize water loss.
- If feasible, implement rainwater harvesting systems to collect and store rainwater for non-potable applications. This can help reduce reliance on freshwater sources for tasks such as landscape irrigation or toilet flushing.
- Establish water consumption targets and regularly monitor and benchmark your facility's performance. This will help you track progress, identify areas for further improvement, and motivate ongoing water conservation efforts.
- Engage with your suppliers and encourage them to adopt sustainable water practices. Encourage the use of water-efficient materials and components in your manufacturing processes, and support suppliers who prioritize water conservation.

Remember, every manufacturing facility is unique, so tailor these recommendations to fit your specific operations and challenges. Conserving water requires a multi-faceted approach involving technological upgrades, process optimization, and employee engagement.

Energy Conservation

Energy conservation in manufacturing refers to the practice of minimizing energy consumption and optimizing energy usage throughout the manufacturing process. It involves adopting various strategies, technologies, and practices to reduce energy waste and improve overall energy efficiency. The primary goal is to reduce the environmental impact of manufacturing operations while also achieving cost savings.

Energy conservation in manufacturing offers several significant benefits. One of the primary advantages of energy conservation in manufacturing is the potential for cost savings. By reducing energy consumption, companies can significantly lower their energy bills and operational expenses. This is particularly important for energy-intensive industries, where energy costs can make up a substantial portion of overall expenditures. By investing in energy-efficient technologies and practices, manufacturers can improve their bottom line and enhance their competitiveness.

Manufacturing processes often consume large amounts of energy, which can lead to a significant carbon footprint. Energy conservation initiatives help reduce greenhouse gas emissions and mitigate the environmental impact of manufacturing operations. By lowering energy consumption, manufacturers contribute to a cleaner and healthier environment, addressing concerns related to climate change and air pollution. Many regions and countries have implemented regulations and standards aimed at reducing energy consumption and promoting energy efficiency. By implementing energy conservation measures, manufacturers can ensure compliance with these regulations, avoiding penalties and legal issues. Additionally, being proactive in energy conservation can enhance a company's reputation and improve relationships with regulatory agencies and the community.

Energy conservation and environmental sustainability are increasingly important factors for consumers and businesses when making purchasing decisions. Manufacturers that prioritize energy efficiency and sustainable practices can differentiate themselves from competitors and attract environmentally conscious customers. Energy conservation initiatives can also contribute to positive brand perception and enhance corporate social responsibility, which can be valuable in attracting investors, partners, and employee talent.

Energy conservation measures often go hand in hand with process optimization and operational improvements. By analyzing energy usage and implementing energy-efficient technologies, manufacturers can identify areas of inefficiency and optimize their processes. This can lead to streamlined operations, reduced downtime, and improved productivity. Energy conservation initiatives may also uncover opportunities for innovation and technological advancements within the manufacturing processes.

Investing in energy conservation measures can provide long-term cost stability for manufacturers. By reducing reliance on volatile energy markets and mitigating the risks associated with energy price fluctuations, companies can better predict and manage their operational expenses. This stability can contribute to improved financial planning and sustainability.

Energy conservation in manufacturing offers a wide range of benefits, including cost savings, environmental sustainability, compliance with regulations, enhanced reputation, improved operational efficiency, and long-term cost stability. By embracing energy conservation practices, manufacturers can achieve both economic and environmental gains, positioning themselves for long-term success.

Tips for Energy Conservation

■ Start by assessing your current energy usage. Identify areas where energy is being wasted or consumed inefficiently. An energy audit will help you understand where improvements can be made.

■ Replace outdated machinery and equipment with energy-efficient models. Look for equipment that has been certified with energy-efficient ratings and features such as variable speed drives, which optimize energy consumption based on demand.

■ Analyze your production processes to identify opportunities for energy conservation. This could involve streamlining workflows, reducing idle time, optimizing production schedules, and minimizing unnecessary process movements or material handling.

■ Switch to energy-efficient lighting systems such as LED bulbs, which consume significantly less energy than traditional incandescent or fluorescent lights. Additionally, utilize natural lighting wherever possible to reduce reliance on artificial lighting during daylight hours.

■ Insulate buildings, windows, doors, and other areas to prevent heat loss or gain. Proper insulation minimizes the need for heating or cooling, leading to significant energy savings.

■ Recover waste heat generated by industrial processes and use it for other purposes, such as space heating or preheating raw materials or water. Heat exchangers or heat recovery systems can capture and repurpose this waste heat effectively.

■ Explore the possibility of integrating renewable energy sources like solar panels or wind turbines to power manufacturing operations. This will help reduce reliance on fossil fuels and lower greenhouse gas emissions.

■ Raise awareness among your employees about energy conservation practices and encourage their active participation. Implement an energy-saving culture by promoting responsible energy use, turning off unused equipment, and properly maintaining machinery.

■ Install energy monitoring systems to track energy consumption in real-time. This data will help you identify patterns, set benchmarks, and pinpoint areas for improvement. Implement automated systems and controls to optimize energy use based on demand.

■ Engage with your supply chain partners to promote energy-efficient practices and sustainable manufacturing. Collaborate with customers to identify opportunities for energy conservation throughout the product lifecycle, including packaging, transportation, and usage.

Tips for reducing energy consumption can be found in the Side Bar at the end of this chapter

Material Conservation

Material conservation in manufacturing refers to the practice of minimizing waste and optimizing the use of resources throughout the production process. It involves strategies and techniques aimed at reducing the consumption of raw materials, energy, water, and other resources, while maximizing the efficiency of manufacturing operations. The goal is to minimize environmental impact and promote sustainability.

Reducing material waste in manufacturing is an important goal that can benefit both the environment and a company's bottom line. Manufacturers can strive to minimize waste generation by implementing measures such as lean manufacturing principles, which focus on eliminating non-value-added activities and optimizing production flows. This reduces the amount of raw materials and resources that end up as waste.

Rather than discarding materials as waste, manufacturers can emphasize recycling and reusing wherever possible. This involves collecting and processing waste materials and reintroducing them into the manufacturing process as raw materials or inputs, reducing the need for extracting and processing new resources.

Manufacturers can also aim to design products and processes that minimize material usage while maintaining or enhancing performance. This can involve lightweighting designs, using eco-friendly materials, and incorporating modular or standardized components that allow for easier repair or upgrades, extending the lifespan of the product. Emphasize designing products that are easy to manufacture, assemble, and disassemble. This approach enables the use of fewer materials, simplifies production processes, and facilitates the recycling or reuse of components.

Manufacturers can implement energy-efficient technologies, such as high-efficiency machinery, optimized heating and cooling systems, and smart controls. This reduces energy consumption, lowers costs, and reduces the environmental impact associated with energy generation. Water is another vital resource in manufacturing, and efforts should be made to reduce its consumption and promote water conservation. Manufacturers can implement water-saving technologies, such as recycling and reusing water within the production process, optimizing water usage through efficient systems, and implementing water management strategies to minimize waste.

Optimize inventory management practices to prevent overstocking or understocking of materials. Implement real-time monitoring systems and utilize predictive analytics to ensure accurate demand forecasting, thereby reducing waste due to excessive raw material purchases or storage. Explore opportunities to replace materials with more sustainable alternatives. For example, consider using recycled materials, bio-based materials, or light-weight materials that require less energy and resources to produce.

Material conservation extends beyond the manufacturing facility itself. Manufacturers should work with suppliers to identify opportunities for waste reduction, recycling, and resource conservation throughout the supply chain. This can involve collaboration on packaging optimization, inventory management, and transportation efficiency. Collaborate closely with suppliers to ensure they understand your waste reduction goals. Encourage them to adopt sustainable practices and provide materials in the precise quantities needed, reducing waste associated with excess packaging or unused materials.

Manufacturers can also conduct lifecycle assessments (LCAs) to evaluate the environmental impact of their products throughout their entire lifecycle, from raw material extraction to end-of-life disposal. By identifying areas of high environmental impact, manufacturers can implement strategies to minimize resource consumption and waste generation at each stage.

Encourage a culture of continuous improvement and involve employees in identifying and implementing waste reduction initiatives. Provide training programs to raise awareness about waste reduction techniques and encourage suggestions from employees to optimize processes and minimize waste.

Material conservation in manufacturing not only benefits the environment but also offers economic advantages. It reduces material and energy costs, improves operational efficiency, enhances the company's reputation, and helps meet regulatory requirements. By adopting sustainable manufacturing practices, manufacturers contribute to a more resource-efficient and environmentally conscious industry.

Alternative Materials

There are several manufacturing materials that are renewable or have a lower environmental impact. The following are some examples.

Bamboo: Bamboo is a fast-growing grass that can be harvested and replenished relatively quickly. It has a high strength-to-weight ratio and can be used as a substitute for wood in various applications, such as furniture, flooring, and packaging.

Recycled plastic: Instead of using virgin plastic, manufacturers can opt for recycled plastic materials. These materials are made from post-consumer or post-industrial plastic waste, reducing the demand for new plastic production and diverting waste from landfills.

Hemp: Hemp is a versatile plant that can be used to produce fibers, textiles, building materials, and biofuels. It requires less water and pesticides compared to other crops, making it more environmentally friendly.

Cork: Cork is obtained from the bark of cork oak trees without harming the trees themselves. It is commonly used as a sustainable alternative to traditional materials in flooring, insulation, and packaging.

Bio-based plastics: Bio-based plastics are derived from renewable sources such as corn, sugarcane, or vegetable oils. These materials can offer similar properties to traditional plastics while reducing reliance on fossil fuels and lowering greenhouse gas emissions.

Recycled metals: Using recycled metals like aluminum, steel, or copper can significantly reduce the energy consumption and environmental impact associated with extracting and refining virgin metals. These materials can be recycled repeatedly without losing their properties.

Biodegradable materials: Biodegradable materials, such as certain types of plastics or natural fibers, can break down and decompose under the right conditions, reducing their environmental impact and potential harm to ecosystems.

Natural fibers: Natural fibers like organic cotton, hemp, flax, and jute can be used as alternatives to synthetic fibers in textiles, reducing the use of petroleum-based materials. These fibers are biodegradable and have a lower carbon footprint.

Recycled paper: Instead of using virgin paper, manufacturers can opt for recycled paper made from post-consumer waste. This helps conserve forests, reduce water usage, and decrease energy consumption in the paper production process.

Mycelium-based materials: Mycelium, the root structure of fungi, can be grown into various shapes and forms to create sustainable packaging materials, insulation, and even building materials. It is biodegradable and requires minimal resources to grow.

When considering renewable or low-impact materials, it's important to evaluate their entire lifecycle, including sourcing, production, use, and disposal, to ensure a holistic approach to sustainability. Additionally, the suitability of these materials will depend on the specific application and requirements of the manufacturing process.

Waste Reduction

Waste reduction in manufacturing refers to the implementation of strategies and practices aimed at minimizing the amount of waste generated during the production process. It involves identifying and addressing inefficiencies, reducing material and energy consumption, and optimizing resource utilization. The goal is to create a more sustainable and environmentally friendly manufacturing system while improving overall efficiency and cost-effectiveness. Let's discuss some key approaches and techniques for waste reduction in manufacturing.

Lean principles focus on eliminating waste in all forms, including overproduction, excess inventory, defects, waiting times, unnecessary transportation, and excessive processing. By streamlining production processes and optimizing workflows, lean manufacturing aims to reduce waste and improve productivity.

Just-in-time (JIT) inventory management involves receiving materials and producing goods as they are needed, minimizing excess inventory, and reducing the risk of waste from obsolete or unused materials. JIT helps prevent overproduction and allows for better inventory control. By optimizing the use of energy, water, and raw materials, manufacturers can minimize waste generation. This can be achieved through measures such as energy-efficient equipment, recycling and reusing materials, and implementing water conservation practices.

Considering sustainability aspects during the product design phase can contribute to waste reduction. Designing products for easy disassembly and recyclability and using eco-friendly materials can minimize waste generation throughout the product's lifecycle. Analyzing manufacturing processes and identifying bottlenecks, redundancies, and inefficiencies can also help reduce waste. By implementing process improvements, such as reducing set-up times, optimizing workflow layouts, and implementing automation where appropriate, manufacturers can minimize waste and improve efficiency.

Proper waste management is crucial for waste reduction. Manufacturers should segregate different types of waste, such as hazardous materials, recyclables, and non-recyclables, to facilitate appropriate disposal and recycling processes. Recycling and reusing materials can help reduce the amount of waste sent to landfills.

Establishing a culture of continuous improvement and involving employees in waste reduction initiatives can be highly effective. Encouraging suggestions and feedback from the workforce can lead to innovative ideas for waste reduction, as they are often the most familiar with the manufacturing processes and potential areas for improvement. By implementing these waste reduction strategies, manufacturers can minimize their environmental impact, improve resource efficiency, reduce costs associated with waste disposal, and enhance overall sustainability.

Recycling and Reuse

Recycling and reuse are two important strategies in manufacturing that aim to reduce waste, conserve resources, and minimize the environmental impact of production processes.

Recycling involves the collection, processing, and transformation of waste materials into new products or raw materials. The goal is to divert waste from landfills and use it as a valuable resource in manufacturing processes. Steps for recycling in manufacturing are as follows:

Step 1 – Collection: Waste materials, such as plastic, glass, paper, metals, and electronics, are collected separately from general waste. This can be done through collection programs and drop-off locations.

Step 2 – Sorting: The collected waste is sorted and separated based on its material composition. This step ensures that different types of materials are properly classified for further processing.

Step 3 – Processing: The sorted materials undergo various processing methods to transform them into usable forms. This may involve shredding, crushing, melting, or refining processes, depending on the material.

Step 4 – Manufacturing: The processed materials are then used as stock in manufacturing new products. For example, recycled plastic can be used to create new plastic items, recycled paper can be turned into new paper products, and recycled metals can be used in metal fabrication.

Step 5 – End-products: The recycled materials are integrated into the manufacturing process, reducing the need for virgin raw materials. The end products made from recycled materials are often similar in quality and functionality to those made from virgin materials.

Recycling not only conserves natural resources but also reduces energy consumption and greenhouse gas emissions associated with the extraction and production of virgin materials. It also helps to minimize pollution and landfill space usage.

Reuse involves extending the lifespan of products or components by using them multiple times instead of discarding them after a single use. This approach aims to maximize the value and utility of materials and products throughout their lifecycle.

Manufacturers can design products with durability, modularity, and repairability in mind. By using robust materials and designing products that are easy to disassemble and repair, the potential for reuse is increased.

Instead of disposing of products or components that are damaged or no longer functional, manufacturers can invest in refurbishment and repair processes. This involves restoring products to a usable condition or replacing faulty components to extend their lifespan.

In some cases, products can go through a remanufacturing process, where used products are disassembled, cleaned, repaired, and reassembled to function as good as new. This approach is commonly seen in industries like automotive, where components like engines or transmissions are remanufactured. Manufacturers can facilitate the resale or redistribution of products through second-hand markets. This allows products to be used by different owners and prolongs their lifespan.

Reusing products and components helps reduce waste generation, conserves resources, and minimizes the energy and environmental impact associated with manufacturing new products from scratch.

Key Points

- Reducing water consumption will allow manufacturers to lower operational costs, improve efficiency, comply with regulations, enhance their corporate sustainability profile, and meet the expectations of environmentally conscious consumers.

- By implementing energy conservation measures, manufacturers can achieve substantial energy savings, lower greenhouse gas emissions, reduce operational costs, and enhance their sustainability performance. Energy conservation in manufacturing is a crucial component of achieving a more sustainable and environmentally responsible industrial sector.
- Companies engaging in recycling and reuse practices in manufacturing can make significant contributions to sustainable production, resource conservation, and waste reduction, ultimately fostering a more circular economy.

SIDE BAR: TIPS FOR REDUCING ENERGY CONSUMPTION

Reducing energy consumption in manufacturing is an important goal for companies seeking to improve their sustainability and reduce costs. The following are some strategies that can help you reduce energy consumption in your manufacturing process.

Conduct an energy audit: Conduct an energy audit to assess your facility's energy consumption patterns, identify areas where energy is being wasted, and prioritize energy-saving opportunities.

Upgrade lighting: Lighting typically accounts for a significant portion of energy usage in manufacturing facilities. Consider upgrading to LED lighting, which is more energy-efficient and longer-lasting than traditional lighting options.

Optimize equipment: Replace older, less energy-efficient equipment with newer, more efficient models. Implement maintenance programs to keep equipment running at optimal efficiency and consider installing variable frequency drives (VFDs) to help control the energy usage of motors.

Improve insulation: Poor insulation can result in significant energy losses. Improve insulation in your facility to reduce heat loss and improve energy efficiency.

Utilize renewable energy: Consider investing in renewable energy options such as solar, wind, or geothermal power to reduce reliance on fossil fuels and decrease your carbon footprint.

Implement a control system: Using a building automation system to control lighting, heating, and cooling can help optimize energy usage based on occupancy and production schedules.

Implement energy management systems: Implement energy management systems to track energy usage and identify areas for improvement. This can include energy monitoring and control systems, building automation systems, and other smart technologies.

Reduce idle time: Turn off machines during idle periods or use sleep mode to reduce energy consumption.

Encourage energy-saving behavior: Encourage employees to adopt energy-saving habits such as turning off lights and equipment when not in use and reducing unnecessary heating and cooling.

Chapter 4.2

Pollution Prevention

Overview

Pollution prevention, in the context of manufacturing, refers to the proactive approach of minimizing or eliminating pollution and waste generation at its source, rather than relying on end-of-pipe treatments or corrective actions. It involves implementing strategies, technologies, and practices that aim to reduce or prevent pollution before it is created, thereby promoting sustainable and environmentally friendly manufacturing processes. This involves optimizing manufacturing processes, materials, and inputs to minimize waste, emissions, and environmental impact. By focusing on source reduction, manufacturers can significantly reduce the need for the treatment or disposal of pollutants.

Pollution prevention starts at the design stage of a product.

Designers can integrate environmental considerations into product design by selecting materials that are less toxic, more recyclable, and require fewer resources during production. Designing products for durability, repairability, and recyclability can also help reduce waste and pollution throughout their lifecycle.

Manufacturing processes can be modified to make them more efficient and environmentally friendly. This may involve adopting cleaner technologies, such as using advanced equipment, energy-efficient systems, and alternative materials. Process modifications can help minimize waste generation, energy consumption, and emissions. In addition, effective pollution prevention requires careful management of raw materials. Manufacturers can assess their material usage and find opportunities to reduce waste generation, such

DOI: 10.4324/9781032688152-19

as implementing recycling and reuse programs, optimizing inventory management, and exploring alternatives to hazardous substances.

Ensuring that employees are trained and aware of pollution prevention measures is crucial for successful implementation. By educating the workforce about environmental impacts, waste reduction techniques, and the importance of pollution prevention, manufacturers can foster a culture of sustainability and encourage employees to contribute to ongoing improvement efforts. Manufacturers can also benefit from collaboration with industry peers, government agencies, and environmental organizations to share best practices, exchange knowledge, and establish industry-wide benchmarks for pollution prevention. These collaborations can drive innovation and foster continuous improvement in pollution prevention strategies.

Regular monitoring and measurement of key environmental indicators allow manufacturers to assess the effectiveness of pollution prevention efforts. By tracking metrics such as waste generation, energy consumption, and emissions, manufacturers can identify areas for improvement and make informed decisions regarding process optimization and resource allocation.

Pollution prevention in manufacturing is a proactive approach that integrates environmental considerations into all stages of the manufacturing process. By implementing strategies and practices that reduce waste generation, minimize resource consumption, and promote sustainable production, manufacturers can achieve significant environmental benefits while also enhancing their operational efficiency and competitiveness. See Figure 4.2.1.

Greenhouse Emissions

Greenhouse gas emissions in manufacturing refer to the release of gases into the atmosphere during the production of goods and materials. These emissions contribute to the overall concentration of greenhouse gases in the Earth's atmosphere, leading to the enhanced greenhouse effect and global warming. Manufacturing processes involve various activities that can generate greenhouse gas emissions.

Manufacturing often requires substantial energy inputs, primarily from fossil fuel sources such as coal, oil, and natural gas. When these fuels are burned to generate electricity or heat for industrial processes, carbon dioxide (CO_2) is released into the atmosphere. CO_2 is the most prevalent greenhouse

Figure 4.2.1 Pollution prevention.

gas and a significant contributor to climate change. Certain manufacturing processes themselves emit greenhouse gases. For example, the production of cement, steel, and chemicals involves chemical reactions that release CO_2 as a byproduct. Similarly, certain industrial activities can emit other potent greenhouse gases like methane (CH_4) and nitrous oxide (N_2O).

Moving raw materials, components, and finished goods within the manufacturing supply chain requires transportation, which often relies on fossil fuel-powered vehicles. The burning of these fuels releases CO_2 and other greenhouse gases, contributing to emissions. Furthermore, manufacturing generates waste materials, such as scrap metal, plastic, and chemicals. Improper disposal or inefficient treatment of these wastes can lead to the release of greenhouse gases. For instance, decomposing organic waste in landfills produces methane, which is a potent greenhouse gas.

Tips for Reducing Greenhouse Gas Emissions

The following are some ways manufacturers can reduce greenhouse gas emissions.

- Improve energy efficiency in manufacturing processes by using advanced equipment, optimizing production layouts, and implementing energy management systems.

- Shift from fossil fuel-based energy sources to renewable sources like solar, wind, or hydropower. Install renewable energy systems on-site or source renewable electricity from the grid.
- Redesign manufacturing processes to minimize the use of energy and raw materials. This may involve recycling or reusing materials, adopting cleaner production technologies, and optimizing process parameters.
- Promote the use of electric or hybrid vehicles, optimize logistics routes, and adopt more efficient transportation methods to reduce emissions associated with the movement of goods.
- Implement proper waste management practices, such as recycling and waste-to-energy technologies to minimize emissions from manufacturing waste.

Governments can play a crucial role by implementing policies, regulations, and incentives to encourage emissions reduction in manufacturing. These can include carbon pricing mechanisms, tax incentives for clean technologies, and industry-specific emission standards. By implementing these strategies and technologies, manufacturers can reduce their greenhouse gas emissions, minimize their environmental impact, and contribute to global efforts to combat climate change.

Air Pollution

Air pollution in manufacturing refers to the release of harmful pollutants into the atmosphere as a result of industrial activities and processes. Manufacturing involves various activities such as production, assembly, and processing of goods, and these activities often rely on the use of raw materials, machinery, and energy sources that can generate pollutants. There are several ways in which manufacturing processes contribute to air pollution. Let's consider a few.

Many manufacturing operations rely on the burning of fossil fuels such as coal, oil, and natural gas for energy generation or as a heat source. This combustion process releases pollutants such as sulfur dioxide (SO_2), nitrogen oxides (NOx), carbon monoxide (CO), and particulate matter (PM) into the air. In addition, certain manufacturing processes involve chemical reactions that can release pollutants. For example, chemical manufacturing may produce volatile organic compounds (VOCs) and hazardous air pollutants (HAPs) during the production of various substances. Metal processing and smelting can release heavy metals such as lead, mercury, and cadmium into the atmosphere.

Manufacturing activities generate waste materials, including solid waste and hazardous substances. Improper disposal of these wastes can lead to air pollution. For instance, incineration of solid waste without proper controls can release pollutants into the air, including toxic gases and fine particles. Dust and particulate matter can also result from manufacturing processes due to the handling, grinding, or cutting of materials. These particles, when released into the air, contribute to air pollution and can have detrimental effects on both the environment and human health. The released pollutants can contribute to the formation of smog, acid rain, and climate change. They can also cause respiratory problems, cardiovascular issues, and other health complications in individuals exposed to polluted air.

To address air pollution in manufacturing, regulatory measures and technological advancements play a crucial role. Governments and environmental agencies enforce emission standards and regulations to limit the release of pollutants. Manufacturing companies are encouraged to adopt cleaner production techniques, use advanced pollution control technologies, and implement waste management strategies to minimize air pollution. Additionally, the development and promotion of sustainable manufacturing practices, renewable energy sources, and improved efficiency can help reduce the environmental impact of manufacturing processes and mitigate air pollution.

Tips to Reduce Air Pollution

The following are some tips to minimize air pollution in manufacturing processes.

- Replace outdated and polluting manufacturing processes with cleaner and more efficient technologies. This may involve upgrading equipment, using advanced pollution control devices, or switching to renewable energy sources.
- Install effective emission control systems, such as scrubbers, filters, and catalytic converters, to capture and treat pollutants before they are released into the air. Regular maintenance and monitoring of these systems are essential for optimal performance.
- Streamline manufacturing processes to minimize waste generation and energy consumption. Implementing lean manufacturing principles can

help identify areas for improvement, reduce emissions, and increase overall efficiency.

■ Encourage the recycling and reuse of materials within the manufacturing process to minimize waste production. Proper waste management practices, such as segregating and disposing of hazardous materials appropriately, can prevent the release of pollutants into the air.

■ Educate employees about the importance of air pollution control and provide training on best practices for reducing emissions. This can include proper handling of chemicals, equipment maintenance, and compliance with environmental regulations.

■ Collaborate with suppliers and encourage them to adopt sustainable practices, such as reducing packaging waste and using environmentally friendly materials. This holistic approach can contribute to reducing pollution throughout the entire manufacturing process.

■ Transition to renewable energy sources, such as solar, wind, or hydro-electric power, to reduce reliance on fossil fuels. Installing on-site renewable energy systems can help offset energy consumption and decrease overall greenhouse gas emissions.

■ Implement a robust monitoring system to track emissions and regularly report them to relevant stakeholders. This ensures compliance with emission standards and helps identify areas for improvement.

■ Invest in research and development to find innovative solutions and technologies for reducing air pollution in manufacturing. Collaborating with academic institutions, industry associations, and government agencies can facilitate knowledge sharing and accelerate progress.

■ Support and participate in the development of stricter environmental regulations and emission standards for the manufacturing sector. Stronger regulations can create a level playing field and drive industry-wide adoption of cleaner practices.

Remember, the combination of multiple strategies and a long-term commitment to sustainability is crucial for effectively reducing air pollution in manufacturing.

Toxic Substances

Toxic substances in manufacturing refer to hazardous materials or chemicals that are used, produced, or released during industrial processes. These substances pose risks to human health and the environment and can have long-term effects if not handled properly. There is a wide range of toxic substances used in manufacturing, including but not limited to:

- *Chemicals*: Various chemicals such as solvents, acids, bases, heavy metals (lead, mercury, cadmium), pesticides, and VOCs are commonly used or produced in manufacturing processes. These substances can cause acute or chronic health effects if workers are exposed to them or if they are released into the environment.
- *Asbestos*: Although its use has significantly declined, asbestos may still be found in older manufacturing facilities. Asbestos fibers, when inhaled, can lead to serious respiratory diseases, including lung cancer and mesothelioma.
- *Radioactive materials*: Certain manufacturing processes involving nuclear power, research, or medical applications may involve radioactive materials that require special handling and containment to prevent radiation exposure.

Exposure to toxic substances in manufacturing can have severe consequences. Short-term effects may include eye and respiratory irritation, dizziness, nausea, or chemical burns. Long-term exposure can lead to chronic health conditions, such as cancer, neurological disorders, organ damage, or reproductive issues. Improper disposal or release of toxic substances can significantly impact the environment due to contaminated soil, water bodies, and air, affecting ecosystems, wildlife, and potentially entering the food chain.

Governments and regulatory bodies are working to enforce standards and regulations to mitigate the risks associated with toxic substances in manufacturing. These measures typically include:

- *Hazard communication*: Employers must provide comprehensive safety data sheets (SDS) that outline the hazards of chemicals, proper handling procedures, and safety precautions to workers.
- *Personal protective equipment (PPE)*: Employers should provide appropriate PPE, such as gloves, masks, goggles, or protective clothing, to prevent direct contact or inhalation of toxic substances.
- *Engineering controls*: Implementing ventilation systems, containment measures, or automated processes can help minimize worker exposure to toxic substances.

- *Waste management*: Proper storage, labeling, and disposal of hazardous materials are essential to prevent environmental contamination. This may involve recycling, treatment, or safe disposal methods.
- *Occupational health and safety programs*: Regular training, monitoring, and health surveillance programs help raise awareness, ensure compliance, and detect potential health issues in workers.

It's crucial for manufacturers to prioritize worker safety, follow regulations, and adopt sustainable practices to minimize the use and impact of toxic substances in their operations.

Tips to Minimize/Avoid Toxic Substances

The following are ways to minimize or eliminate the use of toxic substances.

- Identify and document all the chemicals used in your manufacturing processes. This inventory will help you understand which substances are potentially toxic and need to be addressed.
- Research and explore alternative materials and chemicals that are less toxic or non-toxic. Consider partnering with suppliers and industry organizations to find suitable replacements for hazardous substances.
- Green chemistry focuses on the design and development of chemical products and processes that minimize the use and generation of hazardous substances. Integrate green chemistry principles into your manufacturing practices to reduce the overall toxicity of your products.
- Review your manufacturing processes to identify opportunities for reducing or eliminating toxic substances. This could involve modifying process parameters, optimizing equipment, or implementing closed-loop systems to minimize waste and emissions.
- Establish proper waste management protocols to ensure the safe disposal or recycling of toxic substances. Implement recycling programs, treat hazardous waste appropriately, and comply with all relevant regulations and guidelines.
- Educate and train your workforce on the proper handling and disposal of toxic substances. Implement safety measures, such as PPE, ventilation systems, and regular monitoring, to safeguard employee health.
- Work closely with your suppliers to ensure they understand your commitment to minimizing toxic substances. Encourage them to adopt

sustainable practices, provide eco-friendly alternatives, and prioritize the use of non-toxic materials.

■ Consider obtaining certifications such as ISO 14001 (Environmental Management System) and pursuing compliance with standards like Registration, Evaluation, Authorization, and Restriction of Chemicals (REACH). These certifications and standards demonstrate your commitment to minimizing toxic substances and environmental responsibility.

■ Promote transparency in your supply chain by disclosing the chemicals used in your products. Encourage collaboration and information sharing among industry peers to collectively reduce the use of toxic substances.

Remember, the journey toward minimizing toxic substances in manufacturing is an ongoing process. Continuously evaluate and improve your practices, stay updated on emerging research and regulations, and embrace innovation to advance sustainability in your industry.

Pollution Control Technologies

Pollution control technologies are a wide range of techniques, strategies, and equipment designed to minimize, prevent, or mitigate the release of pollutants into the environment. These technologies aim to reduce the impact of human activities on air, water, and soil quality and promote sustainable development. There are several pollution control technologies available for manufacturing processes to mitigate the environmental impact and reduce pollution. The following are some commonly used technologies.

Air Pollution Controls

■ *Scrubbers*: These devices remove pollutants from industrial exhaust gases by using liquid sprays or other chemical reactions.

■ *Electrostatic precipitators (ESPs)*: They charge particles in the exhaust gas and collect them on charged plates or electrodes.

■ *Fabric filters (baghouses)*: These systems use fabric bags to capture particulate matter from a gas stream.

■ *Catalytic converters*: Typically used in the automotive industry, they help reduce emissions of nitrogen oxides (NOx), carbon monoxide (CO), and VOCs.

■ *Particulate filters*: They capture and remove particulate matter from vehicle exhausts and industrial emissions.

Water Pollution Controls

■ *Sedimentation tanks*: Used to settle out suspended solids from wastewater by gravity.
■ *Filtration systems*: Employ various media, such as sand, activated carbon, or membranes, to remove contaminants from water.
■ *Biological treatment*: Utilizes microorganisms to break down organic pollutants through processes like activated sludge, aerobic and anaerobic digestion, and constructed wetlands.

Waste Management

■ *Recycling and reuse*: Implementing strategies to recycle materials and incorporate recycled content into manufacturing processes.
■ *Waste minimization*: Employing techniques to reduce waste generation and optimize resource utilization.
■ *Landfill gas capture*: Collecting and utilizing the methane gas produced by landfills to generate energy.
■ *Composting*: Promotes the conversion of waste materials into valuable resources, reducing the need for landfill disposal.
■ *Incineration and gasification*: These processes convert solid waste into energy through controlled burning or thermal decomposition, reducing waste volume and generating electricity or heat.

It's important to note that the choice of pollution control technology depends on the specific manufacturing processes, the types of pollutants emitted, and regulatory requirements. Different industries may require tailored solutions to address their unique pollution challenges.

Cleaner Production Methods

Cleaner production methods are vital for future manufacturing due to their positive environmental impact, regulatory compliance, cost savings, reputation enhancement, fostering innovation, and ensuring long-term resilience. By prioritizing sustainability, manufacturers can align their operations with the evolving needs of society and contribute to a more sustainable future.

Using cleaner production methods in manufacturing offers several benefits, including minimizing the environmental impact of manufacturing processes. By reducing resource consumption, waste generation, and emissions, these methods help protect ecosystems, conserve natural resources, and mitigate climate change. Implementing cleaner production practices often leads to cost savings in the long run. By optimizing resource utilization, reducing waste, and improving energy efficiency, manufacturers can lower their operational costs, such as energy expenses and waste disposal fees.

Many countries have stringent environmental regulations and standards in place. Adopting cleaner production methods ensures that manufacturers comply with these regulations, avoiding fines and penalties associated with non-compliance. It also helps companies maintain a positive reputation and build strong relationships with regulatory authorities.

Cleaner production methods often involve process optimization, which can result in better product quality and consistency. By focusing on quality control and waste reduction, manufacturers can minimize defects and variability in their products, leading to higher customer satisfaction and reduced returns or recalls.

As sustainability becomes increasingly more important to consumers, adopting cleaner production methods can also give manufacturers a competitive edge. Companies that prioritize environmentally friendly practices may attract environmentally conscious consumers, gain market share, and differentiate themselves from competitors. Consumers are increasingly demanding products that are produced sustainably and have a minimal environmental footprint. By adopting cleaner production methods, manufacturers can demonstrate their commitment to sustainability, which can also enhance their reputation and brand image.

Cleaner production methods often prioritize worker safety and health. By minimizing exposure to hazardous substances, implementing safer equipment and processes, and promoting a cleaner work environment, manufacturers can improve employee well-being, reduce workplace accidents, and enhance overall productivity. However, implementing cleaner production methods often requires innovation and the adoption of new technologies. This can drive research and development efforts, spur technological advancements, and foster a culture of innovation within manufacturing companies.

Overall, cleaner production methods provide a win-win situation for both manufacturers and the environment by promoting sustainable practices, reducing costs, ensuring compliance, improving product quality, and enhancing competitiveness.

Waste Management Practices

Effective waste management practices are essential for future manufacturing because they promote environmental sustainability, resource conservation, cost savings, regulatory compliance, and the transition to a circular economy. By incorporating these practices, manufacturers can minimize their environmental footprint, optimize resource utilization, and contribute to a more sustainable and prosperous future.

Manufacturing processes generate a significant amount of waste, including hazardous materials and byproducts. Proper waste management practices ensure that these wastes are handled, treated, and disposed of in an environmentally responsible manner. This helps prevent pollution, reduces the release of harmful substances into the air, water, and soil, and minimizes the impact on ecosystems. By adopting sustainable waste management practices, future manufacturing can strive to operate in harmony with the environment, promoting long-term sustainability.

Many manufacturing processes require the extraction and consumption of natural resources, such as minerals, water, and energy. By effectively managing waste, manufacturers can reduce the overall consumption of resources. For example, waste materials generated during production can be recycled or reused, reducing the need for virgin raw materials. This not only conserves valuable resources but also decreases the energy and water requirements associated with the extraction and processing of new materials.

Implementing efficient waste management practices can lead to cost savings for manufacturers. By reducing waste generation, optimizing material usage, and implementing recycling or reuse programs, manufacturers can minimize disposal costs and the need for purchasing new raw materials. Additionally, some waste materials may have economic value if they can be recovered or sold to other industries as secondary resources. By turning waste into a resource, manufacturers can potentially generate revenue and improve their overall financial performance.

Waste management practices play a vital role in transitioning from a linear economy (take-make-dispose) to a circular economy. In a circular economy, waste materials are viewed as valuable resources that can be reintroduced into the production cycle. By designing products for durability, repairability, and recyclability, and by implementing efficient waste management systems, manufacturers can close the loop, minimizing waste generation and maximizing resource recovery. This shift toward a circular economy also encourages innovation in manufacturing processes, product design, and waste management technologies.

Key Points

- Select materials that are less toxic, more recyclable, and require fewer resources during production.
- Design products for durability, repairability, and recyclability.
- Minimize/avoid toxic substances.
- Use renewable energy sources (solar, wind, and hydropower).
- Invest in research and development to find innovative solutions and technologies for reducing air pollution in manufacturing.
- Employ air and water pollution controls.
- Pursue recycling and reuse programs.
- Exercise waste management practices.

Chapter 4.3

Renewable Energy

Overview

Renewable energy refers to energy sources that are naturally replenished and do not deplete over time. These energy sources include sunlight, wind, water, geothermal heat, and biomass. Renewable energy plays a vital role in addressing the challenges posed by climate change and the limited availability of fossil fuels. Renewable energy sources are types of energy that can be replenished naturally and sustainably. The following are some examples of different renewable energy sources.

Solar energy: Solar power harnesses the energy from the sun by using photovoltaic (PV) panels or concentrating solar power (CSP) systems to convert sunlight into electricity or heat.

Wind energy: Wind turbines capture the kinetic energy of wind and convert it into electricity. Large wind farms or individual turbines can generate power.

Hydropower: Hydropower utilizes the energy of flowing or falling water to generate electricity. It typically involves dams or water turbines in rivers, streams, or ocean tides.

Biomass energy: Biomass energy is derived from organic matter such as plants, crop residues, wood, and agricultural by-products. It can be converted into heat, electricity, or biofuels through processes like combustion or fermentation.

Geothermal energy: Geothermal power harnesses the heat generated from within the Earth's core. It involves using steam or hot water from underground reservoirs to drive turbines and produce electricity.

DOI: 10.4324/9781032688152-20

Tidal energy: Tidal energy captures the kinetic energy of ocean tides and currents to generate electricity. It typically involves using turbines placed in tidal basins or near coastal areas.

Wave energy: Wave power utilizes the energy from ocean waves to generate electricity. Various devices, such as floating buoys or submerged turbines, can convert the up-and-down motion of waves into usable energy.

Hydrogen fuel cells: Hydrogen fuel cells convert the chemical energy of hydrogen gas into electricity and heat. It is considered a renewable energy source when produced using renewable sources of hydrogen, such as electrolysis of water using renewable electricity.

These renewable energy sources offer sustainable alternatives to fossil fuels and help reduce greenhouse gas emissions while promoting a cleaner and more sustainable energy future. See Figure 4.3.1.

One of the primary advantages of renewable energy is its minimal environmental impact. Unlike fossil fuels, renewable energy sources do not release greenhouse gases or other pollutants during operation, reducing air pollution and mitigating climate change. They also have a lower water footprint compared to conventional power plants, conserving water resources. Renewable energy plays a crucial role in combating climate change. By displacing fossil fuels, it helps to reduce carbon dioxide and other greenhouse gas emissions. This transition is essential to limit global warming and

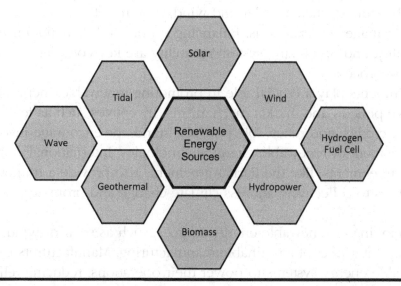

Figure 4.3.1   Renewable energy sources.

its associated negative impacts, such as rising sea levels, extreme weather events, and biodiversity loss.

Diversifying the energy mix by incorporating renewable sources enhances energy independence and security for countries. Since renewable energy sources are typically domestically available, countries can reduce their dependence on imported fossil fuels and mitigate the risks associated with geopolitical conflicts and price volatility. The renewable energy sector also has the potential to generate significant employment opportunities. Jobs in renewable energy range from manufacturing and installation to research and development. The sector's growth stimulates local economies, fosters innovation, and attracts investments.

The development and deployment of renewable energy technologies drive innovation and technological advancements. This progress leads to cost reductions, improved efficiency, and increased reliability of renewable energy systems. As a result, renewable energy becomes more accessible and competitive compared to conventional energy sources. In addition, renewable energy offers a viable solution for expanding energy access in remote and rural areas, where grid infrastructure may be limited or absent. Off-grid renewable energy systems, such as solar home systems and mini-grids, can provide clean electricity to communities, facilitating economic development, improved education, and better healthcare services.

While renewable energy sources have numerous benefits, their integration into existing energy systems presents challenges. The intermittency of some renewable sources, such as solar and wind, requires effective energy storage and grid management solutions. Balancing supply and demand, ensuring grid stability, and optimizing system reliability are key considerations in the integration process.

Governments play a crucial role in promoting renewable energy through supportive policies and market mechanisms. Incentives such as feed-in tariffs, tax credits, and renewable portfolio standards encourage investment and deployment of renewable energy technologies. International collaboration and agreements, like the Paris Agreement, also provide a framework for countries to collectively address climate change and promote renewable energy.

Transitioning to renewable energy sources, such as solar or wind power, is a significant aspect of sustainable manufacturing. Manufacturers can invest in renewable energy systems to power their operations, reducing reliance on fossil fuels and lowering greenhouse gas emissions. It's important to understand energy consumption throughout your manufacturing operations and to implement energy-efficient technologies and equipment, such as LED lighting, high-efficiency motors, and automated systems, that can adjust energy usage based on demand. Additionally, consider investing in renewable energy sources to power your operations.

To maximize the benefits of renewable energy, it is important to integrate it into a broader energy transition strategy, including energy efficiency measures, grid modernization, and supportive policies and regulations. With continued advancements in technology and increased investment, renewable energy holds tremendous potential to drive a sustainable future and combat climate change.

Solar Energy

Solar energy refers to the radiant light and heat emitted by the sun, which is harnessed and converted into usable forms of energy. It is a renewable and abundant source of power that can be used to generate electricity, heat water, and provide heating and cooling for buildings.

The primary technology used to harness solar energy is PV cells, commonly known as solar panels. These panels are made up of semiconducting materials, usually silicon, which absorb sunlight and convert it into electricity through the photovoltaic effect. When photons from sunlight strike the solar cells, they dislodge electrons from their atoms, generating a flow of electricity.

Solar panels are typically installed on rooftops or in open areas where they can receive maximum sunlight exposure. They are connected in series and parallel configurations to form solar arrays, which can generate electricity for residential, commercial, or utility-scale applications. The amount of electricity produced depends on factors such as the size and efficiency of the panels, the angle and orientation of installation, and the local climate and sunlight conditions.

Another way to harness solar energy is through solar thermal systems. These systems use sunlight to heat a fluid, such as water or air, which can then be used for various purposes. Solar thermal technology includes solar water heaters, solar space heating systems, and solar cooling systems. In solar water heaters, sunlight is used to heat water for domestic or industrial use. Solar space heating systems capture and store solar heat to warm buildings, while solar cooling systems use solar energy to drive absorption or adsorption chillers for air conditioning. The following are some advantages to using solar energy:

■ The sun is an inexhaustible source of energy, ensuring a long-term and sustainable power supply.
■ Solar energy is clean and produces no greenhouse gas emissions or air pollutants during operation, unlike fossil fuels.
■ Solar power can significantly reduce or eliminate electricity bills, especially when combined with energy storage systems.
■ Solar energy can be used for electricity generation, heating water, powering appliances, and providing thermal comfort.
■ Solar systems can be tailored to meet different energy needs, from small residential installations to large-scale solar farms.

Despite its numerous benefits, solar energy also has some limitations. Its availability is dependent on sunlight, making it intermittent and subject to weather conditions. Energy storage technologies, such as batteries, are often used to store excess electricity for use during cloudy periods or at night. The initial cost of installing solar systems can be high, although it is decreasing over time as the technology advances and economies of scale are realized.

Wind Energy

Wind energy is a form of renewable energy that harnesses the power of the wind to generate electricity. It is a clean and sustainable energy source that has been used for centuries. The process of generating wind energy involves converting the kinetic energy of the wind into mechanical power and then into electrical power.

The primary technology used to capture wind energy is a wind turbine. A wind turbine consists of a tall tower and large rotor blades. The tower supports the turbine at a sufficient height to capture stronger and more consistent wind currents. When the wind blows, it causes the rotor blades to spin. The design of the blades is carefully engineered to maximize their efficiency in capturing the wind's energy. The kinetic energy of the moving air is converted into rotational energy of the rotor.

The rotating rotor is connected to a main shaft, which is connected to a gearbox. The gearbox increases the rotational speed of the rotor to a level suitable for driving an electrical generator. The mechanical energy from the rotating shaft is used to turn the rotor of an electrical generator. This process converts the mechanical energy into electrical energy. The electrical energy produced by the generator is in the form of alternating current (AC). It is then transmitted through power lines to homes, businesses, and the electrical grid for distribution and consumption.

Wind farms often consist of multiple wind turbines grouped together, forming a wind power plant. These plants are connected to the electrical grid, allowing the generated wind energy to be integrated with other sources of electricity. The grid helps balance the electricity supply and demand, ensuring a reliable power supply.

Wind energy is a renewable resource as wind is a natural occurrence and will not deplete with use. It produces no greenhouse gas emissions or air pollutants, making it environmentally friendly. Wind energy reduces dependence on fossil fuels and foreign energy sources, promoting energy security. As technology has advanced, the cost of wind energy has decreased significantly, making it more economically viable compared to traditional energy sources.

Wind energy also has some limitations. Wind energy production is dependent on the availability and strength of the wind. If the wind speed is too low or too high, turbines may not be able to operate efficiently. Wind turbines can have visual and noise impacts, which can be a concern for nearby communities. Large-scale wind farms require vast land areas, which may impact natural habitats and wildlife migration patterns. However, despite these limitations, wind energy remains a key contributor to global efforts in transitioning to a more sustainable and low-carbon energy system.

Hydropower Energy

Hydropower energy, also known as hydroelectric power, is a form of renewable energy that harnesses the power of moving water to generate electricity. It is one of the oldest and most widely used renewable energy sources in the world. Hydropower plants convert the kinetic energy of flowing or falling water into mechanical energy, which is then converted into electrical energy.

A hydropower plant requires a steady flow of water, which is typically achieved by constructing a dam on a river or diverting a portion of the river's flow. The dam creates a reservoir, which stores water and controls its release. The water from the reservoir is directed through a large pipe called a penstock. The force of the flowing water creates high pressure as it descends from a higher elevation to a lower elevation. The high-pressure water from the penstock is directed onto the blades of a turbine. The water's force causes the turbine to rotate.

The rotating turbine is connected to a generator, which is essentially a large electromagnet. As the turbine spins, it causes the generator to rotate, converting mechanical energy into electrical energy. The electrical energy produced by the generator is sent to a transformer, where it is stepped up to a higher voltage for efficient transmission over long distances. The electricity is then fed into the power grid for distribution to homes, businesses, and industries.

Hydropower relies on the water cycle, which is continuously replenished by rainfall, making it a renewable energy source. It produces no greenhouse gas emissions or air pollution during operation, contributing to a cleaner environment. Hydropower plants can operate continuously, providing a reliable and consistent source of electricity. They can quickly respond to changes in electricity demand and can serve as a backup during peak periods or when other power sources are unavailable.

Hydropower plants can also help with water management by regulating river flows and mitigating floods. Reservoirs created by dams can store water during periods of excess flow and release it during dry spells for irrigation, drinking water supply, or other purposes.

Unfortunately, hydropower does have some potential drawbacks. The construction of dams and reservoirs can have significant environmental impacts. It alters natural river ecosystems, affects fish migration, and may result in the loss of habitats and biodiversity. The flooding of large areas to create reservoirs can also displace communities and lead to social and environmental challenges. However, the suitability of hydropower is dependent on the availability of suitable rivers or water bodies. Not all regions have the necessary topography or water resources to support large-scale hydropower plants. Despite these challenges, hydropower continues to play a significant role in global electricity generation and offers a sustainable energy option for many countries.

Geothermal Energy

Geothermal energy is a form of renewable energy that harnesses the heat generated from the Earth's core and crust. The word "geothermal" comes from the Greek words "geo," meaning Earth, and "thermos," meaning heat.

This energy source is abundant and is derived from the natural heat stored within the Earth.

The Earth's interior is extremely hot, with temperatures reaching several thousand degrees Celsius in the core. This heat is a result of the radioactive decay of elements and the residual heat from the planet's formation. Geothermal energy takes advantage of this heat to generate electricity or provide direct heating and cooling. There are three main types of geothermal resources that can be utilized for energy production.

Hydrothermal systems: These are the most common geothermal resources and occur when groundwater circulates through hot rocks deep within the Earth's crust. The heated water or steam is then extracted using wells, and its energy is used to generate electricity or for direct heating applications.

Geopressured systems: These resources are found in deep sedimentary basins where there is a combination of water, natural gas, and geothermal heat. The heat and pressure trapped within these reservoirs can be tapped to generate electricity or produce natural gas.

Enhanced geothermal systems (EGS): EGS utilizes technologies to create a geothermal reservoir where one does not naturally exist or is not commercially viable. It involves drilling into hot rocks, fracturing them, and then circulating water through the fractures to extract the heat. EGS has the potential to greatly expand the availability of geothermal energy resources.

The extraction of geothermal energy typically involves drilling deep wells into the geothermal reservoirs to access the hot fluids or rocks. The hot water or steam is brought to the surface and used to drive a turbine connected to an electrical generator. After the energy is extracted, the cooled water is reinjected back into the geothermal reservoir to maintain the sustainability of the resource.

Geothermal energy offers several advantages. It is a renewable and reliable source of energy since the Earth's heat is continuously replenished. It produces very low greenhouse gas emissions compared to fossil fuel-based energy sources, contributing to a cleaner environment. Geothermal power plants also have a small physical footprint and can operate continuously, providing a stable source of electricity.

However, there are some limitations to geothermal energy. It is location-dependent, as significant geothermal resources are concentrated in specific regions. Additionally, drilling and exploration costs can be high, making it economically viable only in areas with abundant geothermal resources. The extraction of geothermal fluids can also sometimes release small amounts of gases and trace elements, requiring careful monitoring to minimize environmental impacts. Despite these challenges, geothermal energy has significant potential as a sustainable energy source and is being increasingly utilized around the world to reduce dependence on fossil fuels and mitigate climate change. See Side Bar: Global Geothermal Resource to learn more about the regions of the world with significant geothermal resources.

Manufacturing Benefits of Renewable Energy

Renewable energy use in manufacturing can bring economic benefits in addition to helping protect the environment, comply with regulations, improve brand image, and establish a more sustainable and resilient business model. Renewable energy sources, such as solar and wind power, have become increasingly cost-competitive with traditional fossil fuels. By utilizing renewable energy, manufacturers can reduce their reliance on expensive fossil fuels and, in turn, lower their energy costs over time.

Unlike fossil fuels, which are subject to price fluctuations and supply chain disruptions, renewable energy sources provide a stable and predictable energy supply. This stability enables manufacturers to better plan their production schedules and budget for energy expenses, minimizing risks associated with energy price volatility.

Manufacturing is a significant contributor to greenhouse gas emissions and environmental degradation. By switching to renewable energy sources, manufacturers can significantly reduce their carbon footprint and other harmful emissions. This transition supports environmental sustainability goals and helps mitigate climate change. Many countries and regions have implemented regulations and policies aimed at reducing greenhouse gas emissions and promoting the use of renewable energy. By adopting renewable energy, manufacturers can ensure compliance with these regulations, avoid penalties, and maintain a positive reputation with stakeholders and consumers.

Increasingly, consumers are favoring environmentally conscious companies that demonstrate a commitment to sustainability. Manufacturers that use renewable energy can leverage their green initiatives to enhance their brand image, attract environmentally conscious customers, and differentiate themselves from competitors. In addition, governments and organizations often provide incentives, grants, and tax benefits to encourage the adoption of renewable energy. By incorporating renewable energy sources into their manufacturing processes, companies may become eligible for these financial incentives, which can further offset the costs of renewable energy installations.

Relying on renewable energy sources reduces dependence on fossil fuels, which are finite resources with uncertain availability in the future. By generating their own renewable energy, manufacturers can achieve a greater degree of energy independence and reduce vulnerability to energy price shocks or supply disruptions.

Key Point

- Renewable energy offers a sustainable and environmentally friendly alternative to fossil fuels. Its benefits encompass mitigating climate change, enhancing energy security, fostering economic growth, and improving access to electricity. Continued investments, technological advancements, and supportive policies are essential to accelerate the transition to a renewable energy future.

SIDE BAR: GLOBAL GEOTHERMAL RESOURCE

Significant geothermal resources can be found in various areas around the world. Geothermal energy is harnessed from the Earth's natural heat, typically derived from volcanic activity or the radioactive decay of minerals in the Earth's crust. The following are some regions known for their substantial geothermal resources.

The Ring of Fire: This is a horseshoe-shaped region encircling the Pacific Ocean, known for its high seismic and volcanic activity. Countries in the Ring of Fire such as Iceland, New Zealand, Japan, Indonesia, the Philippines, and parts of the western coasts of North and South America have notable geothermal resources.

The United States: The US is a significant player in geothermal energy production, with several states having notable resources. California,

Nevada, Oregon, and Utah are some of the leading states with geothermal power plants and potential for further development.

Italy: Italy has a considerable number of geothermal power plants, especially in the Tuscany region, where the Earth's natural heat is readily accessible due to its geological characteristics.

Mexico: Mexico is also home to several geothermal power plants, with the Los Azufres and Cerro Prieto fields being among the most prominent.

Kenya: This East African country has tapped into its geothermal resources and hosts one of the largest geothermal power plants in the world, the Olkaria Geothermal Complex.

Iceland: As a highly geologically active country, Iceland derives a significant portion of its energy from geothermal sources. It has a vast geothermal capacity compared to its small population.

The Philippines: This archipelago nation is rich in geothermal resources and has been utilizing them for electricity generation for several decades.

Indonesia: With its numerous volcanic regions, Indonesia has substantial geothermal potential, although it has only tapped a fraction of it so far.

New Zealand: This island nation is actively utilizing geothermal energy for electricity generation and heating applications.

Central and South America: Several countries in this region, such as Costa Rica, El Salvador, and Nicaragua, have significant geothermal resources and have started to develop them for sustainable energy production.

It's important to note that the utilization of geothermal resources can vary significantly depending on factors such as local geology, technological capabilities, and government policies. As technology advances and renewable energy becomes more crucial, more regions around the world may explore and develop their geothermal potential.

Chapter 4.4

Design for Sustainability

Overview

Design for sustainability in manufacturing refers to the practice of integrating environmental and social considerations into the design and production processes of manufactured goods. It involves minimizing the negative impact of manufacturing activities on the environment, conserving resources, and promoting social responsibility throughout the product's lifecycle. Key aspects of design for sustainability in manufacturing include using sustainable materials, practicing energy efficiency, reducing waste, creating durable goods, and considering the human factor in manufacturing designs.

Choosing sustainable materials that have a minimal environmental impact is crucial. This involves considering factors such as renewable resources, recyclability, toxicity, and energy requirements during extraction, production, and disposal. Additionally, designing products and manufacturing processes that are energy-efficient helps reduce the carbon footprint associated with manufacturing. This can include optimizing energy use during production, utilizing renewable energy sources, and implementing energy-saving technologies.

Minimizing waste generation is essential for sustainable manufacturing. Designing products with a focus on reducing material waste, implementing recycling programs, and utilizing waste as a resource through techniques like remanufacturing or recycling are effective approaches.

An organization can consider conducting a comprehensive lifecycle assessment to evaluate the environmental impact of a product from raw

DOI: 10.4324/9781032688152-21

material extraction to disposal. This assessment considers factors such as energy consumption, emissions, resource depletion, and waste generation, enabling designers to make informed decisions to minimize the overall environmental impact. Designing products that are also durable and long-lasting helps reduce the need for frequent replacements, thereby conserving resources and reducing waste. Considering factors like material durability, repairability, and modularity can extend the lifespan of a product.

Sustainable design also involves minimizing packaging waste and optimizing logistics to reduce transportation-related emissions. Designers can focus on using eco-friendly packaging materials, reducing packaging size, and optimizing transportation routes to minimize environmental impact. Designing products with end-of-life considerations in mind can also contribute to sustainability. This involves creating products that are easy to disassemble and separate into recyclable components or that can be effectively repurposed. Implementing take-back programs or establishing partnerships with recycling facilities facilitates proper disposal and reduces environmental impact.

Designing for sustainability also entails considering social aspects such as fair labor practices, human rights, and community welfare. Manufacturers can prioritize the ethical sourcing of materials, safe working conditions, fair wages, and community engagement to promote social responsibility.

By integrating these principles into the manufacturing process, companies can reduce their ecological footprint, conserve resources, and contribute to a more sustainable future.

Environmental Footprint

The environmental footprint in manufacturing refers to the overall impact that manufacturing processes have on the environment, including the consumption of resources, generation of waste, and emissions of pollutants and greenhouse gases. Manufacturing activities can have a significant environmental footprint due to their energy-intensive nature and the extraction and processing of raw materials. Let's take a moment to review some aspects of manufacturing that influence its environmental footprint.

Manufacturing processes often require substantial energy inputs, primarily from non-renewable sources such as fossil fuels. The extraction, processing, and transportation of raw materials, as well as the operation of machinery and equipment, contribute to energy consumption and associated emissions. Furthermore, manufacturing typically relies on the extraction of natural resources, such as minerals, metals, and timber. Extractive activities can result in habitat destruction, soil erosion, water pollution, and biodiversity loss. Sustainable sourcing and responsible extraction practices can help mitigate these impacts.

Manufacturing processes generate various types of waste, including solid waste, wastewater, and air emissions. Solid waste includes packaging materials, scrap materials, and manufacturing byproducts. Proper waste management, recycling, and waste reduction strategies can minimize the environmental impact. In addition, manufacturing processes often require significant water usage for cooling, cleaning, and chemical processes. Excessive water consumption can strain local water supplies, deplete aquatic ecosystems, and lead to water pollution through the discharge of untreated wastewater. Implementing water-efficient technologies and recycling water can reduce the environmental footprint.

Manufacturing activities can release various pollutants into the environment, such as volatile organic compounds (VOCs), particulate matter, sulfur dioxide (SO_2), nitrogen oxides (NOx), and greenhouse gases (GHGs) like carbon dioxide (CO_2). These emissions contribute to air pollution, climate change, and negative health impacts. Adopting cleaner production technologies, improving energy efficiency, and utilizing renewable energy sources can help minimize emissions.

The environmental footprint of manufacturing extends beyond the factory walls. It includes the entire supply chain, from the extraction of raw materials to the distribution and disposal of products. Manufacturers can collaborate with suppliers to promote sustainable practices, reduce transportation-related emissions, and implement circular economy principles to minimize waste and maximize resource efficiency.

To address the environmental footprint in manufacturing, several strategies and initiatives have emerged. These include adopting cleaner production processes, implementing energy-efficient technologies, promoting resource conservation, utilizing renewable energy sources, implementing waste reduction and recycling programs, and integrating sustainability into product design and lifecycle analysis. Additionally, regulatory frameworks, environmental certifications, and consumer demand for sustainable products can incentivize manufacturers to reduce their environmental impact.

Eco-Friendly Materials

Eco-friendly materials in manufacturing refer to materials that have a minimal negative impact on the environment throughout their lifecycle, from sourcing and production to use and disposal. The use of such materials aims to reduce resource consumption, waste generation, and pollution, while promoting sustainable practices. The following are some commonly used eco-friendly materials in manufacturing.

Recycled materials: These include recycled metals, plastics, paper, and textiles. By using recycled materials, the need for raw material extraction is reduced, saving energy and resources while preventing waste accumulation.

Sustainable wood: Wood sourced from responsibly managed forests certified by organizations such as the Forest Stewardship Council (FSC) is considered eco-friendly. These forests follow sustainable practices, ensuring the replenishment of harvested trees and protecting biodiversity.

Bamboo: Bamboo is a highly renewable resource that grows quickly without the need for pesticides or fertilizers. It can be used in various applications, including furniture, flooring, and packaging, as it is strong, lightweight, and biodegradable.

Natural fibers: Natural fibers like organic cotton, hemp, and flax are considered eco-friendly alternatives to synthetic fibers. They require fewer chemicals and pesticides during cultivation and have a lower environmental impact during production and disposal.

Bioplastics: Bioplastics are derived from renewable resources such as corn, sugarcane, or cellulose. They offer a more sustainable alternative to traditional petroleum-based plastics, as they reduce dependence on fossil fuels and have a lower carbon footprint.

Low-VOC paints: Conventional paints often contain VOCs that contribute to air pollution and can be harmful to human health. Low-VOC or VOC-free paints use water as a base and have reduced levels of harmful chemicals, making them more environmentally friendly.

Recycled aggregates: In construction and building materials, the use of recycled aggregates, such as crushed concrete or reclaimed asphalt, reduces the need for new resource extraction. This practice minimizes waste and energy consumption associated with traditional materials like gravel or virgin aggregates.

Energy-efficient insulation: Eco-friendly insulation materials, such as cellulose, wool, or recycled denim, provide effective thermal insulation
while reducing energy consumption. They are often made from recycled materials and have low embodied energy.

Green concrete: Traditional concrete production generates a significant
amount of greenhouse gas emissions. Green concrete incorporates recycled materials, industrial by-products like fly ash or slag, and alternative
cementitious materials to reduce its environmental impact.

3D printing filaments from sustainable sources: Filaments used in 3D
printing can be made from renewable resources like bioplastics or
recycled materials, promoting a circular economy and reducing plastic
waste.

Implementing eco-friendly materials in manufacturing processes offers
several benefits, including reduced carbon emissions, decreased waste
generation, and improved resource conservation. By choosing sustainable
alternatives, manufacturers can contribute to a more environmentally conscious and sustainable future. Using eco-friendly materials in manufacturing offers several benefits for businesses and the environment. Eco-friendly
materials are sourced and produced in a manner that minimizes harm to the
environment. They often have lower carbon footprints, require fewer natural
resources, and generate less waste compared to traditional materials. This
contributes to the preservation of ecosystems, reduces pollution, and helps
combat climate change.

Many eco-friendly materials are designed to be more energy-efficient
during their production, use, and disposal phases. They often require less
energy to manufacture, which can lead to significant energy savings and
reduced greenhouse gas emissions. They also tend to be safer for human
health since they contain fewer toxic substances, such as VOCs and heavy
metals, which can be harmful to workers and end-users. By using these
materials, manufacturers can create safer working environments and produce
products that are healthier for consumers.

Eco-friendly materials are often derived from renewable resources, such
as bamboo, hemp, or organic cotton. These resources can be replenished
over time, ensuring a sustainable supply. Additionally, many eco-friendly
materials are recyclable or biodegradable, allowing for reduced waste generation and the potential for a circular economy.

Consumers are increasingly conscious of environmental issues and
are more likely to support businesses that prioritize sustainability. By

incorporating eco-friendly materials into their products, manufacturers can enhance their brand image, attract environmentally conscious consumers, and differentiate themselves in the market. The use of eco-friendly materials also aligns with evolving regulations and policies aimed at promoting sustainability and reducing environmental impact. By adopting these materials, manufacturers can ensure compliance with environmental standards and avoid potential legal or reputational risks associated with non-compliance.

While eco-friendly materials may sometimes have higher upfront costs, they can result in long-term cost savings. For example, energy-efficient materials may reduce operational expenses through lower energy consumption. Additionally, some eco-friendly materials can be sourced locally, reducing transportation costs and dependence on global supply chains.

By embracing eco-friendly materials, manufacturers can contribute to a more sustainable future while reaping the benefits of reduced environmental impact, improved brand reputation, and potential cost savings.

Durable, Repairable, and Recyclable Products

Durable, repairable, and recyclable products are considered eco-friendly due to several reasons. Durable products are designed to last longer, reducing the need for frequent replacements. This, in turn, reduces the consumption of raw materials and energy required to manufacture new products. By minimizing the demand for resources, durable products contribute to the conservation of natural resources and help mitigate the environmental impact of extraction and production processes.

Repairable products are designed with the intention of fixing them when they break or become faulty, rather than immediately discarding them. Repairing a product extends its lifespan and reduces the amount of waste sent to landfills or incinerators. This helps minimize the environmental issues associated with waste disposal, such as pollution, greenhouse gas emissions, and the depletion of landfill space. Manufacturing new products from scratch requires significant amounts of energy and often results in the release of greenhouse gas emissions. By opting for repairable and durable products, the need for frequent manufacturing is reduced, leading to energy savings and lower emissions. Repairing existing products typically involves less energy and emissions compared to producing new ones.

Every product has an "embodied energy" or "embodied carbon" footprint, which represents the energy and carbon emissions associated with its entire lifecycle, including extraction, production, transportation, and disposal. Durable products ensure that the initial embodied energy is maximized over a longer lifespan. Repairing and recycling further extend the utilization of embodied energy, as existing materials are utilized rather than starting from scratch.

Recyclable products are designed to be disassembled and their components or materials reused in the production of new products. By incorporating recycled materials, the demand for raw resources is reduced, leading to energy savings, and minimized environmental impacts. Additionally, a circular economy approach, where products are recycled and reused instead of discarded, helps create a more sustainable and resource-efficient system.

Overall, durable, repairable, and recyclable products promote a shift towards a more sustainable and circular economy. They contribute to resource conservation, waste reduction, energy savings, and a reduced ecological footprint, making them environmentally friendly choices. See the Side Bar: What Is a Circular Economy? for more information on a circular economy.

Supply Chain Management

Supply chain management (SCM) in the context of design for sustainability refers to the strategic coordination and integration of various activities, processes, and stakeholders involved in the production, distribution, and disposal of products or services with a focus on minimizing negative environmental impacts and maximizing social and economic benefits throughout the entire supply chain.

Design for sustainability emphasizes the incorporation of environmentally friendly practices and principles into the design phase of products or services. It involves considering the entire lifecycle of a product, from raw material extraction and manufacturing to distribution, use, and end-of-life disposal or recycling. SCM plays a crucial role in implementing and optimizing sustainable design principles within the supply chain. The following are some aspects of supply chain management to consider when designing for sustainability.

■ Encourage collaboration among various stakeholders, including suppliers, manufacturers, distributors, retailers, and consumers. By involving these parties in the design process, sustainability goals can be jointly established and integrated throughout the supply chain. Collaboration fosters the sharing of knowledge, resources, and best practices for sustainable design and production.

■ Focus on identifying and sourcing sustainable materials that have a reduced environmental impact, such as renewable resources, recycled materials, or low-impact alternatives. This involves working closely with suppliers to ensure transparency, traceability, and adherence to sustainable sourcing practices.

■ Seeks to optimize energy consumption throughout the supply chain by identifying opportunities for energy efficiency improvements. This can include using energy-efficient manufacturing processes, optimizing transportation routes to minimize fuel consumption, and implementing energy-saving technologies in warehouses and distribution centers.

■ Promote waste reduction and recycling by implementing strategies to minimize waste generation during manufacturing processes. This involves designing products with minimal packaging, encouraging reuse and recycling, and establishing reverse logistics systems to manage product returns and end-of-life disposal in an environmentally responsible manner.

■ Integrate product lifecycle assessment (LCA) into the design process. LCA analyzes the environmental impact of a product from cradle to grave, including raw material extraction, production, transportation, use, and disposal. By considering LCA data, designers can make informed decisions to minimize environmental impacts at each stage of the product's life.

■ Supply chain transparency and ethical practices are core to design for sustainability. This includes ensuring fair labor practices, human rights, and worker safety, as well as verifying and auditing suppliers to ensure compliance with sustainability standards. Transparency enables the identification and mitigation of potential risks and allows consumers to make informed choices.

■ An important aspect of sustainable design practices is creating a culture of continuous improvement and innovation. This involves monitoring key performance indicators (KPIs), benchmarking against industry standards, and seeking new technologies, materials, and processes that can further enhance sustainability within the supply chain.

Integrating these principles into supply chain management will help organizations achieve a more sustainable and resilient supply chain by reducing their environmental footprint, enhancing their brand reputation, and meeting the growing consumer demand for environmentally responsible products and services.

Sustainable Sourcing Practices

Sustainable sourcing practices in manufacturing refer to the adoption of environmentally and socially responsible methods to acquire raw materials and components for production processes. These practices aim to minimize the negative impact on the environment, conserve resources, promote social well-being, and ensure the long-term viability of the manufacturing industry. The following are some sustainable sourcing practices in manufacturing.

Manufacturers prioritize transparency throughout their supply chain, ensuring visibility and traceability of materials from their origin to the final product. This transparency helps identify potential environmental and social risks, such as deforestation, unethical labor practices, or excessive resource consumption.

Sustainable sourcing involves selecting materials that have a reduced environmental impact. Manufacturers prioritize materials that are renewable, recyclable, or biodegradable, minimizing the use of non-renewable resources. Additionally, they may favor materials with lower carbon footprints or those obtained through ethical and fair-trade practices.

Manufacturers strive to reduce transportation distances and associated carbon emissions by sourcing materials locally whenever possible. They may also foster regional collaboration to share best practices, reduce duplicate efforts, and support local economies. Manufacturers actively engage with their suppliers to encourage sustainability practices. They assess suppliers based on environmental and social criteria, such as energy efficiency, waste management, labor conditions, and human rights. Collaborative partnerships with suppliers can foster continuous improvement and help drive sustainable practices throughout the supply chain.

Sustainable sourcing often involves seeking certifications and adhering to recognized standards. For example, manufacturers may obtain certifications such as FSC for responsibly sourced wood or Leadership in Energy and Environmental Design (LEED) for sustainable building materials. Compliance with such certifications ensures adherence to specific environmental and social criteria.

Sustainable sourcing practices involve minimizing waste generation and promoting recycling. Manufacturers may implement measures like lean manufacturing principles, waste management systems, and closed-loop processes that prioritize the reuse or recycling of materials and by-products. Furthermore, manufacturers are increasingly transitioning to renewable energy sources to power their operations. This includes investing in solar, wind, or hydroelectric power to reduce reliance on fossil fuels and minimize greenhouse gas emissions.

Sustainable sourcing practices require a commitment to ongoing improvement and innovation. Manufacturers should strive to identify and implement new technologies, processes, and materials that can enhance sustainability throughout the production lifecycle. By embracing sustainable sourcing practices, manufacturers can contribute to a more environmentally conscious and socially responsible manufacturing sector, addressing the challenges of climate change, resource depletion, and social inequality.

Reducing Transportation Impacts

Reducing supply chain transportation can have several positive impacts on sustainability starting with carbon footprint reduction. Transportation, especially through fossil fuel-powered vehicles, contributes significantly to greenhouse gas emissions. By reducing supply chain transportation, companies can lower their carbon footprint and help mitigate climate change. Shorter transportation routes, consolidation of shipments, and optimizing logistics can all contribute to reducing emissions.

Transportation requires significant energy consumption, primarily in the form of fossil fuels. By minimizing the distance and frequency of transportation in the supply chain, less energy is consumed overall. Additionally, alternative modes of transportation such as electric vehicles or renewable energy-powered logistics can further enhance energy conservation.

Transportation activities also release pollutants into the air, leading to poor air quality, particularly in urban areas. Reducing transportation distances and employing cleaner transport methods can result in improved air quality, benefiting both human health and ecosystems.

Supply chain transportation involves the use of various resources such as fuel, packaging materials, and vehicles. By optimizing transportation routes, reducing packaging waste, and implementing efficient practices, companies can minimize resource consumption and waste generation. In addition, transportation infrastructure, such as roads and highways, can disrupt ecosystems and wildlife habitats. By reducing the need for extensive transportation networks, the negative impacts on natural environments can be minimized, preserving biodiversity and ecological balance.

While sustainability is a significant motivation for reducing supply chain transportation, it can also lead to cost savings for businesses. Optimizing logistics, consolidating shipments, and implementing efficient transportation practices can reduce fuel and maintenance costs, ultimately benefiting the bottom line. Overall, by reducing supply chain transportation, businesses can contribute to sustainability goals by reducing carbon emissions, conserving energy and resources, improving air quality, preserving ecosystems, and achieving cost savings. It is important for companies to consider sustainable practices throughout their supply chains to maximize the positive impact on the environment and society as a whole.

Ethical Labor Conditions

Ethical labor conditions in sustainable manufacturing refer to the practice of ensuring fair and safe working conditions for employees throughout the production process. These conditions prioritize the well-being and rights of workers, promoting social responsibility and sustainability in the manufacturing industry. The following are some key aspects of ethical labor conditions in sustainable manufacturing.

Fair wages: Workers are paid fair and living wages that meet or exceed local industry standards. This ensures that employees can sustain themselves and their families without facing undue financial hardship.

Safe working environments: Sustainable manufacturers prioritize worker safety by maintaining safe and healthy working conditions. They implement safety protocols, provide proper training, and adhere to local and international safety standards to prevent accidents, injuries, and occupational hazards.

Reasonable working hours: Workers are not subjected to excessively long working hours or forced overtime. Sustainable manufacturers recognize the importance of work-life balance and limit the number of hours employees are expected to work each day and week.

No child or forced labor: Ethical labor conditions strictly prohibit the use of child labor and forced labor. Manufacturers ensure that all employees are of legal working age and that their employment is voluntary.

Respect for workers' rights: Sustainable manufacturing companies uphold the fundamental rights of workers, including freedom of association, collective bargaining, and the right to form and join trade unions. They promote an inclusive and supportive work culture that encourages open communication and employee empowerment.

Non-discrimination and equal opportunities: Ethical labor conditions promote diversity and equality in the workplace. Manufacturers maintain a non-discriminatory environment where all employees are treated with respect and provided equal opportunities for employment, promotion, and professional development.

Supply chain transparency: Sustainable manufacturers prioritize supply chain transparency by ensuring that their suppliers also adhere to ethical labor conditions. They conduct thorough audits and assessments to verify compliance and address any issues or violations promptly.

Social and community impact: Ethical labor conditions extend beyond the workplace and encompass the social and community impact of manufacturing operations. Sustainable manufacturers engage in philanthropic activities, support local communities, and contribute positively to the social and economic development of the regions where they operate.

Overall, ethical labor conditions in sustainable manufacturing prioritize the dignity, rights, and well-being of workers. They aim to create a responsible and equitable manufacturing ecosystem that values people, planet, and profits in equal measure.

In summary, design for sustainability in manufacturing not only benefits the environment but also enhances the brand reputation, reduces manufacturing costs in the long run, and fosters innovation and competitiveness in the market. See Table 4.4.1 for tips on how to design for sustainability.

Table 4.4.1 Design for Sustainability Tips – What to Do and How to Do It

Design for Sustainability – *What to Do and How to Do It...*	
Choose Sustainable Materials	**Packaging and Logistics**
> Use renewable resources	> Minimize packaging waste
> Use recyclable materials	> Reduce transportation emissions
Optimize Energy Efficiency	> Use eco-friendly packaging materials
> Optimize energy use during production	> Reduce packaging size
> Use renewable energy sources	> Optimize transportation routes
> Implement energy-saving technologies	
Reduce Waste	**End-of-Life Impacts**
> Reduce material waste	> Create easy to disassemble products
> Implement recycling programs	> Create products that easily separate into recyclable components
> Remanufacture and recycle	
Durability and Longevity	> Create products that can be effectively repurposed
> Consider material durability	
> Consider product/process modularity	> Implement take-back programs
> Consider product/process repairability	> Establish recycling partnerships

---

SIDE BAR: WHAT IS A CIRCULAR ECONOMY?

A circular economy is an economic system that aims to maximize resource utilization and minimize waste and environmental impact. It is a departure from the traditional linear economy, which follows a "take-make-dispose" model, where resources are extracted, transformed into products, used, and then discarded as waste.

In a circular economy, the focus is on designing out waste and keeping products, materials, and resources in continuous circulation. The aim is to create a closed-loop system where resources are reused, repaired, and recycled, extending their lifespan and reducing the need for new resource extraction. There are several key principles that underpin a circular economy.

Design for durability and longevity: Products are designed to be durable, repairable, and upgradeable, ensuring they have a longer lifespan.

This reduces the need for frequent replacements and minimizes waste generation.

Emphasize recycling and reuse: Materials and components are recovered from products at the end of their life and recycled or reused in the manufacturing of new products. This reduces the demand for virgin resources and minimizes waste disposal.

Regenerate natural systems: A circular economy aims to minimize the impact on natural resources by using renewable energy sources and promoting sustainable practices. It seeks to restore and regenerate ecosystems to ensure long-term environmental sustainability.

Embrace the sharing economy: Sharing platforms and collaborative consumption models are encouraged to optimize resource utilization. This includes shared mobility services, co-working spaces, and the sharing of tools and equipment, reducing the overall consumption of resources.

Shift from ownership to access: Instead of owning products, the emphasis is on providing access to goods and services through leasing, renting, or subscription models. This approach encourages manufacturers to design products for durability and repairability, as they retain ownership throughout the product's lifecycle.

Enable digitalization and data utilization: Utilizing digital technologies and data analytics can optimize resource allocation, enable efficient logistics, and support the tracking and tracing of materials throughout their lifecycle. This allows for better resource management and waste reduction.

By adopting a circular economy approach, businesses and societies can reduce environmental degradation, conserve resources, create new economic opportunities, and promote sustainable development. It requires a shift in mindset, collaboration among stakeholders, and the integration of sustainable practices across industries and sectors.

Chapter 4.5

Sustainable Manufacturing Culture

A Culture of Sustainable Manufacturing

A culture of sustainable manufacturing refers to a set of values, practices, and principles adopted by an organization or society that prioritizes environmentally conscious and socially responsible approaches to manufacturing processes. This culture promotes the efficient use of resources, minimizes waste generation, reduces pollution, and emphasizes the well-being of workers and local communities.

Sustainable manufacturing places a strong emphasis on minimizing environmental impact. This involves using renewable energy sources, implementing energy-efficient technologies, and reducing greenhouse gas emissions. Manufacturers actively seek to conserve water, minimize waste generation, and promote recycling and reuse practices. A sustainable manufacturing culture focuses on optimizing resource utilization. This includes the efficient use of raw materials, energy, and water throughout the production process. Manufacturers employ techniques such as lean manufacturing and process optimization to minimize waste and increase overall efficiency.

Adopting a circular economy model is a fundamental aspect of sustainable manufacturing. Instead of following a linear "take-make-dispose" approach, this culture promotes the design of products with a focus on durability, reparability, and recyclability. Manufacturers strive to close the material loop by using recycled or renewable inputs and implementing take-back programs for end-of-life products.

DOI: 10.4324/9781032688152-22

Sustainable manufacturing culture encourages collaboration and transparency among stakeholders. Manufacturers actively engage with suppliers, customers, and local communities to foster dialogue, exchange ideas, and find innovative solutions. Transparent reporting of environmental and social performance enables accountability and builds trust with stakeholders.

A culture of sustainable manufacturing places a strong emphasis on ethical and fair practices throughout the supply chain. This includes ensuring safe working conditions, fair wages, and respecting human rights. Manufacturers seek to eliminate the use of hazardous substances, child labor, and other exploitative practices.

Embracing innovation and promoting a culture of continuous improvement are vital for sustainable manufacturing. Companies invest in research and development to develop eco-friendly technologies, explore alternative materials, and improve manufacturing processes. They also actively seek feedback from employees, customers, and stakeholders to drive ongoing improvements.

Building a culture of sustainable manufacturing also requires education and training initiatives. Manufacturers invest in training programs to enhance the skills and knowledge of their workforce in areas such as environmental management, waste reduction, energy efficiency, and sustainable design. These programs help instill a sustainability mindset throughout the organization.

In essence, a culture of sustainable manufacturing is focused on creating a balance between economic growth, environmental responsibility, and social well-being. By integrating sustainability principles into their operations, organizations can contribute to a greener future while meeting the needs of present and future generations.

Employee Awareness and Collaboration

Manufacturing processes can have significant environmental consequences, such as resource depletion, pollution, and greenhouse gas emissions. By understanding the importance of sustainability, employees can make informed decisions, adopt responsible practices, and actively participate in minimizing the ecological footprint of manufacturing operations. Collaboration among employees is essential for identifying and implementing waste reduction strategies. When employees are encouraged to communicate and share ideas, they can collectively identify areas of waste generation and develop innovative solutions to minimize waste. By fostering a culture of collaboration, manufacturing organizations can tap into the collective knowledge and creativity of their employees, leading to more effective waste reduction practices and increased operational efficiency.

Energy consumption is a significant aspect of manufacturing operations. Employee awareness regarding energy-saving practices, such as turning off lights and equipment when not in use, optimizing production schedules to avoid peak energy demand, and using energy-efficient technologies, can significantly contribute to reducing energy consumption. Collaborative efforts within the organization can further enhance energy efficiency by identifying areas for improvement and implementing energy-saving initiatives.

Sustainability is an ongoing process that requires continuous improvement and innovation. Employee awareness and collaboration are vital for driving this process. By encouraging employees to stay informed about emerging sustainability trends, technologies, and best practices, organizations can tap into their expertise and enthusiasm to implement positive changes. Collaborative problem-solving and knowledge-sharing initiatives can facilitate the identification of opportunities for improvement, enabling the organization to stay ahead in sustainability efforts.

Developing a sustainable manufacturing culture relies on the active participation and engagement of employees. When employees are aware of the organization's sustainability goals and are involved in collaborative initiatives, they feel a sense of ownership and pride in their contributions. This positive culture fosters employee satisfaction, motivation, and loyalty, which in turn translates into increased productivity and improved overall performance.

Employee awareness and collaboration are essential for driving sustainability in manufacturing. By promoting a culture of awareness, collaboration, and continuous improvement, organizations can harness the collective efforts of their employees to reduce environmental impact, enhance operational efficiency, and create a positive sustainable manufacturing ecosystem.

Acronyms

ABS	Acrylonitrile butadiene styrene
AC	Alternating current
AGC	Automated guided cart
AGV	Automated guided vehicle
aAGV	Autonomous automated guided vehicle
API	Application programming interfaces
AR	Augmented reality
AS/RS	Automated storage/retrieval system
BOM	Bill of material
CAD	Computer-aided design
CH$_4$	Methane
CMM	Coordinate measuring machine
CNC	Computer numerical control
CO	Carbon monoxide
CO$_2$	Carbon dioxide
CO$_2$e	Carbon dioxide equivalents (standard of measurement)
CSP	Concentrating solar power
DApps	Distributed applications
DCS	Distributed control systems
DfC	Design for circularity
DfE	Design for the environment
DLT	Distributed ledger technology
EGS	Enhanced geothermal systems
EOL	End of line
ESP	Electrostatic precipitator
FSC	Forest Stewardship Council
GHG	Greenhouse gas
GPS	Global positioning system

GWP	Global warming potential
HAP	Hazardous air pollutants
HMD	Head-mounted display
HMI	Human machine interface
IIoT	Industrial Internet of Things
IP	Intellectual property
JIT	Just in time
KPI	Key process indicator
LCA	Lifecycle assessments
LCE	Lifecycle engineering
LEED	Leadership in Energy and Environmental Design
LGV	Laser guided vehicle
MES	Manufacturing execution systems
MQTT	Message Queuing Telemetry Transport
MR	Mixed reality
N_2O	Nitrous oxide
NUD	New, Unique, Difficult
NOx	Nitrogen oxides
OEE	Overall equipment effectiveness
PCB	Printed circuit board
PETG	Polyethylene terephthalate glycol
PFMEA	Process Failure Mode and Effects Analysis
PLA	Polylactic acid
PLC	Programmable logic controller
PM	Particulate matter
PV	Product validation
PV	Photovoltaic
REST	Representational state transfer
RFID	Radiofrequency identification
RPA	Robotic process automation
RPS	Renewable portfolio standard
SCADA	Supervisory Control and Data Acquisition (system)
SCARA	Selective Compliance Assembly Robot Arm or Selective Compliance Articulated Robot Arm
SCM	Supply chain management
SO_2	Sulfur dioxide
SOP	Start of Production or Standard Operating Procedure
TCP/IP	Transmission Control Protocol/Internet Protocol
TPE/TPU/TPC	Thermoplastic elastomer/polyurethane/co-polyester

TQM	Total quality management
VFD	Variable frequency drive
VOCs	Volatile organic compound
VR	Virtual reality
WBS	Work breakdown structure
WIP	Work in progress
WMS	Warehouse management system
XR	Extended reality

Index

Page number followed by *f* indicate figure and **bold** indicate table respectively

Printed in the United States
by Baker & Taylor Publisher Services

Printed in the United States
by Baker & Taylor Publisher Services